PARTHIBAN'S DREAM

Praise for *Parthiban's Dream*

'Kalki Krishnamurthy's historical novels have achieved this incredible distinction of multiple translations. His *Ponniyin Selvan* has even been translated into Sanskrit. *Alai Osai*, which was posthumously awarded by the Sahitya Akademi, has seen a Russian translation. *Parthiban Kanavu* too has been translated into English and published decades ago ... A translator's task is often thankless and punishingly hard. Additionally, a historical canvas poses its own challenges of word choice. But the thirst to share and express in another language what one has experienced reading, is as compelling as writing one's own story. Nandini Vijayaraghavan's translation of *Parthiban Kanavu* as *Parthiban's Dream* is testimony to this.'

Seetha Ravi

'Lucid prose and glitch-free translation, with beautiful illustrations by late S. Gopalan – this classic is an interesting read, a page turner.'

Divya Shankar (review on Amazon)

'An element that enhances the English *Parthiban's Dream*, is the evocative monochromatic illustrations in the book from one of Tamil Nadu's most respected artists from a bygone era, Gopulu, who was a household name as an illustrator and cartoonist ... The drawings are redolent of the period being written about, inducing an inescapable whiff of nostalgia.'

Suresh Subrahmanyan, *Deccan Chronicle*

'*Parthiban Kanavu* is a swashbuckling story of a young prince keeping alive his father's dream of establishing a glorious kingdom. The storyline is marked by palace intrigues, betrayals, and love at first sight. Vijayaraghavan faithfully follows the plot, omitting no digressions or descriptions. Nor does she editorialise to explain plot complications. Her choice of words is impeccable, the polysyllabic and slightly archaic language reflecting Kalki's Sanskritised Tamil, which is not easily accessible to contemporary readers ... *Parthiban's Dream* features exquisite artwork by Gopulu which was part of the Tamil original when it was serialised. The volume will be a treasured addition to any bookshelf.'

Hema Ramanathan, *The Hindu*

'Nandini Vijayaraghavan has done a remarkable job of translating *Parthiban Kanavu* into English ... I read the novel twice, which is proof enough that I enjoyed being transported to a different century.'

Sabita Radhakrishna, *The Book Review*

'Nandini Vijayaraghavan's English translation of Kalki's *Parthiban's Kanavu* as *Parthiban's Dream* is a timely recall of Kalki's dexterity in weaving history, fiction, romance and nationalist aspirations in a riveting prose that is at once simple and stately.'

B. Mangalam, *Indian Literature*

Shortlisted for the Valley of Words Award 2022 for translation

PARTHIBAN'S DREAM

— A NOVEL —

KALKI KRISHNAMURTHY

TRANSLATED FROM THE TAMIL BY

NANDINI VIJAYARAGHAVAN

ILLUSTRATIONS BY S. GOPALAN AKA GOPULU

RATNA BOOKS

HARPERPERENNIAL

An Imprint of HarperCollins *Publishers*

First published as *Parthiban Kanavu* in Tamil in India 1942
First published in English in India by Ratna Sagar P. Ltd. 2021, 2023
This edition co-published in India in 2026
by
Harper Perennial
An imprint of HarperCollins *Publishers* India
Cyber City, Building 10-A, Gurugram, Haryana-122002, India
www.harpercollins.co.in
and
Ratna Sagar P. Ltd.
Virat Bhavan, Mukherjee Nagar Commercial Complex
Delhi 110009, India
www.ratnabookseries.wordpress.com

2 4 6 8 10 9 7 5 3 1

P-ISBN: 978-93-6989-711-7

Printed and bound at
Nutech Print Services Pvt. Ltd.

This book is printed on FSC® certified paper which ensures responsible forest management.

HarperCollins *Publishers*, Macken House, 39/40 Mayor Street Upper, Dublin 1, D01 C9W8, Ireland

Contents

Part I

1. Quay

The iridescent rays of the rising sun lent a golden hue to the river Kaveri, the lifeline of Chola Nadu. No wonder the serene river was also called Ponni, the golden hued woman! The gentle zephyr played mischief with the swirls of the river, creating an ethereal scene. Countless water drops sprang forth, sparkling like jewels, as waves bumped into each other, rendering a surreal look to the river.

The banyan trees on the banks with their widespread roots sported new sprouts announcing the advent of spring. These young offshoots shone brilliantly in the rays of the morning sun. In the distance, amidst the vast expanse of water in the north-east, lay a verdant island. At the centre of the island, towering over the green trees, stood a majestic palace with its golden turret glittering in the sun.

Against the backdrop of the tranquil and serene river in full flow, there was enough movement caused by the chirping of birds. The melodious cooing of the birds filled the air, welcoming the rising sun. It was as though the gurgling of the river set the background score for the melody spouted by the birds. Some were cajoling their chicks to stay put, before leaving in search of food; others flapped their wings joyously as they took off!

The peepal tree, towering over the banyans, rustled its leaves to register its presence. The river tried assiduously to push away the boats tied to the aerial roots of the banyan trees. Unsuccessful at doing this, the river continued along its course, vowing to unsettle the boats one day.

Under a banyan tree, a little away from the riverbank, a small hut was visible. Wood smoke mixed with the fragrance of kambu adai, a pancake made of pearl millets, emanated from within the hut. A buffalo was lying near the hut, chewing cud while her calf watched her with wonder.

Taktak, taktak, taktak!

Suddenly, the sound of horse hooves shattered the serenity of the riverside.

Taktak, taktak, taktak!

The progressively amplifying sound indicated the movement of a horse towards the riverbank. What a sight to behold! A well-built warrior was riding a statuesque steed, and both were drenched in sweat. On reaching the quay, the horse halted and the warrior leapt to the ground.

❖

A young lady was cooking adais inside the hut, while a sturdy youth sitting beside her was eating the adai from a plate made with tender banyan leaves sewn together.

He smacked his lips in appreciation of the kambu adai and keerai kuzhambu, spinach cooked in tamarind sauce. He said, 'For how long I will be fortunate enough to relish your adai, Valli?' Pat came the reply from the woman, 'You keep repeating this every day. I will break this stove and fling it into the Kaveri if you speak thus again!'

'I am not joking, Valli. I heard the Maharaja and Maharani converse yesterday. A war is most certainly imminent,' stated the youth.

'Why should an imminent war concern you? Who invited you

to enlist in the army? Why don't you continue plying the boat?'

'Most certainly not! I will prostrate before the Maharaja and entreat him to take me along to the battlefield.'

'I will fall at your feet and request you to take me along with you. If you are unwilling to do so, push me into the Kaveri and head to the battlefield! After all, it was you who rescued me when the river had swept me away.'

'That's right, Valli! This is the current state of our Chola Desam (country). Women will enlist for war while men will cower in their homes... Wait, I can hear a horse approaching.'

Yes, that was when the warrior was riding towards the boat quay.

The youth felt a shiver of excitement and rushed towards the entrance without even washing his hands. On seeing the youth, he exclaimed, 'Ponna, I have a message for the Maharaja. Row the boat fast!'

'I'll come quickly!' responded Ponnan as he rushed inside.

Valli was about to pour the batter into the pan to make another adai. 'Valli, he is carrying an urgent message from Uraiyur. I need to leave now,' said Ponnan. 'Fie the urgent message! Your stomach is not even half full. I don't like this,' snapped Valli as she turned her face away.

Ponnan said in a placatory tone, 'What can be done, Valli? This is to be expected when one is in the service of the Maharaja.' He walked towards her and drew her angry visage towards him. Valli smiled as she swept away a lock of hair from her face. She looked up to Ponnan and enquired, 'You'll return early, won't you?' Without replying, Ponnan lowered his face towards hers.

Just then, the warrior shouted, 'How much longer will you take, Ponna?' Startled, Ponnan rushed out without looking back.

2. Royal Family

Ponnan left with the horseman; Valli started her household chores. She mopped the floor of the hut and then milked the buffalo tethered to a tree. Wishing to bathe, she chose a secluded spot of the Kaveri covered by the tree branches that bent low. After bathing, she returned home and draped herself in a fresh sari. Then, she lit the stove again and started cooking. All along she was agitated and restless. She went to the entrance of the hut several times and scanned the area with her wide, dark eyes. She had a premonition, an anticipation of exceptional events in the near future.

In a short while, ten to fifteen cavalry men approached the quay from the direction of Uraiyur. In the entourage were two caparisoned white steeds and an ivory palanquin. The steeds were riderless just as the palanquin was empty. Eight sturdy men carried this beautiful palanquin.

The retinue halted on nearing the quay. The palanquin was lowered to the ground. The cavalry men tied their horses to the trees. Standing at the door, Valli observed the scene in rapt attention. One of the men saw Valli and said to another, 'Anna (elder brother)! Let's ask Valli for some water.'

'Velappa! Why do you want to ask Valli for water when you are in front of the Kaveri in full flow?'

'Anna, can it be as tasty as the water that Valli serves us?' Speaking thus, they sauntered towards the hut.

'Valli, we are thirsty. Can you give us some water?' asked Velappan.

Valli rushed inside and returned with two earthen pots of mor, the buttermilk cherished in the region. While they were relishing the drink, she enquired, 'Is it true that the Maharaja is leaving for Uraiyur today? Why is he in such a hurry? Isn't it customary that he stays this whole month at the Vasantha Maligai?'

'Why are you quizzing us and not your husband, Valli? Can there be any state secret which boatman Ponnan is not privy to?' shot back Velappan.

'A messenger came with an urgent missive to be delivered to the Maharaja this morning. He rushed out without finishing his breakfast! How do I ask him?' complained Valli.

'How concerned she is! A model wife!' said Velappan.

Valli's cheeks dimpled as she smiled coyly. She mumbled, 'Go away! Enough of teasing!'

'Valli, henceforth we may not be able to tease you often,' said Velappan.

'Why do you say so? Won't you divulge the truth to me?' asked Valli earnestly.

'Aren't you aware of the impending war?'

'Yes, I know there is a lot of talk about war. But I can't comprehend the need for a war now.'

'Our Maharaja has not paid tribute to Kanchi Narasimha Varma Chakravarthi for the last four to five years. Apparently, the Chakravarthi, on his return after his invasion in the North, had sent emissaries to enquire about this non-payment of the tribute. They may reach Uraiyur today,' explained Velappan.

'Why should a war break out for this? The matter can be settled if the tribute for four years is paid!' said the innocent Valli.

'Our Maharaja is not in favour of paying the tribute. He refuses to change his stand.'

They then noticed a boat sailing towards them. Velappan and his comrade quickly strode away to join the others. The boat reached the pier soon after.

This boat was unlike Ponnan's modest boat. It was an ornate royal float fitted with a mast at one end. Three royals were seated in the boat – the king, Maharaja Parthiba Chola, his consort, Maharani Arulmozhi, and their son, Ilavarasar Vikraman or Prince Vikraman.

Two men stood guard at the two ends of the boat. In addition to the swords fastened to their waists, they also held spears. Ponnan and yet another man manoeuvred the boat towards the bank.

No sooner the boat touched the bank than the guards disembarked and announced the arrival of the king. 'Here comes Rajadhi Raja, Raja Marthanda, Raja Gambeera, Chola Mandaladhipathi Parthiba Maharaja – the King of Kings, Descendent of the Sun God resplendent like the sun, the majestic awe-inspiring King, Sovereign of the Chola realm!' All the warriors on the riverbank stood with their arms folded and echoed, 'Victory to the Maharaja!'

The Maharaja on alighting from the boat, looked towards Ponnan's dwelling. His gaze fell upon Valli, who was standing at the entrance of the hut looking in their direction. He beckoned her. Valli rushed and prostrated before him as a mark of obeisance. When the Maharaja asked her to get up, she complied and stood meekly behind Ponnan.

'Valli, does Ponnan take good care of you?' enquired the Maharaja.

Valli smiled slightly with her head lowered. She was tongue-tied. The Maharani said, 'You ought not to have asked her thus. She would have replied had you enquired if she took good care of Ponnan.'

The Maharaja laughed and then said, 'Valli, did you hear what the Maharani said? Be watchful of Ponnan. Don't allow him to wander around. He may rescue yet another woman from the flood and bring her home!' Overcome by embarrassment and happiness, Valli contorted her body.

But all this humour was lost on Ponnan. He brought his palms together and said, 'Maharaja! Kindly grant me a boon. Please allow this servant to accompany you to the battlefield.' The king regained his composure and stated, 'Though I understand your feelings, Ponna, I'm unable to bestow this boon. You must remain here. In the event of my not returning from the battlefield, it is you who have to teach the Ilavarasan swimming. Do you understand?' On hearing this, Ponnan's and Valli's eyes brimmed with tears. Maharani Arulmozhi heaved a sigh. It was impossible to fathom the thoughts that assailed her.

It is only after the Maharaja and his retinue traversed a long distance did Valli return to normalcy. She joked, 'Did you hear what the Maharaja said? You ought not to budge anywhere without my permission!'

'In that case, I seek your consent right away to head to Uraiyur this afternoon,' said Ponnan.

'What is transpiring at Uraiyur?' asked Valli.

'Today is going to be eventful. Emissaries from Kanchi are expected to arrive at Uraiyur today, asking for the unpaid tribute. Our Maharaja is likely to refuse to pay. I must be there,' said Ponnan.

Valli brought her palms together and mimicked Ponnan, 'Maharaja! Kindly grant me a boon. Please allow this servant to accompany you to the battlefield.'

'Leave me alone! I will not go if you were to mock me thus,' remonstrated Ponnan.

Having decided not to go to Uraiyur, Ponnan started swimming languidly, cavorting around the Kaveri.

But the agitation he felt within was indescribable once he

heard the horse hooves. He swam swiftly to the bank to ascertain what was happening. Valli too stepped out of their hut.

They could see a horse followed by four others approaching swiftly from the east. The man mounted on the first horse held aloft a flag bearing the lion insignia. The horses were headed to Uraiyur.

'Who are these men bearing the flag with the lion insignia?' asked Valli.

Ponnan, who appeared to be hypnotized, snapped back to his senses. 'Valli! These are the Pallava emissaries. I must go to Uraiyur today. Why don't you accompany me? We can also visit your grandfather,' he said.

3. Pallava Emissaries

Ponnan and Valli locked up their hut and headed towards Uraiyur, which was about one *kaada*[1] to the west of the quay. During those days – around one thousand three hundred years ago, before the advent of automobiles and trains, royalty and nobles used elephants, horses and horse-drawn chariots while commoners used bullock carts for travel. To facilitate this, wide roads were laid. Chola Nadu was renowned for its network of roads flanked by canopies of trees. The highway adjoining the southern bank of Kaveri was not only wide but also scenic with many shade-giving trees all along its course.

Ponnan and Valli took this highway to reach Uraiyur, the capital of Chola Nadu. The kingdom had lost its glory and pre-eminence and by 7th century CE was reduced to a vassal state. The Pandyas from the south and the Pallavas from the north repressed Chola Nadu. But they could not rob the natural wealth and prosperity of Chola Nadu. Neither the Pandyas nor the Pallavas could change the course of the Kaveri, the reason for its prosperity and fertility.

The highway to Uraiyur bore testimony to Chola Nadu's abundant water resources; it was flanked by the majestic Kaveri on one side and green fields on the other. Across the river, mango orchards and coconut plantations extended till the horizon, caressing the blue sky.

Planting had been completed in most paddy fields. It was the season when the shade of paddy saplings deepened to green-black from emerald green. Water gurgled down the narrow channels that irrigated the fields. White storks that stood on one leg in a meditative posture in these channels accentuated the greenery. Plantain, coconut and sugarcane groves dotted the paddy fields.

What will become of these tranquil, lush green scenic fields should war break out! As they walked towards Uraiyur, Ponnan and Valli tried to fathom the distress and turmoil that would afflict the Chola denizens in case of a war. On seeing the couple, farmers who were working in the fields and the women folk who were pulling out the weeds abandoned their chores midway and came running towards them.

'Ponna! What news do you have to convey?' asked a few eagerly. 'Will there be a war, definitely?' quizzed some.

'What message did the emissaries bring?' yet another curious group wanted to know.

Ponnan responded to everyone, but differently.

He said to a group, 'War is certain. How will our Maharaja agree to pay tribute to the Pallava King? Keep your swords and spears sharp and be ready to enlist in the army.'

To others he said, 'What do I know? I know nothing more than you do.'

'Don't talk like that, Ponna! How can the de facto Prime Minister of Chola Nadu be in the dark! Is there a state secret you are unaware of?'

Pride was writ large on Valli's beaming face on hearing that. But, within a moment, annoyance took over when someone asked, 'Ponna, won't you accompany the Maharaja to the battle front?'

Ponnan said, 'It's for the Maharaja to decide.'

After they crossed the village, Ponnan told Valli, 'Did you hear that, Valli? It will be cowardly to desist from enlisting. I will become a laughing stock!'

Valli shot back saying, 'I do not stop you from enlisting in the army. You may go if the Maharaja commands you to do so but please take me along with you.'

Ponnan had to answer many more on his way. By dusk, the couple reached the entrance of the Uraiyur Fort and, precisely at that moment, through the gates of the fort came out a few horsemen. The warrior leading the group was holding the flag with the lion insignia. Ponnan understood that they were the emissaries who headed to Uraiyur that afternoon. The couple stepped aside and waited till the dust kicked up by the speeding horses settled down.

Entering the city, they could see people standing in groups, conversing animatedly. The couple stood at the periphery of one such group. A man who was in the Royal Assembly during the visit of the Pallava emissaries was recounting what he witnessed there. 'Aha! Words are inadequate to describe what transpired at the Assembly today! Our Maharaja was seated majestically on the throne. The Ilavarasar, ministers and general were occupying their designated places. There was absolute silence.

'The Maharaja commanded in a voice that reflected his alacrity, "Summon the Pallava emissaries." The emissaries were ushered in. Their leader took one step forward and bowed to the Maharaja. Our Maharaja asked, "Emissary! What news do you bear?" The emissary unnerved by the regal tone of the Maharaja, could not bring himself to speak.

'He stammered as he announced, "We are the emissaries of Triloka Chakravarthi, Kanchi Mandalathipathi, Shatru Samhari – Emperor of the three realms, the Sovereign of Kanchi, the decimator of foes – Narasimha Varma Pallavarayar..."

'The palace jester interjected, querying, "Emissary! Stop!

Which three realms is he the Chakravarthi, the emperor of? Are these the three realms of the nether world or Indra Loka, Chandra Loka and Yama Loka?"

'Everyone in the Assembly burst out laughing. The emissary was embarrassed; he trembled and was tongue-tied. He slowly regained composure and said, "The customary tribute paid since Your Majesty's grandfather's time remains unpaid for the past six years. Our Chakravarthi has commanded us to ascertain the reason from you."

'Aha! One ought to have seen our Maharaja then.

'"You may inform your Chakravarthi that the reason will be revealed on the battle front."

'I felt goosebumps…'

When the narrator paused, everyone asked in unison, 'What happened then?'

'The emissary was stunned for a few moments. He gathered his wits and then said, "In that case, our Chakravarthi asked you to be prepared for war. The Pallava army would have left Kanchi by now. Our Chakravarthi said that you may choose the date and the location of the battlefield."

'Our Maharaja replied, "We will meet on Puraṭṭāsi (mid-September to mid-October) Pournami (full moon day) on the banks of Vennaru."

'Immediately, all those present at the Assembly hailed, "Vetri Vel! Victory to the spear! Veera Vel! The valorous spear!" (The spear is the weapon of the Hindu God of war, Muruga.)'

On hearing this, everyone in the crowd cheered, 'Vetri Vel! Veera Vel!' Ponnan also joined the crowd in cheering loudly before walking ahead with Valli.

By then, night had set in. The moon, covered by white clouds, radiated a dull glow. Big earthen lamps, placed atop the stone pillars at street corners, were lit. They started burning, emitting smoke.

Suddenly, the sound of a trumpet was heard. It resonated

in all directions across Uraiyur's mandapams, public halls, mansions, towers and fort entrances. It sounded like a war cry. Ponnan was charged, his hair stood on end, his heart beat faster and nerves stiffened on hearing the thunderous sound!

Valli shivered as she exclaimed, 'What noise is this? I have never ever heard one like this!'

Ponnan replied, 'That is the war bugle.'

Valli, who was taken aback by Ponnan's tone, asked, 'Aiyyo! What happened to you?'

'Nothing, I am fine,' replied Ponnan. A little later, as if in a trance, he said, 'Valli, I must certainly head to the battlefield!'

4. Grandfather and Granddaughter

Ponnan and Valli came to a halt outside one of the houses on Uraiyur's Kammala (blacksmith) Street. The doors were shut. Valli called out, 'Thatha!' (grandfather). A few moments elapsed before an elderly man opened the door and welcomed them, 'Come in, Valli. Welcome mapillai (son-in-law).' He then looked inside the house and said loudly, 'Come here, kizhavi (old woman)! Look, we have visitors.' The three of them entered the house. The elderly woman who stepped out of the kitchen asking, 'Who has come?' shot a wide toothless smile at Valli and Ponnan. She embraced Valli and enquired, 'Are you happy, my dear? How is your husband doing?'

Ponnan said, 'Thatha, I am handing over your granddaughter to you. I need to step out.'

'You've just arrived. Where are you off to now?' asked the elderly man.

'I'm going to see our Maharaja,' replied Ponnan.

'The Maharaja is not at the palace. He has gone to the temple on the hill. Come here, I'll show you,' stated the elderly man as he ushered Ponnan to the muttram or the courtyard of the house. The illuminated lamp of the Ucchi Pillaiyar temple, the Ganesha temple atop the hill, was visible from there. A few people were descending the hill holding torches. They stopped their descent midway. 'What are they looking at?' asked Valli. 'The statue of Mahendra Chakravarthi, Narasimha Varma Pallavar's father is there. I think our Maharaja is pointing it out to the Ilavarasar,' stated the old man.

'Since they are on their way down, I'll wait for them at the palace entrance, thatha. I must somehow meet our Maharaja tonight,' said Ponnan as he walked out of the house.

The old man followed him to the door and whispered, 'Ponna, you must convey an important message to our Maharaja in confidence. Ask him to be wary of Marappa Bhupathi.'

'What about Marappa Bhupathi?' asked Ponnan. 'I will tell you about him later. You must somehow convey this message to our Maharaja,' said the elderly man. His wife went to the kitchen to prepare dinner for the guests.

The grandfather and granddaughter sat at the muttram. At one corner of the muttram, beside the forge, were heaped swords, spears and lances. As soon as she saw them, Valli screamed, 'Aiyo thatha! What is all this?'

'Don't you know what these are? These are weapons. It is unlikely you would have seen these. Those days…'

'Why do we need these weapons, thatha?'

'I propose to keep them in a temple and worship them! What a silly question! The swords will be used to decapitate our foes. Our soldiers will use spears to pierce our adversaries' abdomens, extract their intestines and wear them as garlands!'

'Aiyayo! I'm scared!' shrieked Valli.

'Soon enough, even our menfolk will become cowardly like you and will wonder how to use swords and spears. Heed this, Valli. Do you know what it was like during my grandfather's times? Those days, blacksmiths' forges used to churn out swords, spears and lances non-stop. In every city, the Kammala Street used to be abuzz with activity. Kings, princes and generals used to frequently visit the blacksmiths. The situation changed during my father's time. Blacksmiths now forge scythes to harvest plantains and goads and axles for bullock carts to earn their livelihoods. I am seeing swords and spears for the first time at my advanced age . . . aha! If only my arms possessed their youthful vigour! If only this war had broken out twenty years ago!'

'Oh no, thatha! I was hoping that you would advise my husband against going to the battlefield! He speaks continuously of enlisting in the army . . .'

'Who, Ponnan?! How will he be able to leave you and head to the battlefront, Valli? The arms that wield oars will not be able to brandish a sword. Will a besotted man engage in aggression?'

'Don't mock him, thatha! He has been raring to enlist in the army. But the Maharaja did not permit him to do so as he wanted him to teach the Ilavarasar swimming.'

'Ah! Had your father and uncles been alive today, I would have handed them a sword and spear each and have sent them to the battlefield. Why did Kaveri Amman, Mother Kaveri, have to decimate all of them in a single day?' moaned the elderly man as he heaved a deep sigh. Valli recollected the horrific incident.

Four years ago, all family members save her grandparents had rowed across the Kaveri river to attend a wedding. When they had traversed half the distance, cyclonic winds suddenly cropped up and the boat capsized. Ponnan, who was then on the riverbank, immediately jumped into the river and tried to rescue the people who were flung off the boat. By God's grace, he was able to rescue Valli. Everyone else was washed away.

The grandfather said, 'You are the only one who can sustain my clan. Had you borne a child by now, I myself would have held Ponnan by his neck and coerced him to join the army.'

'I am unable to understand why wars break out, thatha,' said Valli.

'We need to wage this war to uphold our honour. The tiger flag ought not to be subdued by the bull flag. How can Chola Nadu be subjugated to Thondai Nadu (another name for the Pallava nation)? We need to wage this war to wipe away this ignominy.'

'Whose insignia is the bull?'

'Aren't you aware that the bull is the insignia of the Kanchi Pallava King?'

'His insignia is the lion.'

'No, it is indeed the bull.'

'I saw the flag today, thatha. The flag the emissaries carried bore the lion insignia.'

'Yes, they changed the insignia from a bull to a lion. But will the bull morph into a lion on defeating the pig?' asked the old man.

'I don't understand, thatha! Please explain what happened,' said Valli.

'Fine, I'll explain everything from the beginning!' The grandfather started narrating the Pallava history. 'This happened during the year of your birth. Mahendra Chakravarthi ruled the Pallava Empire from Kanchi. The entire nation used to laud his valorous acts. He had also visited Uraiyur once. A statue was instated at the hill to commemorate his visit. It was then that the King of Vatapi, Pulikesi, mobilized a large army and invaded Thondai Nadu from the north. Mahendra Chakravarthi did not muster courage to wage war with the ocean-like Chalukya army. So, he, along with the Pallava army, remained cloistered within the Kanchi Fort. Pulikesi laid siege to the Kanchi Fort for some time. As his efforts were futile, he progressed further south. He had reached the northern banks of the Kollidam River. Appappa! You ought to have seen the turmoil in Uraiyur then! Our Parthiba Maharaja had ascended the throne just a few months ago. He was preparing assiduously to wage war with Pulikesi.

'By then, Pulikesi's kingdom itself was facing danger, due to which he retreated without crossing Kollidam. While returning to his kingdom, that tyrant and his demonic forces wrought unspeakable atrocities. They plundered and set villages ablaze. These incidents cast a shadow on Mahendra Chakravarthi's fame. People started commenting on how the Chalukya's pig insignia had frightened the Pallava's bull insignia. Mahendra Chakravarthi did not live long after this humiliation; he was succeeded by Narasimha Varma Chakravarthi. Ever since he ascended the throne, he worked relentlessly to avenge the humiliation at Pulikesi's hands and to erase the slur cast on the Pallava dynasty. Finally, six years ago he mobilized a large army and marched northwards.

'He returned to Kanchi only after slaying Pulikesi at the battlefield, setting Vatapi ablaze, and reducing the city to ashes. Narasimha Chakravarthi replaced the bull with the lion as the Pallava insignia to commemorate this momentous victory. It is barely a month since he returned, Valli. He has already...'

Valli, who was listening till then with rapt attention, asked, 'Why does our Maharaja have to wage war with such a powerful Chakravarthi, thatha? Why doesn't he maintain a cordial relationship?'

The old man started responding, 'You, ignorant girl...' when the sound of horse hooves was heard. The horse came to a halt outside their house. A man with an authoritative tone called out, 'Veerabhadra Achari!'

Immediately the old man said, 'It is the vile Marappa Bhupathi! Valli, you go to the kitchen; he must not see you. I will call you once he leaves.'

5. Marappa Bhupathi

The visitor was a sturdy youth, around twenty-five years of age. His attire and jewellery betrayed his senior position in the government. His physiognomy revealed his predilection for earthly pleasures and miracles. The old man welcomed the visitor saying, 'Please come in, Senathipathi (general),' and led him inside.

'Henceforth, do not address me so! I am not the Senathipathi! Neither am I Marappa Bhupathi, nor am I the son of my father!' snapped Marappan as he entered the house. He occupied the seat at the muttram that was previously occupied by the old man.

'The Yuvaraja (crown prince) appears to be very angry!'

'Who is the Yuvaraja? Me? Don't you know that the useless boy is the Ilavarasar! Long live Ilavarasar Vikrama Singar! Jaya Vijayi Bhava, Victory be ours!' exclaimed Marappa Bhupathi sarcastically and laughed aloud. Little later, he said, 'Never mind, Achari! Tell me what your cowries foretell!' Veerabhadra Achari was not only a blacksmith but was also an astrologer of repute, who could predict future, using cowries for calculations.

The old man responded, 'Yuvaraja! Why do you harbour such illusions…?'

Marappan interjected, 'Don't beat around the bush! Do you genuinely foresee occurrences or are you unnecessarily making me run around?'

'I do, Yuvaraja! Please ask me what you want to know. I'll tell you.'

'The key event at the current juncture is war. What will be the outcome of this war? Your astrology is of no use if you're unable to foretell this. I will fling your cowries into the Kaveri!' said Marappan.

'Please do so, Yuvaraja. That will be very helpful to me. My knowledge of astrology was of no use to me in my personal life. I lost my entire family in one day. There is only a young girl alive now to sustain my clan.'

Marappa Bhupathi's face appeared grotesque when he asked, 'How is Valli doing, Achari?'

'She is alright,' replied the old man.

'What will Valli do when Ponnan heads to the war front?'

'That is not an issue, Yuvaraja! God will protect Valli; so, will this old man!' stated Veerabhadra Achari firmly.

'True, why should she worry when you are around? Never mind; we digressed. What will be the outcome of this war? Do tell me what you deduced from your calculations using your cowries. If you were unable to deduce anything, you ought to cease practising astrology!'

'I quit practising astrology long ago, Yuvaraja. I resumed making predictions only because of your insistence.'

'What did you foresee on resuming your practice?'

'The planetary positions point to a horrific outcome. One army will be annihilated. Not even one person will survive. But I'm unaware which of the two armies will be devastated.'

'I know which army will be wiped out. Neither you nor your cowries are required to predict this. It is the Chola army that will be obliterated. The credit for that destruction will go to your Parthiba Chola Maharaja!'

'Yuvaraja! Is it becoming of you to speak thus? We may have differences of opinion amongst us; but in the face of our foes...'

'Is the Pallava Chakravarthi our foe? No, never! The greatest enemy to Chola Nadu today is Parthiban. He is incapable of wielding a sword or a spear. Such a peerless warrior is embarking on an expedition against the Pallava army! The Pallava army is no laughing matter. It is possible to count the grains of sand on a seashore; but not the number of soldiers in the Pallava army.

'The palm-sized Chola Nadu is no match for the expansive Pallava Empire, which spans from the Kaveri to the Godavari river. Can Narasimha Chakravarthi be taken lightly? He marched a hundred *yojanai*[1] northwards, vanquished the demonic Pulikesi, set Vatapi to fire and returned victoriously. How can we confront him? We Cholas are like mosquitoes in the presence of elephants!'

'Yuvaraja! Why do you tell me all this? Why don't you speak to our Maharaja?'

'Do you think I did not tell this to the Maharaja, old man? I was stripped of my Senathipathi post for being outspoken. The Maharaja has assumed the role of the Senathipathi too. Apparently, he is going to personally lead the army to the battlefield! Let him do so. I do not regret losing my post as the Senathipathi of the illustrious Chola army!'

'Yuvaraja! Won't you go to the battlefield?'

'Who me? I will go if I'm asked to do so. If not, I will refrain. Repeat what you had just said about the outcome of the war, old man.'

'Yes, Yuvaraja. All the warriors of one army will be killed. Not even one person will return alive.'

'They won't return alive! Then, will their lifeless bodies return? Ha ha!' laughed Marappa Bhupathi. He then said, 'Yes! If I die in the battlefield, I will return as a ghost, possess Valli and torment her!' and laughed horrendously.

Valli, who was listening to this conversation from the kitchen,

snapped her knuckles and muttered, 'I will strangle you to death!' The elderly woman, who was slightly hard of hearing, asked, 'What are you saying, Valli?' Valli closed her grandmother's mouth with her palm and hissed, 'Keep quiet!'

Marappa Bhupathi asked, 'Who is speaking inside?'

'The old ghost who has possessed me must be speaking to herself!' said the old man referring to his wife.

'Alright, I'm getting delayed. I must leave. Are your predictions about me true? If it turns out that you lied...'

'How do I benefit by lying to you, Yuvaraja?'

Marappa Bhupathi stood up and looked around. He laughed aloud when his glance fell on the swords, spears and shields stacked at the muttram.

'Aha! So, you are working diligently. Look at the knives, swords, spears and shields! Is your Parthiba Maharaja going to vanquish the Pallava Chakravarthi using these blunt knives and scythes meant to cut grass? That's so funny.' Marappa Bhupathi laughed loudly as he kicked the swords stacked on one side of the muttram. He then stepped out of the house.

The old man's eyes glowered like fire sparks from the forge.

6. Bugle Calls

Valli came to the muttram of the house after the trot sound receded. She grabbed a sword from the stack Marappan had kicked and exclaimed angrily, 'Thatha! Of what use are these swords and shields that you have forged? You spared the man who spoke so disparagingly of our Maharaja!'

'Why are you so enraged, Valli? Didn't our erstwhile Senathipathi echo the same sentiments as yours when he advised the Maharaja to refrain from war?' asked the elderly man.

'Oh no! I did not imply that we ought to eschew wars. I questioned the purpose of wars out of my ignorance!' responded a teary-eyed Valli.

'True, Valli. That sinner visited our house just as I was about to explain the cause of war. Didn't I mention that the Vatapi Chakravarthi, Pulikesi, wrought several atrocities when he invaded Dakshina Bharata (southern India)? Narasimha Chakravarthi, to avenge this ignominy, was engaged in intense battle preparations for long. He finally invaded Vatapi six years ago. He had then sent a missive asking Parthiba Maharaja to join him.

'Parthiba Maharaja assured his participation and said that,

in exchange, Uraiyur would cease paying tribute and that the tiger flag must be treated on a par with the Pallava flag. Why Narasimha Chakravarthi did not acknowledge or send a reply is not known. Nevertheless, he embarked on his expedition! From that day, Parthiba Maharaja ceased paying tribute to Kanchi. That is the reason for this war, Valli. You tell me. Should Parthiba Maharaja retract his stance and surrender to the Chakravarthi? Should we lower the tiger flag hoisted on the Chirapalli Mountain and hoist the Pallava's bull flag again? Should the denizens of Chola Desam continue to live enduring this disgrace?'

'I am unaware of the logic, thatha. Our Maharaja is a just man…'

'Yes! Our Maharaja was indeed upright. That's why he gave so much latitude to and showered immense affection on this low-born Marappa Bhupathi!'

'What are you saying, thatha?

'Marappa Bhupathi is our Maharaja's half-brother. Our older Maharaja, blinded by lust when he was over fifty years old, married an obscure gold-digger. The denizens disliked this marriage. Marappan was born to the gold-digger. Apparently, the elder Maharaja had, on his death-bed, said that Marappan ought to succeed Parthiba Maharaja in the event of the latter not bearing a son. Marappan was the Yuvaraja till Vikrama Ilavarasar was born. Parthiba Maharaja was very fond of him, accorded him respect, and appointed him Senathipathi. Characteristic of his lineage, he turns out to be an ungrateful wretch.'

'Why do you associate with him, thatha? Why do you foretell his future?'

'It was an association formed because of you, Valli,' said the elderly man.

A surprised Valli exclaimed, 'Because of me? That's impossible!'

'It is indeed because of you. I will now relate the story I had not divulged to you so far, Valli. These are treacherous times. One does not know what will befall our Maharaja and our kingdom. But I'm confident that Marappa Bhupathi will not head to the battlefront. You must be very wary of him.'

'Why are you scaring me, thatha? Why should I be scared of this dark-faced man?' asked Valli.

'Heed me, my child. A few years ago, Marappa Bhupathi had asked me for your hand in marriage.'

'May thunder strike his head!' remarked Valli.

'Well, the thunder struck my head and not his! Unfavourable planetary positions foretold the occurrence of a calamity in our family. I came to know that Marappa Bhupathi intended to come to our house with his men and abduct you. I thought there will be bloodshed if you and your brothers were in our house then. So, I sent you all away to attend a wedding being solemnized on the opposite bank of the river. Yaman struck mid-river as a cyclone. All your elder brothers died. God spared you for me...' After speaking thus, the elder man heaved a deep sigh. He looked skywards, lost in thought.

'Why did you hide this from me all these days, thatha? Was he the cause of my elder brothers' death? What happened afterwards?' enquired Valli.

'After all of you had sailed away in the boat, Marappan came with his men as I had expected. He created a commotion on realizing that you were not at home. I resorted to astrology to placate him. I said, "You are destined to become a powerful Chakravarthi's son-in-law. Rid yourself of such base desires." Since then he started building castles in the air. He annoys me frequently by asking me to foretell his future.'

'I now understand the import of his reference to me, thatha! What will become of me if the boatman heads to war?' said Valli as she grasped her grandfather's hands tightly. She was trembling.

The elderly man said, 'You crazy girl! Why are you trembling thus? Ponnan will not enlist for war. The Maharaja will not take him along. The Maharaja is aware of the tragedy that befell our family. He also knows that you are the sole person alive to sustain our clan. This is why he forbade Ponnan from enlisting in the army. He will definitely not take Ponnan along!'

The sound of the bugle was heard at the entrance. The herald announced, 'Vetri Vel! Veera Vel! War is imminent! War is imminent! We need to fight a war to uphold Chola Desam's honour! All able-bodied males may enlist in the army. Everyone except the lame, the blind, the maimed, and the sole progeny may join! Vetri Vel! Veera Vel!'

The sound of the bugle pulsating across the city followed the announcement. Valli and her grandfather headed to the entrance of the house. An elephant bearing the herald and the man who blew the bugle surrounded by a few soldiers passed their house.

The grandfather and granddaughter watched this procession without batting an eyelid till it reached the end of their street. When the procession disappeared from their sight, the elderly man heaved a sigh and said, 'God and Ponnan will protect you, Valli. There is no one but me in my family to fight in this war and embrace a heroic death.'

In the southern horizon, a star suddenly moved. It twinkled brightly for a moment, moved swiftly and mysteriously disappeared the next instant. Valli shivered as she witnessed the occurrence. Ponnan, who also happened to observe this phenomenon, trembled. He was then walking down the royal thoroughfare of Uraiyur. It was four days before Pournami, the full moon. The waxing moon in all its radiance was gliding across the firmament like a royal swan. Bathed in the moonlight, Uraiyur's mansions appeared to be part of a dream world.

The fortunes of not just humans, but also cities, wax and wane. Today, Tiruchirappalli is a big city while Uraiyur is a suburb. In the ancient times, the situation was reverse. While Uraiyur was the Chola capital, Tiruchirappalli was a suburb.

Ponnan wanted to reach the palace entrance before the Maharaja had climbed down the Chirapalli Mountain. He was able to deduce what the Maharaja, after offering his prayers at the temple located on the mountain peak, had shown the Ilavarasan on his way down. That was the site of the ignominy of the Chola dynasty – a painting depicting Parthiba Maharaja's father placing his sword and spear in front of Mahendra Varma Chakravarthi, supplicating before him, and offering precious gems and jewellery as tribute.

The very recollection of that painting caused Ponnan's blood to boil. He often pondered, 'For how long will Chola Nadu tolerate this disgrace? Shouldn't we wipe away this ignominy with the blood shed by the Pallavas on the battlefield? How can I be at home when such an opportunity has arisen?' Ponnan walked swiftly thinking thus.

7. Arulmozhi Devi

Just as Ponnan and Valli were entering the Uraiyur Fort, Rani Arulmozhi Devi was walking into the palace garden. The palace attendants had informed her of the Maharaja's response to the Pallava emissaries. The Rani decided to spend time at the palace garden till the King arrived. She headed to a corner of the garden where champa flowers abounded and sat on the marble bench there. She could see the sun setting in the western horizon through the trees. The sky was glowing like molten gold. Even as she was watching, the golden hue of the sky became progressively dull, the sun dipped. Soon the sky assumed a blood red hue. Reminded of bloodshed in a battlefield, Arulmozhi shivered as she closed her eyes.

When she opened her eyes again, the silver rays of the moon were peeking through the branches of the trees. Past memories assailed the Rani then. She had come to this palace twelve years ago after her marriage with Parthiba Maharaja. On several such moonlit nights, she and Parthiban had strolled arm in arm in the palace garden and had sat on this very marble bench, losing track of time. Sometimes, Parthiban used to play the flute for her. Engrossed in his music, Arulmozhi would think that Lord

Krishna had assumed the form of Parthiban to wed her and would become ecstatic! Their joyous life reached its acme when Vikraman was born. Arulmozhi recollected the instances of her cuddling Vikraman, seated on the very same marble bench.

Even through these blissful days, an intense, indescribable sorrow gnawed at Parthiban's heart. Arulmozhi became aware of his very private sorrow much later. She partook of his sorrow since then and despaired thinking that she was the root cause for that. Arulmozhi was the daughter of a Chera vassal king. She was renowned as the most beautiful princess in the southern country. After her marriage with Parthiban was arranged, the emissaries of Kanchi Mahendra Chakravarthi had met the Chera King. The Chakravarthi sought Arulmozhi's hand in marriage for the Crown Prince Narasimhan. Arulmozhi's family found this proposal acceptable but she did not consent to this. Instead, she definitively informed them that she considered Parthiba Cholan her husband and hence, would not marry any other man.

Mahendra Chakravarthi, very graciously, did not pursue the proposal. He got Ilavarasar Narasimha Varmar married to the Pandya princess. Parthiban came to know of this incident only after his marriage with Arulmozhi. He sometimes rued, 'You ought to have been a Chakravarthini of an empire, seated on the Kanchi throne. On the contrary, you have become the Rani of this palm-sized Chola kingdom!' Arulmozhi initially thought that he was joking. She realized with the passage of time that this thought tormented her husband. Her efforts to erase this sorrow were futile. Parthiban's sorrow seemed to intensify after Vikraman's birth. He occasionally lamented, 'Your son could have been the Chakravarthi of an expansive empire. It is because of me that he is destined to be a tribute-paying vassal!' Once, he remarked, 'Arulmozhi! I will not be able to crown your son as the Chakravarthi of an empire. But I will ensure that he is renowned as the son of a valorous father!'

The time was ripe for him to fulfil his vow. Arulmozhi was

immersed in sorrow, torn between her husband's demand of her garnering courage to raise Vikraman as a valiant son and her desire of sacrificing her life along with his like the heroic women of yore in case of any misfortune on the battlefield. Alas! How could she bear to live in his absence? Such thoughts ripped Arulmozhi's heart apart and she felt an intense urge to cry. She started weeping. She turned around when she heard a

harsh voice ask, 'Arulmozhi! I thought you were a courageous wife. Are you so cowardly?' Parthiba Maharaja was standing behind her. Her tears immediately dried up. 'Come! Let's go to the palace. This is not the time to weep and be consoled,' stated the Maharaja. They both returned to the palace in silence with their arms locked. When Parthiban and Arulmozhi entered the palace's prayer chamber, the priest was about to perform the deeparadhanai – to rotate the lamp in the vertical clockwise direction in front of the deity.

At the centre of the prayer chamber was a Shiva lingam, with an exquisite statue of Goddess Parvathi to the right. Statues of Vinayaka and Murugan flanked that of Goddess Parvathi. Statues of Mahavishnu and his consorts, Sridevi and Bhudevi, were in another part of the chamber. All the deities were adorned by champa, paneer and parijatham flowers. Ilavarasar Vikraman was at the sanctum with his hands folded, observing the prayers. After the prayers were over, the priest distributed the prasadam to those present and left the chamber. Vikraman asked the Maharaja, 'Appa, didn't you say that you will take me to the Chitra Mandapam (painting gallery)?' 'Vikrama, you go ahead. I'll come in a short while!' said the Maharaja.

As soon as Vikraman left the chamber, the Maharaja pointed to a rectangular wooden casket at the base of the Mahavishnu idol and said to his wife, 'Devi, you have enquired about the contents of that casket several times. I promised to tell you at the opportune moment. Now is the apt time. This casket contains the hoary treasures of the Chola dynasty. Let me show you.' The Maharaja opened the casket as he spoke to reveal a glittering sabre and a bunch of palm manuscripts. The sabre's handle was made of gold and embedded with gems. The blade was well-oiled and sharp. The gleaming sabre and its handle were in stark contrast to the ancient manuscripts that had turned black.

Parthiban said, 'Devi, this sword has been handed down from the times of our renowned ancestors, Karikal Vallavan and

Nedumudi Killi. Thirukkural, the work of Tamizhagam's divine scholar (Thiruvalluvar), is inscribed in these palm manuscripts. This sabre and the manuscripts are the cherished treasures of the Chola dynasty. You have to safeguard them and hand it all over to Vikraman when he comes of age.

'My father wielded this primal sword, but I refrained from doing so. I, a mere vassal, do not wish to carry the sword once used by Karikal Vallavan and Nedumudi Killi. You must instruct Vikraman that only when he becomes an independent king of at least a small territory, may he wield this sword and rule the kingdom in accordance with the precepts of the divine Thirukkural. I entrust you with this responsibility. You must give me your word at this sanctum, Arulmozhi. You must bring up Vikraman to be a valorous son.' Arulmozhi replied in a choked voice, her eyes brimming with tears, 'As you command, Maharaja!' Parthiban embraced his wife and blessed her, 'May the Almighty bestow upon you the courage to execute this mission!' He wiped away her tears with his angavastram (upper cloth).

8. Chitra Mandapam

The Chitra Mandapam located on Uraiyur's southern royal thoroughfare was renowned across Dakshina Bharata. People often remarked that even Mahendra Chakravarthi's fabled Chitra Mandapam at Kanchi did not measure up to the one at Uraiyur. Ponnan arrived at the Chitra Mandapam just when Parthiba Maharaja and Ilavarasar Vikraman reached the gallery on white steeds. Ponnan was worried that he would not be able to meet the Maharaja at that untimely hour. He felt tongue-tied on running into the Maharaja unexpectedly. He stuttered as he called out, 'Maharaja…' The Maharaja and Ilavarasar turned around on hearing his muffled voice.

'Ponna! Why are you here?' enquired the king. As he got down from the horse, he deduced the reason for Ponnan's visit from his silence. The crown prince, Vikraman, too adroitly jumped off the horse. The Maharaja gestured in the direction of the usher holding the torch and said, 'Take the torch and follow us, Ponna.' Ponnan did not comprehend the reasons for the Maharaja coming to the Chitra Mandapam at this hour but he was ecstatic that the Maharaja had not sent him back and hastened to carry the torch.

The Maharaja and Ilavarasar walked into the gallery,

followed by Ponnan who held the torch aloft. First time visitors to the gallery were bound to wonder, 'Are two eyes adequate to appreciate the beauty of these paintings? Even two thousand would not suffice!' Numerous colourful paintings adorned not just the walls of that expansive gallery but also the sculpted pillars and the ceiling of the building's spire. Scenes from mythology such as Indra obtaining his thunderbolt from Sage Dadhichi, his routing Virudasuran, his return to his abode, Indra Loka, the Gods and Goddesses welcoming him back and celestial nymphs dancing were majestically portrayed.

A splendid painting of the devas and asuras churning the ocean using Mount Mandara as the churning rod and the snake, Vasuki, as the rope covered a wall. Adjacent to this were a series of paintings depicting the incidents that led to the birth of Kumara Peruman or Lord Muruga, starting from Kama Deva stringing together an arrow of flowers to distract Paramasivan (Lord Shiva) from his penance. These paintings were life-like and Ponnan felt they were all alive.

The paintings appeared divine and the realistic postures and facial expressions rendered them striking, despite not conforming to Samudrika Lakshanam – the Vedic tradition that focuses on the study of the face, aura and body. The Chitra Mandapam was open to denizens for three weeks every month. Ponnan had visited the gallery on multiple occasions; each time the paintings held him spellbound. But this time he was unable to tarry and view the paintings leisurely as the Maharaja and Ilavarasar strode ahead of him briskly. After crossing two to three sections of the Chitra Mandapam, the Maharaja came to a halt in front of a locked door. During one of his earlier visits to the gallery, Ponnan had stood at this very spot and had pondered what lay beyond the locked door. The guards had informed him that they had strict instructions from the Maharaja not to unlock the doors for anyone else.

Ponnan's eagerness knew no bounds when the Maharaja

inserted a key into the lock and started unfastening it. His heartbeat accelerated and he was tremendously excited at finally being able to behold what lay behind those doors. The Maharaja commanded, 'Ponna! You step in first! Hold the torch aloft and do not take it too close to the walls! The smoke from the torch will ruin the paintings.'

Ponnan entered the chamber holding the torch aloft. Paintings adorned the walls of this chamber too. But he was unable to comprehend the import of these paintings. The Maharaja followed Ponnan and led Vikraman by his hand into the dark chamber. 'My child! You have asked me several times what lay inside this locked chamber. I had intended to show you these paintings when you were slightly older. But it has become imperative for me to show them now. I had intentionally kept this chamber locked, Vikrama. No one but me has ever entered this chamber or has viewed the paintings. Hold the torch high, Ponna!' said the Maharaja. Ponnan, who was attentively listening to the Maharaja, immediately held the torch up.

'Look at the first painting, my child! What do you deduce from it?' asked the Maharaja.

'An army is headed to the battlefield! Aha! What a massive army! I see several elephants, chariots, horses, foot soldiers,' stated a bewildered Vikraman. He then turned to his father and seemed to hesitate.

'What is it Vikrama? Ask me,' said the Maharaja.

'It's nothing, appa! I was wondering about the artist who painted these portraits.'

'Your presumption is correct, my child. It is, indeed, I who painted these portraits. These paintings are an outpouring of all that I have dreamt in my sleeping and waking hours during the last twelve years. Observe closely, my child! Do you recognize the kingdom this army owes allegiance to?'

'Aha! Isn't that the tiger flag? This is the Chola army. But appa...' said Vikraman as he hesitated again.

'Go ahead Vikrama'

'Only a mahout is seated on the majestic royal mount. The ambari (howdah) on the back of the elephant is empty, appa!'

'That's a good observation. I intentionally left the ambari empty. The likeness of that Chola warrior, who one day will mobilize a gargantuan army and embark on a digvijayam, a victory march, across the country with his army to exercise his suzerainty, ought to be painted in the ambari, my child! The Chola kingdom is, today, a vassal state that can fit on the palm of a hand. The Pallavas in the north, Pandyas in the south and the Cheras in the west are constricting the Chola kingdom. But our country has not always been in this situation.

'Our dynasty reigned supreme during times of yore, Vikrama. Karikal Vallavan and Nedumudi Killi were your ancestors. The other kings trembled on hearing the name "Chola", courtesy their valorous deeds. The Pallavas were then inconspicuous rulers. The Chola territory covered a vast area to the north. Those days the Pandyas and the Cheras paid tribute to the Chola kings. The kings of distant nations that lay across the ocean used to send gifts and emissaries to the Chola Chakravarthis.

'Kaveri Pattinam, like Kadal Mallai of today, used to be a prominent port those days. Huge merchant ships used to ply from Kaveri Pattinam to far-flung nations and fill the coffers of Chola kings with gold and gems. My child! I fervently wish that the Chola kingdom reclaims the eminence and glory of the bygone era. This is what I dream of, day and night!'

The Maharaja, like one possessed, pointed out to the pictures in the chamber and explained their meaning. The next portrait depicted the Chola army crossing a wide river. Then those forces scaled a tall mountain. This was followed by the portrayal of a fierce war. The vanquished surrendered to the victorious Chola forces and paid tribute. The Chola army, after crossing many rivers, scaling several mountains and annihilating numerous kings, reaches the Himalayas. The Cholas hoist their tiger flag at the zenith of the Himalayas, the king of mountains. Jubilant scenes of the Chola army returning to the capital and being given a traditional welcome by the denizens followed.

Exquisite depictions of imposing ships sporting the tiger flag sailing from the port were found in another part of the chamber. These ships reach distant shores. The kings of those nations, accompanied by their retinues, receive the Chola emissaries. The tiger flag majestically flutters in those island countries. Large temples, whose towers graze the skies, are built in all those nations where the tiger flag is hoisted.

Wondrous paintings such as these filled that chamber.

9. Vikraman's Vow

After viewing all the paintings, Vikraman hesitantly called out, 'Appa...' The Maharaja looked at him affectionately and responded, 'Ask me whatever you want to, my boy. Don't hold back your thoughts; it is unlikely that we will get one more opportunity to talk things over.'

'I just want to tell you that all these paintings are exquisite, appa. When did you learn to paint so well? The paintings in our Chitra Mandapam outside are not as poignant as these,' Vikraman blurted out.

The Maharaja embraced his son and said, 'My dear son! I am happy that you have seen my works of art and are impressed. I don't require anyone else's appreciation. I feel gratified that my artistic abilities are recognized; I don't yearn for anything more.'

'But, appa, what is the necessity to keep your talent under wraps? Why aren't you proud of such fine paintings? Aha! These paintings are so realistic, and soul stirring. Who else can paint like you? Why should you lock up these paintings in a dark chamber? Everyone must be allowed to view and appreciate these paintings,' said an agitated Vikraman.

Parthiba Maharaja responded, 'Listen to me, Vikrama.

The world will appreciate and laud the talents of only those in power. Several artists congregated and conferred the title of "Chithrakara Puli" or the "Tiger among artists" upon Kanchi Mahendra Chakravarthi.

'Mahendra Varman's paintings are actually mediocre; yet everyone praises his paintings profusely. His son, Narasimha Chakravarthi has been conferred several titles. A lion amongst painters! His music has been compared to that of Narada and his sculptures with those of Viswakarma. Why do you think the world showers such praise on him? It is because he commands a gargantuan army. My child, God does not discriminate between the indigent and affluent. A Chakravarthi and a cobbler are on a par in the Almighty's presence. But most "representatives of God" believe that He is only on the side of the powerful.

'Mahendran practised Jainism for long. He subjected sivanadiyars, the Saivite ascetics, to untold misery. He suddenly attained enlightenment and then started masquerading as a devotee of Lord Shiva. Vikrama, both Mahendran and his son Narasimhan are extremely talented actors. They assume several disguises and betray those who have reposed their trust in them. The world is deceived by their pretence of being devoted to Lord Shiva.

'It is the Chola dynasty that has helped Saivism and Vaishnavism to flourish from days of yore. The Cholas were devoted to their dynastic deities – Chirapalli Peruman (Lord Shiva) and Sriranganathar (Lord Vishnu). But to whose court do the sivanadiyars and the Vaishnava elders flock? At the court of the sovereign of the three worlds, Kanchi Narasimha Chakravarthi.

'Do you know why I am averse to showcasing my paintings to the outside world? As long as Chola Nadu is a vassal state, people will mock me saying, "Now Parthiban also has started to paint..." Vikrama, you ought not to forget one more thing...' The Maharaja paused.

'What is it, appa?' asked Vikraman.

'These paintings are not mere expressions of my artistic ability, my son! These are the reflections of my deep desires, dreams and hopes. Won't those who see these pictures now taunt me as one who desires for things beyond his stature and as one who builds castles in the air? This is the reason for my hiding these paintings in a dark chamber. It is only when the scenes depicted in these paintings become a reality should light be allowed to enter this chamber. It is only then that all denizens may view these paintings. I know I am not destined to witness these events during my lifetime, Vikrama. I fervently hope that

you fulfil my aspirations. Do you now understand why I forbade you from accompanying me to the battlefield?'

'I understand, appa.'

'You must live to transform my dreams into reality. You must dedicate your life to the betterment of Chola Nadu. The aspiration of Chola dynasty regaining its glory must consume

your thoughts, day and night. The tiger flag of the Cholas must flutter proudly, grazing the skies, and must be subservient to none. This must be the aim of your life.

'I am leaving for the battlefield the day after tomorrow. There is no certainty that I will return. The Puranas state that the souls of those who perish in the battlefield go to heaven. But my soul will not go to heaven; it will return to Chola Nadu. The lush green Chola Nadu through which the Kaveri flows is my heaven. My soul will wander around the paddy fields, temples, ponds, riverbanks and coconut groves of Chola Nadu. I must then hear people say, "Parthiban's son brought glory to the Chola dynasty." Nothing can make me happier than this. This is your filial duty. Will you accomplish this, Vikrama?'

Ilavarasan Vikraman uttered in a choked voice, 'I will, appa! I promise I will!' The tears that brimmed his eyes and subsequently overflowed glistened like pearls. Ponnan, who was a witness, also shed copious tears.

The Maharaja then turned to him and asked, 'Did you listen to our conversation, Ponna? I want at least a few who are loyal and genuinely affectionate towards the Ilavarasar to be with him. I will be far more content if you stay back with the Ilavarasan rather than if you accompany me to the battlefield. Will you do so?'

Ponnan choked as he replied, 'I will, Maharaja!'

10. The Army Marches Forth

Uraiyur appeared to be animated as it prepared itself for the unfolding event. People swore that the city was not so beautifully decorated even for Parthiba Maharaja's coronation or for Mahendra Chakravarthi's state visit. The denizens residing along the army's proposed route had decorated their houses with festoons of coconut leaves and mango leaves. The portico walls lining the street had received a fresh coat of quick lime, drying into brilliant whiteness, with columns of red for relief. The women folk had risen much before dawn to sweep their forecourts, sprinkle water and create exquisite kolams. The forecourts were also lit by brass oil lamps adding to the festive look. Having decorated their houses, the women proceeded to deck themselves up, hoping to catch glimpses of the proceedings from the porticos or from the balustrades on the upper floors.

Rumblings of the war drums could be heard right from the pre-dawn hours. The neighing of the horses, the soldiers calling out to one another, the clanking of weapons and the rousing war cries rented the air. Mothers blessing their warrior sons and lovers bidding farewell could be heard along with the chirping of birds that woke up before their usual time.

Soldiers started assembling in front of the palace well before daybreak. The army chiefs ensured the infantry, cavalry and elephant forces were placed in formation. The tiger flag of the Cholas was held aloft ahead of the formations. It fluttered majestically against the clear sky. Conch blowers, trumpet players and kettle-drum beaters were placed at strategic points along the formations. So were the sturdy bulls on whom the huge war drums were mounted. The beautifully caparisoned royal elephant was brought to the palace entrance. As the forces were being organized, soldiers often cheered, 'Vetri Vel! Veera Vel!' Soon there was a flurry of activity at the palace entrance.

People whispered amongst themselves, 'The Maharaja is coming! The Maharaja is coming!' As if it were a prediction, immediately two heralds walked out of the palace announcing, 'Here comes the Chola Mandalathipathi Parthiba Maharaja!' The elders and brahmins who had congregated on the street-side cheered, 'Jaya Vijayi Bhava!' The Maharaja walked out of the palace clothed in yellow robes with an armour fastened to his chest and a sword to his waist. The Rani and Ilavarasar followed him.

At the palace entrance, the Maharani placed a garland made of aatthi flowers on the Maharaja's shoulders. A lady-in-waiting, then handed over a plate filled with turmeric water that held an illuminated lamp placed in the centre. The Maharani, moved the plate in front of her husband thrice in a vertical circular motion to ward off evil spirits. She then moistened the tip of her index finger with the turmeric water and placed a tilakam on the Maharaja's forehead. The sound of people cheering 'Jaya Vijayi Bhava!' and 'Vetri Vel! Veera Vel!' reached a crescendo. The din made by conches, trumpets and drums increased a few more decibels. The Maharaja scanned the multitude flocking the street. An usher approached. Prostrating before the king, he stood in a supplicating posture.

'What news do you carry?' asked the Maharaja.

'Marappa Bhupathi fell off his horse as he was leaving the palace this morning and he fainted. We took him back to the palace and he has not yet regained consciousness.' The Maharaja smiled imperceptibly and told the usher, 'Good! You may return to the palace. Inform Bhupathi when he regains consciousness that I had asked him to take good care of his health.' Only a few people who were in the Maharaja's vicinity heard this conversation. Nevertheless, the news of Marappa Bhupathi facing a mishap and not heading to the warfront spread like wildfire.

Then, the Maharaja lifted Vikraman up, hugged him and kissed his forehead. Lifting his chin up, he said endearingly, 'My boy! Did you understand everything that I told you? You must fulfil all that I expect of you.'

Vikraman replied, 'I remember, appa! I will never ever forget.'

The Maharaja, in a symbolic gesture, then placed his son's hands in Arulmozhi's and said, 'You must be courageous, Devi. I am handing over the future of the Chola dynasty to you. You, as my valorous wife, must fulfil my request. Now bid me a joyous farewell as I set forth on my mission.'

Tears welled in Arulmozhi's eyes and her voice choked as she said, 'May the Almighty be with you at every step of yours. May you return to us victorious!'

The Maharaja then got on to the royal elephant. Amidst the thunderous din of conches, trumpets and drums, the Chola army started marching.

❖

The banks of the Vennaru river presented a gory sight on that full moon night of Puraṭṭāsi.

The luminous moon floating across the firmament disappeared behind the silver clouds as though she was unable to behold the bloody river. The blood shed by those decimated in the fierce battle fought during the day mingled with the waters of the river, which appeared to have turned into a river of blood.

The full moon too did not shine as bright on the river that

was now red in colour. The aftermath of the ferocious clash extended up to the western bank of the river. The corpses of the innumerable warriors who had laid down their lives lay scattered across the fateful battlefield. Heaps of cadavers, slain horses and corpses with their limbs dismembered dotted the landscape. Black figures resembling hillocks were visible at a distance. One could guess that they were actually the dying or already dead elephants.

Thousands of rapacious vultures were circling the battlefield. Their widespread wings cast shadows, accentuating the eeriness of the war zone. The gentle cadence of the river was often interrupted by the harsh noises made by the birds of prey. A man was walking slowly across that ghastly battlefield on which the moonlight, dimmed by clouds, cast a pale glow and the carrion seeking birds cast their shadow.

The man carefully scanned his surroundings as he walked

ahead. He was a sivanadiyar whose forehead was smeared with *thiruneeru*[3] (Vibhuti, the sacred ash) and who sported matted locks. His long beard had just started greying. The sivanadiyar wore a rudraksha malai, a neckpiece made of the holy rudraksha seeds. His body was covered in ochre robes and he wore a vest made of tiger skin. He carried a kamandalam, a spouted vessel. His uncommonly luminous visage, enlightenment-filled wide eyes, his statuesque appearance and majestic gait made one wonder if he was indeed a sivanadiyar or an incarnation of Lord Shiva himself. What was this elderly man doing in this gory battlefield? Whom or what was he searching for?

Just then a large form resembling a granite hillock appeared

to move towards the sivanadiyar. This was the Chola King's elephant. The sivanadiyar stopped in his tracks on seeing the elephant. The animal, which had sustained several injuries, was bleeding. It was evident that the Goliath was struggling to walk. Nevertheless, it was careful not to stamp the corpses of the vanquished warriors as it trudged ahead. The way in which the elephant swayed its trunk and caressed the dead bodies indicated that it was in search of something.

Shortly thereafter, the royal elephant came to halt in front of a heap of corpses. It gently lifted and placed aside one corpse after another. The sivanadiyar, on observing this, started walking towards the elephant. He hid himself behind a solitary karuvella tree and observed the elephant. After placing all except the last corpse aside, the elephant stared at the body that lay at the bottom of the heap.

The quadruped gently caressed the body thrice. It then moved away from that spot, lifted its trunk towards the sky and cried out in a tone that conveyed indescribable grief and agony. That shriek echoed across the battlefield, the river and the paddy fields that lay beyond the river, rose up to the skies and faded out. Then the elephant dropped to the ground like a felled tree. Its body shook a couple of times like a mountain trembling during an earthquake. Then there was absolute stillness! Peace prevailed. The sivanadiyar emerged from behind the karuvella tree and walked towards the body the elephant had sought out. He closely observed that body for a few moments and realized that it was Parthiba Maharaja.

The sivanadiyar immediately sat on the ground and felt Parthiban's forehead and chest. He then lifted Parthiban's head and placed it on his lap. He took some water from his kamandalam and sprinkled it on Parthiban's face. Signs of life were evident in the seemingly dead body. Parthiban's eyes fluttered open. Parthiban viewed the sivanadiyar with his half-open eyes and asked in a weak tone, 'Swami . . . who are you?'

'I serve the adiyars of the Lord who dances at Ambalam! I witnessed your awe-inspiring acts of gallantry at today's battle. I came to seek an audience with a great warrior. Parthiba, the world will always remember your blemishless bravery,' said the elderly man.

'What was the outcome of today's war, swami!' asked Parthiban in a feeble voice. Unbridled eagerness was evident in his pale eyes.

'Do you harbour any doubts about the outcome, Parthiba? Listen to the Pallava army's exultations on the other bank!'

Parthiban flinched. 'I did not ask about their victory. Swami! Did anyone in the Chola army...' He hesitated to speak further.

'No, no. Not a single person from the Chola army is alive. Not even one person surrendered. All of them attained martyrdom,' said the sivanadiyar. Parthiban's eyes widened in joy.

'Aha! Good times have dawned for Chola Nadu. You have conveyed such good news, swami. How may I reward you?'

'I don't need a reward, Parthiba. I consider it my beholden duty to be of service to illustrious warriors like yourself. Please tell me if you feel any regret or have any unfulfilled desire; I will fulfil it,' said the sivanadiyar.

'Is that so? How fortunate I am, swami! Chola Nadu's loss of ancient pre-eminence pains me. Chola Nadu must become an independent state, like it was during the times of yore. I dreamt that the tiger flag will be hoisted in far-off nations. This remained a dream during my lifetime. I wish that my dream is fulfilled at least during my son's lifetime. Vikraman ought to be groomed to be a brave warrior. The betterment of Chola Nadu must be his life goal. He must realize that honour and bravery supersede life and luxuries. He must despise a life of subjugation. Swami, will you grant me this boon that I ask of you?' asked Parthiban.

It is difficult to comprehend how his limp body garnered the stamina to speak so animatedly. The sivanadiyar responded in a serene tone, 'I will fulfil your desire if I continue to live.'

'How fortunate I am! Now, I harbour no regret. But, but... who are you, swami? Are you the Shiva Peruman who I have worshipped day and night? Aha! Your visage exudes a divine aura! Has my dynasty's deity, Sri Ranganathar, assumed human form...?'

The sivanadiyar interrupted him saying, 'No, Parthiba, no. Don't speak sacrilegiously. I am a mere mortal like you. Is it essential for you to know of my identity? If so, behold me.' He then lifted the matted locks and took off his beard.

Parthiban took in his luminous countenance without batting an eyelid. He stammered, 'Aha! Is that you?' His eyes widened in indescribable wonder. Moments later his eyes closed. Parthiban's soul was liberated from his mortal body.

Part II

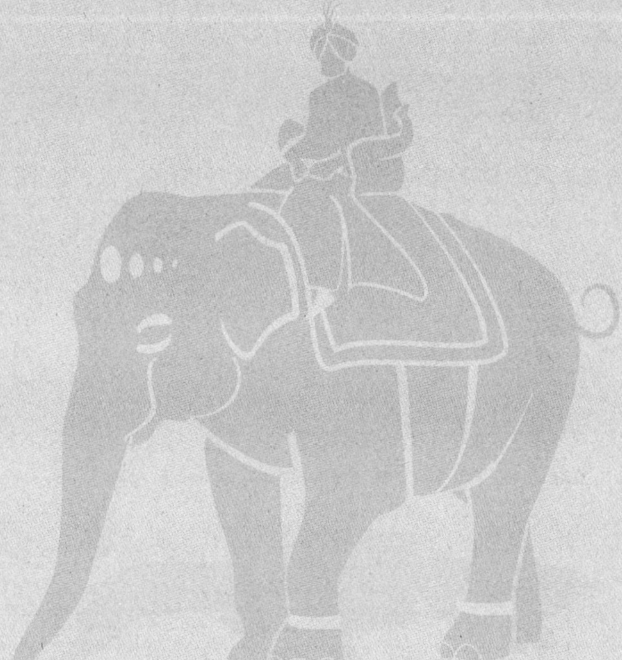

1. Sivanadiyar

It must have been half a *jaamam*[2] before dawn. The moon and the morning star glowed beside each other in the horizon. The stars in the firmament glittered like scattered diamonds. The Saptarishi Mandalam (Ursa Major) adorned the northern sky like a kolam. The uncharacteristically luminous Swati (Arcturus) star illuminated the southern sky. Venus and the moon glowed next to each other and Saturn was resplendent in the south, the other stars in the firmament were still visible and shone brightly. The only sound heard during that scenic dawn was the flow of river Kaveri.

There was no other audible sound but for the rumblings of the Kaveri as it sped along its course. The silence was shattered by the sound of an approaching horse. A majestic high-breed stallion was gently trotting from west to east on the highway abutting the Kaveri. A well-built warrior could be seen sitting on the horse. The ambient light being inadequate, it was impossible to ascertain his identity or demeanour. Having travelled a great distance swiftly, the rider appeared to be resting the horse a bit by letting it trot leisurely. It also seemed that he was not far from his destination.

The road was flanked by the Kaveri on the right and woods with dense foliage on the left. The warrior kept his eyes open to the passing foliage on his left and unerringly turned his horse into it at a precise spot. One could guess that the horse too was not unfamiliar with the locale. As the horse and the rider turned into the bushes, the going got tough. The path was narrow and winding. Both the horse and the rider had to twist and turn to avoid the unruly growth and the suddenly descending branches of trees. Often the rider had to flatten himself on the body of his ride to progress at all.

The path led to a clearing with a modest-sized temple. The massive statues of horses and elephants outside the temple indicated that it was an Ayyanar (a guardian folk deity in Tamil Nadu and Kerala) temple. The statues left there were the votive offerings from devotees. Some of these clay horses and elephants were quite old, while others were definitely new for the paint on them had not yet started fading. A balipeetam (sacrificial altar) and dhwajasthambam (flagstaff) were also seen in the clearing.

By the time the warrior reached the temple, the sky had lightened with the scattered light of the imminent sunrise. He jumped off his horse and set about tasks which would appear very strange to anyone observing him. He and his horse stood amidst the votive offerings and he untied a bundle fastened to the back of the horse. He rid himself of the trappings of a warrior and put on what was in the bundle – a tiger skin, rudraksha malai, a fake beard, and equally fake matted locks. Soon, he transformed himself from a warrior to a sivanadiyar, exuding a divine aura!

He was the same sivanadiyar who had granted a boon to Parthiba Maharaja at the battlefield on the banks of Vennaru. He bundled the soldierly garments and ornaments along with his weapons and hid the bundle behind a broken statue of an elephant.

He fondly caressed the horse, which seemed to have understood the import of that gesture and neighed softly. The sivanadiyar then retraced his steps to the banks of the Kaveri. He began walking westwards.

After walking for about a *nazhigai*[2] (~24 minutes), the sivanadiyar reached the riverside quay – the location at which this chronicle began. He halted outside the dwelling of Ponnan, the boatman, and called out, 'Ponna!' From within the hut, one could hear Ponnan say to his wife, 'The samiyar has come, Valli! The ascetic is here!'. The next instant Ponnan stepped out of the hut and prostrated at the feet of the sivanadiyar. Valli followed Ponnan and bowed. Then the three of them entered the hut. The sivanadiyar sat on a manai (a low wooden stool) that Valli devotedly placed on the floor.

He adjusted the manai and asked, 'Ponna! Are the Maharani and Ilavarasan staying at the Vasantha Maligai?'

'Yes, swami…please tell me that the day when everyone will address our Ilavarasar as Maharaja is not far!'

'Yes, if everything progresses well. Why don't you fetch them here immediately!' remarked the sivanadiyar.

'I will leave right away. Valli, please attend to the needs of the Swamigal,' said Ponnan as he stepped out. Shortly thereafter the sound of a boat rowing across the river was heard.

2. Combative Valli

Once Ponnan left, Valli whole-heartedly attended to the needs of the sivanadiyar. After the ascetic had said his morning prayers, she served him a breakfast of hot kambu adais. As the tasty adais went down, the sivanadiyar became chatty, 'What news of your Maharani?'

'Oh! She puts up a brave face while the Ilavarasar is around and turns teary-eyed whenever he is out of sight. What is in store for the Ilavarasar, swami? If some harm were to befall the Ilavarasar, the queen won't be able to bear it and would give up her life for certain.'

'What do I know, my child? It is all God's will! By the way, what do people say?'

'Everyone supports our Ilavarasar. They are all desirous of putting an end to the Pallava reign. Even a young child is aware of Parthiba Maharaja's heroic death. Swami! Weren't you the one who conveyed that news to us six years ago? The boatman and I must have shared it with at least with a lakh of people,' said Valli.

'I too have narrated that incident to numerous people. But tell me, how is Marappa Bhupathi doing? Does he still seek astrological guidance from your grandfather?' asked the sivanadiyar. Valli replied, 'Aha! He often visits my grandfather for predictions.' She then burst out laughing as she was reminded of some past event. The sivanadiyar asked, 'What is so amusing, Valli? Is it my face?'

'Not at all, swami! Aren't you aware of Marappa Bhupathi's desire? He wishes to marry the daughter of the Kanchi Chakravarthi! Only the *muhurtham*[2], the auspicious time, for the wedding needs to be decided!' replied Valli.

The sivanadiyar's face darkened just for an instant. He brought himself to smile and enquired, 'Why are you so amused by that?'

'Will the Chakravarthi's daughter deign to marry Marappa Bhupathi? It's not as though the men on this earth are facing extinction. Why should Narasimha Pallavar's daughter marry this coward?' observed Valli.

'But isn't it true that your grandfather has made a fool of Marappan with such fabricated predictions?' observed the sivanadiyar.

'Had he not done so, that scoundrel would have been after my life. Never mind my story, swami. Is it true that the Chakravarthi's daughter is very beautiful? Have you seen her?' asked Valli eagerly.

The sivanadiyar smiled as he replied, 'I have indeed seen her, my child. But what do I know of beauty? I'm an ascetic!'

'Tell me if she is more beautiful than our Maharani?'

'Is your Maharani so beautiful?'

'Our queen? Not at all! Our Maharani is not at all beautiful. She looks hideous. Your Chakravarthi's daughter is beauty nonpareil…'

'Why are you so sarcastic, Valli?'

'Why won't I be if you ask thus despite having seen our Rani several times? There is no woman in this cosmos who is more beautiful than Arulmozhi Devi…'

'Didn't I tell you, my child? How will a monk like me be able to distinguish beauty from ugliness?'

'Isn't it obvious that you are incapable of perceiving beauty? But do ask the Kanchi Chakravarthi should you meet him sometime. He will tell you. Do you know what transpired before Arulmozhi Devi married Parthiba Maharaja? Narasimha Varmar, on hearing of Arulmozhi Devi's loveliness, insisted that he would marry only her; failing which he would tonsure his head and become a Buddhist bikshu. But Arulmozhi Devi's wedding with Parthiba Maharaja was arranged even earlier. She asserted that she would not even think of any man besides Parthiba Maharaja and finally wedded our Maharaja.'

The sivanadiyar queried in a mocking tone, 'What did

Narasimha Varmar do subsequently, my child? Did he tonsure his head and become a bikshu?'

'Swami, aren't you aware how fickle men, especially Rajas

and Chakravarthis, are? He then married the Pandya princess. Who knows how many times he has wed? If I were to be born as a princess, I would not marry a king. I would rather be the only wife of a man in a thatched hut than be one among his many consorts in a gilded palace!'

The sivanadiyar laughed merrily and said, 'What you say is true, my child! But Narasimha Varman is not as vile as you make him out to be...'

Valli interjected, 'Swami, if he were as virtuous as you make him out to be, why don't you arrange for the Chakravarthi's daughter to marry our Ilavarasar? All conflicts will be amicably resolved.'

'That's a good idea, Valli! But not something I will be able to mediate. Why don't you meet the Chakravarthi and suggest this?'

'I will definitely mention this if I were to ever meet the Chakravarthi. Why should I be scared?'

Just then, the sound of the boat reaching the riverbank was heard. Valli exclaimed, 'They have come!' and stepped out of the hut.

3. The Plot Thickens

Soon, Arulmozhi Devi and Ilavarasar Vikraman stepped into the hut. 'Swami!' they uttered as they paid their obeisance to the sivanadiyar. The sivanadiyar lifted Vikraman up, and then embraced and blessed him. Vikraman, who was a naïve boy six years ago, had grown into a tall and well-built youth. Vikraman's face exuded his bravery and his eyes reflected exuberance. He started speaking animatedly, 'Swami, my father appeared in my dream last night. He led me to the peak of the Chirapalli mountain and pointed out to the Pallava flag bearing the lion insignia. I cannot wait any longer, swami. You must bless me!'

'You always have my blessings, Vikrama! I merely asked you to wait for the opportune moment. What do you plan to do? You know you will not achieve anything by being hasty. You need to exercise forethought before embarking on any venture. Do you recollect the couplet from the divine Thirukkural your father had bequeathed you?

'Think and act;
For action sans thought paves way to ignominy.'

'True, swami! I am indeed daring but prudent. This Puraṭṭāsi pournami, this full moon night, I am going to remove the Pallava flag fluttering on the peak of the Chirapalli Mountain and hoist the tiger flag in its place. I am steadfast in my resolve notwithstanding the dissent I may face!'

'I am very happy to hear that, Vikrama. I am not going to ask you to give up your resolve. I have been waiting for this day. But do let me know the measures you have taken to convert your resolve into action. Would it suffice to hoist the tiger flag? Don't you need forces to stand guard? Will the Pallava general, Achuta Varmar, remain a mute witness?'

'You do not have to worry on that count, swami. The denizens of Chola Nadu are well prepared. Ponnan will confirm what I say. A large contingent of warriors will gather at Uraiyur on Puraṭṭāsi pournami. They will voluntarily join my army once the tiger flag is hoisted. We will decimate the Pallava forces stationed in Uraiyur and imprison Achuta Varmar…!'

'Who is assisting you in this perilous initiative? Who is mobilizing the forces for you? You yourself never venture out of the Vasantha Maligai…'

'My chithappa… my uncle, Marappa Bhupathi, is making all the preparations. He has secretly mobilized a large army…'

The sivanadiyar's face darkened on hearing Marappa Bhupathi's name. He interrupted Vikraman asking, 'Who? Marappa Bhupathi? When did you inform him of your intention?'

'He is no longer the person he used to be! You need not be concerned about his motives. He has turned over a new leaf. He repents for his actions during my father's time. As atonement, he is now prepared to lay down his life for the liberation of Chola Nadu!' said Vikraman effusively.

The sivanadiyar asked Arulmozhi, 'Devi, is this true?'

'Yes, swami. Marappa Bhupathi indeed appears to be a changed man,' stated Arulmozhi.

'I am very happy to hear this Vikrama! May your efforts bear fruit! May the divine general, Karthikeyar, protect you! May

Parasakthi endow strength to your shoulders and sword! I will visit you again at the appropriate juncture. Now, I take your leave,' said the sivanadiyar as he stood up.

'Swami, my chithappa mentioned that he would visit you here. He is keen to gain an audience with you. Do stay here a little longer,' said Vikraman.

'No, Vikrama, I have no time to tarry... As I leave, I urge you remember your father's advice to you. You must strive towards your goal regardless of any opposition to your efforts.'

Arulmozhi Devi interjected, 'Please accompany the Ilavarasar to the boat, Ponna. I will join you shortly.'

After Ponnan and Vikraman left the hut, the queen prostrated and held the sivanadiyar's feet. She said, 'Swami, I don't know your antecedents. I have had a lot of misgivings about you in the past. I am now convinced that you are our well-wisher. So now, I don't even wish to ascertain your identity. I beseech you to grant me a boon. I have no one else to turn to. You are my sole refuge.'

Tears welled in the sivanadiyar's eyes. He said, 'I assure you that I will do anything within my capacity for you. Please ask.'

'You are a great soul! Nothing is impossible for you. I have only one request. You must protect my son's life. Swami, I do not believe Vikraman will be successful in the initiative he is about to undertake. How can a young man oppose the might of the Pallava Chakravarthi? You, who are omniscient, are goading him to undertake this venture. Perhaps you have your reasons for doing so, swami. I want you to assure me that you will safeguard his life no matter what your plans are,' beseeched the queen in a choked voice.

'Only the Almighty is capable of safeguarding lives, amma. Even then, I promise you that the soul of Vikraman's valorous father will protect him. Please do not worry. Rise!'

Just then, along the riverbank, the sound of an approaching horse could be heard. The sivanadiyar hurriedly took leave and walked away in the direction opposite to that of the approaching horse. Soon after, Marappa Bhupathi reached the spot on his horseback. As he jumped off the horse, he enquired, 'Vikrama, you had mentioned that the sivanadiyar will be visiting. Has he arrived?'

'He left moments ago, chithappa! You ought to have come earlier,' remarked Vikraman, looking in the direction the sivanadiyar had left.

Observing this, Marappan said, 'So he walked down this road? I will go meet him and come back!' He mounted his horse again and rode off swiftly. Despite riding a long distance along the riverbank, he was unable to sight the sivanadiyar. The monk had vanished into thin air!

4. Mamallapuram

All the traditional sounds and signs of festivity were apparent in the seaside city of Mamallapuram. The mango leaf festoons and coconut palm saplings interspersed with the fluttering lion standard of the Pallavas adorned the buildings along the main street. The streets themselves were decorated with intricate kolams drawn to represent chariots, elephants, horses and temple towers. One could see the lion insignia all over the city adding importance to the events of the day. The sound of trumpets and ceremonial instruments rented the air. Since daybreak, denizens of Mamallapuram clad in fine silks and jewellery were seen standing along the streets or in the front of their houses. Curiosity and expectation filled the air as they were conversing incessantly: 'It is being said that the Chakravarthi has left Kanchi!', 'Now it is confirmed that he has traversed half the distance', 'Princess Kundavai is accompanying him' and so on.

Mamalla Narasimha Chakravarthi's visit was the cause for much exuberance among the residents of Mamallapuram. The heralds had announced that the Chakravarthi, during his visit, will initiate the sculpture works that had come to a halt eight years ago. The denizens had been made aware that the apple of the Chakravarthi's eye, his dear daughter – Kundavai Devi, will also be with him. The city looked forward to their arrival with joyous expectations and bated breaths.

These were the heady days of Pallava rule. Kanchi Narasimha Varma Chakravarthi was famous not just across Bharata Kandam, but also in other countries across the seas. The Pallavas exercised their suzerainty from the river Kaveri in the south to the river Krishna in the north. People living in this region were extremely loyal to Narasimha Varmar. His subjects took immense pride in his wisdom, valour, gentle nature, impartial dispensation of justice, his concern for the denizens' welfare and patronage of arts, especially sculpting, painting and music. Their regard for him increased manifold after he led his army northwards up to the Narmada river, vanquished the wicked Pulikesi in war and set the city of Vatapi ablaze.

The denizens of Pallava Nadu firmly believed that 'never in the history of Dakshina Bharata has there been a Chakravarthi of Narasimha Varmar's stature; nor is one likely to emerge in the future!' Who could have foreseen the rise of the mighty Raja Raja Chola and Rajendra Chola three centuries later! While all subjects of the Pallava Empire were devoted and loyal to Narasimha Varma Chakravarthi, the residents of Mamallapuram shared a special bond with him. The city, after all, literally and figuratively owed its fame to him.

During the times of Mahendra Varma Chakravarthi, the then young Narasimhar had vanquished all the renowned wrestlers or mallar. It was then that his father, Mahendra Varmar, bestowed upon him the title 'Mamallar', the great wrestler. Little later, this seaside city too inherited that title!

The royal entourage was on its way. Princess Kundavai was seated on the royal elephant beside her father. Soldiers armed with spears and swords marched ahead of and behind them. Some of them also carried the trophies won by the Chakravarthi. Sturdy bulls mounted with drums could be seen in the forefront

of the royal procession. Sounds of the periodic drum beats filled the area.

Narasimha Chakravarthi and Kundavai, seated on the ambari, looked as if the rising sun and the full moon had decided to appear side by side on the firmament! Their glittering crowns and gem-studded ornaments dazzled the eyes of the onlookers. The tall and well-built Pallava Chakravarthi looked majestic. His face lined with scars bore testimony to his valour and royal lineage. He appeared strong, dexterous, handsome and, at the same time, tender and compassionate. Kundavai Devi, in contrast, was an epitome of feminine beauty and grace.

Renowned sculptors and painters of the Pallava kingdom acknowledged that their artistic skills had come to naught while trying to portray Kundavai Devi. 'The magnetic charm of Kundavai Devi's dark kohl-lined eyes mesmerizes us and renders us incapable of painting portraits and crafting sculptures!' they said. Some artists remarked, 'Brahma must have created Kundavai Devi with the explicit intention of humbling our pride!'

As the procession moved towards Mamallapuram, Kundavai Devi who was known also for her irrepressible nature turned to the Chakravarthi and said, 'Appa! Why is this city named after you? You had promised to tell me why but have been procrastinating. Now, you must tell me without further delay.' Her tone made it clear that she would not allow any more deflections.

'In that case, we must climb down from this elephant,' responded the Chakravarthi.

'May I leap to the ground from here?' teased Kundavai.

'You may very well jump from atop an elephant and injure your leg, if only you were a commoner, my child! You are not at liberty to do so as you are the Chakravarthi's daughter!' stated the Chakravarthi.

'Why is that so, appa? Why should a Chakravarthi's daughter be denied the liberty to jump off an elephant's back and break her leg?' Kundavai asked playfully.

'That's the way it has to be! If you were to do so, the news of the Kanchi Chakravarthi's daughter, Kundavai, jumping off an elephant and injuring her leg would spread far and wide. Then none of the princes of the fifty-six kingdoms including Anga, Vanga and Kalinga will seek your hand in marriage. Subsequently, I should take recourse to a ruse like Janaka did to get Sita married.'

'What ruse did Janaka resort to, appa?'

'Aren't you aware of that? Sita, as a young girl, inadvertently lifted a holy bow. What a sacrilege! As a result of that, the princes of fifty-six kingdoms refused to marry her. Do you know what Sita's father, Janaka, then did? He schemed to have Vishwamitra rishi to fetch a nincompoop prince called Rama. Janaka then broke a large bow into two and placed the broken bow in a box, camouflaging the fact that it was broken. When Rama casually lifted the bow, it split into two parts. Immediately Janaka exclaimed, 'Aiyyo! You broke the bow, which is our dynasty's treasure! You ought to either fuse the broken bow or marry my daughter, Sita!' Rama did not know how to mend the bow and so had no option but to marry Sita.'

Kundavai burst into peals of laughter and commented, 'Appa! I too have heard the Ramayana. The version you just narrated is blasphemous!' Once her laughter subsided, she said, 'But you do not have to worry about finding an idiot prince as I am not going to marry at all!'

An amused Chakravarthi asked, 'Am I allowed to ask why is that so? What do you have against the time-honoured institution of marriage? Why do you reject it so flippantly?'

Kundavai replied, 'The answer is very simple . . . I will be separated from you if I were to marry. I do not wish to leave you. I will always be with you.'

'Is that so, Kundavai? Do repeat what you just said,' said the Chakravarthi.

'I will not, appa. Everyone knows that you are so sharp that you comprehend everything that is once uttered in your presence. Why are you asking me to repeat what I just said?'

'Oh! May the Lord above have mercy on us! Please save the prince who ends up marrying this cantankerous girl!' said the Chakravarthi as he raised his joined palms skywards.

'Appa, stop mocking me! Will you ask our elephant to be halted or not! If you fail to do that, I will surely jump off. Then no prince will marry me. I will be around only to trouble you for the rest of my life,' remarked Kundavai as she stood up in the ambari and pretended to be on the verge of jumping down.

The Pallava Chakravarthi looked alarmed, 'No, my child! Don't do such dangerous things!' He immediately instructed the mahout to bring the elephant to a halt. Once the elephant ceased walking and sat down, father and daughter climbed off it. The Chakravarthi then gestured for the horse and palanquin to be brought. Once they were fetched, he instructed his retinue, 'You may proceed and wait for us at the entrance of Mamallapuram. We will join you there.' He then climbed on to the horse and started riding down a narrower road that branched off the highway. The palanquin bearing the Ilavarasi followed him.

As it was normal practice for the Chakravarthi to behave in this impulsive manner, his retinue continued on unperturbed, marching down the highway.

5. The Uraiyur Emissary

The Chakravarthi and Kundavai reached a spot where naturally occurring knolls had been sculpted into exquisite chariots and towers. Adjacent to a temple tower were an elephant and lion carved from rocks indigenous to the region.

The Chakravarthi approached the elephant and said, 'Kundavai! Do you observe this elephant? Doesn't it seem as though a live elephant is standing here? Thirty years ago, a bare boulder stood in the place of this elephant!'

'Weren't all these temples carved out of hillocks?' enquired Kundavai.

'Yes, my child! Thirty years ago, I had accompanied my father to this place just as you have today. You are aware that your thatha was obsessed with sculpture and paintings?'

'Are you any less obsessed?' interjected Kundavai.

The Chakravarthi smilingly remarked, 'His passion far exceeded mine. He commissioned a thousand temples to be built of bricks and wood. Yet he was not content. He was desirous of building indestructible temples for the immortal Almighty. He wanted temples to be carved out of mountains.

'While the search was on to choose the right place for such

a rock temple, one day we reached this place. I must have been your age then! When I casually looked skywards, I saw small white clouds floating on the firmament assuming different shapes – some meaningful and others not so meaningful. One of them appeared to resemble an elephant. Struck by that, I started sketching the outline of an elephant on this rock with a piece of the chuna stick, the chalk, I was carrying with me. My father who was observing me exulted on my completing the sketch. He embraced me and said, "Narasimha! What a magnificent idea! We will carve these rocks into temples. Small rocks will be chiselled into horses, elephants and chariots; large ones can become temples! We will create such marvels which will exist as long as the world exists!" He sounded like one possessed. His dream started taking shape soon after. For twenty long years from that time, the whole place echoed the sounds of the numerous chisels engaged in sculpting the temple and the accompanying statues. Work stopped when I invaded the northern country.' Saying so, the Chakravarthi was lost in a reverie!

Kundavai waited for some time and commented, 'Appa! Was this city named after you to commemorate the sculpting works coming to an end after twenty years?' She shot a mischievous smile.

The Chakravarthi burst out laughing and said, 'No, my child! My father named this city after me as I was instrumental in the creation of this city of sculptures. Several kings bearing the name "Narasimhan" may reign in future. My father reasoned that future sovereigns are unlikely to assume the title "Mamallan" and hence christened this city "Mamallapuram". My father's love for me was boundless!' He was again lost in thought.

'True. But why is it that your love for annan, my elder brother, is not even a fraction of that which thatha bore for you? If only you possessed an iota of love for annan, you wouldn't have dispatched him off to Singhala (Sri Lanka) on a ship,' commented Kundavai.

'Heed me, Kundavai! I had several desires during my youth. While many of them were fulfilled, only one was not. I fervently wished to travel by ship to far-flung nations across the seas. My father forbade me from doing so. Sea travel became an impossibility after I ascended the Pallava throne. I sent your brother to the island of Singhala as I was keen that your brother experience the joy that I was unable to – the joy of overseas travel. I shall also send any other youth for whom I bear deep affection across the high seas,' concluded the Chakravarthi.

When Kundavai remarked, 'In that case, it appears that you don't love me,' the Chakravarthi interjected. 'I am agreeable to your boarding a ship and travelling overseas, my child. But my hands are tied as you are a woman. Sometimes I wish you were born a male and your brother, a female,' stated the Chakravarthi.

Kundavai retorted, 'Had I been born a man, I wouldn't have permitted you to reign for so long. I would have, like Kamsa did, imprisoned you and ascended the throne. Since anna is docile and naïve, he complied with your command and boarded the ship.' She then started running around the temples to view them.

Little later, the Chakravarthi called out, 'Come, my child! We'll view this place in a leisurely manner another day. People will be expecting us at Mamallapuram.'

Kundavai immediately approached him and enquired, 'Appa! These temples are half complete. Will these temples be completed as part of the sculpture works you're about to commission? Which deities will be instated in these temples?' The horse and palanquin were stationed under a tree a short distance away. The duo started walking towards that tree.

The Chakravarthi responded, 'My child! These temples will remain incomplete. Sculpture works will resume at all other places barring this one. A great sculptor named Aayanar resided here. The sculpting of these temples was initiated under his supervision. He was the one responsible for sculpting the temples up to their current state. Misfortunes befell him and he passed away. No sculptor is dexterous enough to complete the works he had undertaken; neither is one likely to emerge in the future!'

'I have heard of Aayanar, appa! His daughter…' Mamallar interrupted Kundavai and said, 'Look there! I wonder who the man riding towards us on horseback is.' Though he had said so to deflect their conversation, a horseman was indeed approaching them at a distance. The rider brought his horse to a halt by the tree just when the Chakravarthi and Kundavai reached there. He quickly jumped off the horse, deferentially walked towards the Chakravarthi and presented a missive. 'Salutations! I come from Uraiyur. Achuta Pallavarayar commanded me to rush without tarrying a moment and submit this epistle to Your Majesty!'

The Chakravarthi received the scroll from the messenger and without reading it instructed, 'You may leave! I have despatched the instructions relating to this communique yesterday.' The emissary prostrated and hurried away.

'Appa! The manner in which you govern this kingdom is truly spectacular! Don't you even have to read a message addressed to you?' asked the princess.

'It appears that you don't trust my clairvoyance! Shall I divulge the contents of this manuscript? The Chola prince, Vikraman, intends to hoist the Chola flag this Puraṭṭāsi pournami. General Achuta Pallavarayar awaits my order on the action to be taken against the prince. You may read the manuscript!' He handed over the missive to Kundavai.

Kundavai looked at the Chakravarthi with amazement after reading the manuscript. 'You do possess some miraculous prowess, appa! Won't you impart it to me?' The Chakravarthi climbed on to the horse, while Kundavai sat in the palanquin. The retinue resumed its journey. Kundavai suddenly put her head out and asked, 'Appa! Why is that prince so arrogant? Isn't he fortunate to be a tribute paying vassal to Mamalla

Chakravarthi? You ought not to spare him; you must mete out a suitable punishment.'

'Yes, my child! I am not going to spare him. I am going to fetch him to Kanchi and ensure that he is punished aptly.'

6. Festival of Arts

Mamallapuram wore a festive look on the three days Narasimha Varmar and Kundavai were there. The city was brimming with gaiety and exuberance. On the first day was the pattina pravesam – the royal procession. The residents witnessed the Chakravarthi and his daughter passing by their houses, offered traditional welcome and extended hospitality. The second day being Saraswati poojai, they performed Vani Poojai at home in the morning and gathered at public places later, to join the festivities dedicated to the Goddess of Arts. Temples, monasteries, art galleries and schools wore a festive look to celebrate the occasion.

That day, the Chakravarthi and Kundavai visited the Shiva and Vishnu temples, offered worship and rewarded the temple priests. They stopped by at art and academic schools and gifted teachers with gold and new clothes. People thronged the streets to watch them travel from one spot to another and cheered them enthusiastically. But, the full extent of the adulation of the residents of Mamallapuram was evident on the third day – Vijayadasami. On that day, festivities were held on the outskirts of the city. The hillocks and rocks that dotted a vast area to the south of Mamallapuram seemed vibrant. Colourful depictions of stories from the puranas adorned the hillocks and rocks.

The pranks of Balagopala at Gokulam were beautifully portrayed on one large piece of rock. Be it Krishna decimating Butaki or dancing on Kalinga or his pleading for butter with his arms around the neck of Yashoda, who was churning curd, captured the undivided attention of the onlooker! Another rock which was split into two, bore the Bhagirathan Tapas. The intensity and devotion of Bhagiratha observing penance to bring river Ganga and the awe and respect felt by the devas and rishis congregated around him bore testimony to the expertise of the artist. That he was also a man of humour was evident from his corner portrayal of a cat pretending to be in meditation!

Several such paintings adorned the rocks. Men, women and children strolled around in groups viewing those paintings. All of them sported fine silks and lustrous ornaments. While the women adorned their hair with flowers, the men wore garlands.

A sense of celebration and euphoria was pervasive. There were other attractions besides paintings to buoy peoples' festive spirit. The area was dotted with pandals decorated with plantain trees and festoons, where music concerts were underway. A veenai concert, a flute performance, brahmins chanting samaganam, and a musician rendering Appar Peruman's Thevaram could be heard from different pandals. People flocked to view the paintings and listen to concerts that interested them. They also flocked the thanneer (water) pandals, which offered sweetened puffed rice and panagam – a beverage made of water and jaggery.

Though an ocean of humanity appeared to stretch up to the horizon, the density of people was particularly high in one area. This multitude was not stationary; it was moving, akin to the continuous motion of a large wave in the ocean amidst the ebb and fall of smaller waves. The moving multitude was following the Chakravarthi and his beloved daughter.

Narasimha Varmar was seated on a high-breed stallion, while Kundavai Devi was seated in a palanquin. A few warriors walked ahead of and behind the duo to pave the way amidst the crowd. The royal retinue was led by heralds who announced the Chakravarthi's arrival and a large bull with a drum fastened to its back. The drum was beaten frequently. This procession stopped often as it made its way amidst the throng. Whenever the Chakravarthi and Kundavai stopped to view the paintings, people showered flowers and sprinkled fragrant rose water and sandalwood paste on them. There were cheers of 'Jaya Vijayi Bhava!', 'Long live the just king of kings!', 'Long live the Chakravarthi of the three realms!', 'Long live Narasimha Pallavendrar!' and 'Long live King Mamalla!'

The Chakravarthi viewed each of the paintings keenly and complimented the artists and sculptors who stood deferentially beside their works. The retinue finally reached the Durga temple. Though the temple was carved out of a hill during the reign of Mahendra Varmar, it remained unfinished. The Durga temple was the focus of the day's festivities.

A spacious pandal with its roof lined in blue silk, creating an illusion of the star specked sky of the new moon night, was erected opposite the rock-cut temple. While the supporting poles of the pandal were wrapped in multi-coloured silk, festoons made of tender palm leaves adorned the edges of the pandal. Flags with the lion insignia fluttered on the top edge of the pandal. At the centre of the pandal facing the Goddess' sanctum were placed two ornamental thrones for the Chakravarthi and his daughter. There were several rows of seating arrangements for other dignitaries.

The sculpture work that was interrupted on account of Pulikesi's invasion was to resume on Vijayadasami from the Durga Devi temple. Long before the Chakravarthi's arrival, members of the Ministers' Council and officers had already reached the pandal and were seated at their appointed seats.

When the Chakravarthi and Kundavai Devi entered the pandal, the assembled courtiers stood up. The crescendo of victory chants, cheering and musical instruments rent the air.

7. Resumption of Sculpting

The Chakravarthi and Kundavai first visited the temple and worshipped Goddess Ambika (another name for Parvati). After they sat down on their thrones, the temple priests distributed thiruneeru, and applied kumkumam, vermillion, to everyone and garlanded them. Amidst the blowing of trumpets, the Chakravarthi fastened a silk parivattam (a rectangular piece of cloth worn as a turban) around the acharya sthapathi's head. He then handed over a tray lined with fine silk cloth, carrying a hundred gold coins. The acharya sthapathi received the tray and touched it with his eyes as a mark of devotion.

Silk parivattams were fastened to the heads of the hundreds of sculptors, ministers and officials present; silk clothes and gold coins were also presented to them. Then the head of the Ministers' Council, Vishnu Sharma, stood up and addressed the audience. He narrated the valorous exploits of the Pallava kings, lauding Narasimha Varmar's father, Mahendra Varmar's acumen.

Vishnu Sharma further stated that Mamalla Chakravarthi's fame had spread overseas and a testimony to this was the visit of the representatives of Shenbaga Theevu, the island of Shenbaga.

They had come to Mamallapuram to request the Chakravarthi that their nation be made a vassal state of the Pallava kingdom. Those assembled cheered, on hearing this announcement, with much gusto. The leader of the Ministers' Council continued, 'Esteemed audience! Kanchipuram and Mamallapuram are the two eyes of the Pallava kingdom. The eminence of the harbour city of Mamallapuram was at par with the capital city of Kanchipuram for long! But ever since the late Mahendra Chakravarthi commissioned sculpture works here, Mamallapuram's eminence has eclipsed that of Kanchipuram!

'Eight years ago, it had become imperative to halt the work on sculptures when our Chakravarthi had embarked on a campaign to invade the north. You are aware that when the Chakravarthi returned after decimating the vile Pulikesi and setting Vatapi ablaze, he had to resolve the intense famine that had gripped the nation and quell domestic strife. By the grace of Parasakthi and the blessings the Pallava dynasty earned for always upholding justice, the Chakravarthi could overcome the challenges.

'The sculpting works are to resume today in this city, which has been named after our Chakravarthi. The Chakravarthi has promised to visit this city often and oversee the work.' Hearing this, those assembled were delirious with joy. The representatives from the Shenbaga Theevu were then escorted to the Chakravarthi's assembly. The Tamil that the leader of the contingent spoke sounded somewhat different causing amusement to those assembled.

The emissary said, 'The current residents of Shenbaga Theevu are the descendants of Tamils who had migrated to the island half a millennium ago during the reign of Karikala Chola. The dynasty that ruled the island came to an end a few years ago as the last king had no progeny. So, Shenbaga Theevu is currently a kingdom devoid of a sovereign. People from the neighbouring nations, particularly those of the flat-nosed clan, frequently attack and loot the Shenbaga Theevu and create chaos.

'The Denizens' Council of Shenbaga Theevu arrived at a unanimous decision to counter this threat. They implore the foremost emperor of their homeland, Narasimha Pallavendrar, to make their island part of the Pallava kingdom and to dispatch

a brave person of royal lineage to rule Shenbaga Theevu on behalf of the Chakravarthi.'

The Chakravarthi did not immediately respond to the entreaty. He informed the emissaries that he will deliberate over

the matter and will inform the emissaries of his decision within a week. In the meantime, he invited the emissaries to visit the cities of his kingdom, including Kanchi.

The Chakravarthi and Kundavai Devi, followed by the Ministers' Council and the sculptors, entered the Durga temple again. The walls of the temple's outer mandapam were bare. The Chakravarthi took a piece of red mud stick that Kundavai was holding and started sketching a figure. Those in the vicinity watched with rapt attention. Soon a vivid portrait of Durga Devi dressed as a warrior and seated on a lion emerged.

Kundavai Devi exclaimed in a terrified tone, 'Appa! The Devi's wrath is unbearable. Please sketch the image of the demon with whom the Goddess Ambika is engaged in combat.' The Chakravarthi instantly sketched the figure of Mahishasura armed with a mace. Kundavai remarked, 'Only now can one view the sketch without fear.'

The Chakravarthi then addressed the acharya sthapathi, who stood nearby, 'Respected sthapathi! Goddess Ambika slaughtered Mahishasura on Vijayadasami. May we resume our sculpture works with a depiction of that incident?' The acharya sthapathi bowed in agreement and handed over a chisel to the Chakravarthi, who tapped the sketch he had just drawn with the tool a few times.

The sthapathi took the chisel from the Chakravarthi with respect, bowed to the image of Goddess Ambika and the Chakravarthi and started sculpting. Since that day the sounds of thousands of chisels were incessantly heard at Mamallapuram for several years.

8. Kundavai's Consternation

Kundavai Devi was traversing in a palanquin the main thoroughfares of Kanchi, a city that Sanskrit poets had eulogized as

'Jasmine, the most enticing amongst flowers,
Vishnu, the most adored amongst men,
Rambha, the most alluring amongst women,
Kanchi, the most vibrant amongst cities.'

She had intended to witness the ucchi kala poojai, the noon prayer service, at the temples. But her heart dwelt on the Vijayadasami festivities she had participated in at Mamallapuram a week ago. She imagined that the sculpture works that had resumed on Vijayadasami would ensure that her father's fame remained intact for eternity. She thought that she was indeed blessed to be born to such an illustrious father. Then the thought that the subjects who lived during such a Chakravarthi's reign were fortunate occurred to her. She was preoccupied with such thoughts and when the palanquin turned around a street corner, she witnessed a curious sight.

A regal looking youth was approaching her on horseback. His body and arms were shackled by iron chains. The horse was surrounded by warriors who marched along holding the iron chains. Though the youth was extremely fatigued, his face did not betray an iota of trepidation. He appeared to be a fearless warrior.

His nonchalant expression seemed to enquire, 'My body may be fettered with chains. But, how can anyone imprison my spirit?' Kundavai Devi's large eyes widened further on seeing this sight. At that instant, the youth's eyes met with those of the Chakravarthi's daughter. Her divine beauty must have dumbfounded him for an instant. The next moment the palanquin and the horse crossed each other. Kundavai, while still seated in the palanquin, looked around a few times. She may have expected the youth seated on horseback to act likewise. But the young man did not even move his head slightly. Was it the iron chains that bound him or his steely resolve that prevented him from looking back?

Kundavai Devi was as renowned for her devout nature as she was for her beauty. Whenever she visited Shiva, Vishnu or Parasakthi temples, she lost her self and surrendered totally to the Almighty. But, Kundavai was unable to meditate undistractedly that day.

Even at the temple, she was only thinking of the imprisoned youth seated on the horse. However much she tried, she was unable to wean her mind away from the youth. The chance encounter made her experience a novel sensation mixed with joy and fear, hitherto unknown! Kundavai somehow managed to utter her prayers and returned to the palace. By then, she had abandoned her attempts to stop thinking about the youth. On the contrary, her mind was focusing on him! She wondered, 'Who could the regal looking youth be? Where was he being taken and why? What crime could he have committed?'

She suddenly recollected the missive that had reached Mamallapuram bearing the news that the Uraiyur prince was planning to revolt against the Chakravarthi. The Chakravarthi had responded that he had already made the necessary arrangements. Was the young man the Chola prince? Kundavai felt angry with the young man the moment the possibility struck her. She thought: 'How arrogant and defiant of him! He was seated on the horse so unflappably without any fear or shame despite committing such a treacherous act! How dare he revolt against Narasimha Pallavendrar? The denizens of far-flung nations are keen to be Narasimha Chakravarthi's subjects. The residents of Shenbaga Theevu even sent a delegation for this purpose! What came over this insignificant prince? I must ask my father to mete out a harsh sentence if he had indeed engaged in revolt. Only then will he come to his senses.'

The next instant, Kundavai's mind vacillated. She sympathized with him and thought, 'Poor man! He doesn't appear to be evil. He wouldn't have acted thus on his own accord. He must have been misguided by malevolent advisors! It is they who ought to be punished! What good will come of penalizing this prince? The iron chains fastened around his chest, shoulders and hands must have caused him much pain. It may be a good idea to caution and counsel him and then free him. I must tell this to appa tonight. But isn't he omniscient and renowned for his just rule? He will never waver from the path of justice. He may pardon and spare the young prince...'

Kundavai was assailed by such conflicting thoughts and every passing moment seemed to be an eon as she eagerly awaited sunset and her father's return from the court.

9. Father and Daughter

Kundavai was just seven years old when her mother, the Pandya princess and Narasimha Varmar's queen, Vanama Devi, passed away. Sivakami Ammai raised her affectionately and for some time, Kundavai did not feel the grief of losing her mother much. Sivakami was the daughter of the renowned sculptor, Aayanar. Narasimhar had freed her from her captivity at Vatapi and had brought her back to Kanchi. There was talk of Narasimhar marrying Sivakami after the demise of the Queen Consort. But that did not happen. A few years later, Sivakami Devi also passed away. Then it was the Chakravarthi who assumed the roles of both the father and the mother and raised Kundavai.

Kundavai's grandmothers – Mahendra Varmar's wives – resided at the anthapuram. But Kundavai did not really bond with them. Kundavai, as a young girl, had heard them scornfully refer to her mother as a 'southerner' and speak ill of Sivakami Devi. Hence, Kundavai was not particularly attached to her grandmothers. Kundavai's demeanour, style of dressing and certain activities that she unwittingly engaged in, did not endear her to her grandmothers. They also thought that Narasimha Varmar was spoiling the girl by giving her excessive leeway.

Thus, Kundavai's natural affection for her father grew manifold. She was the happiest in his company and revelled in arguing and squabbling with him. Whenever Narasimha Varmar left Kanchi to attend to matters of the state, time weighed heavily upon Kundavai.

The Chakravarthi, in turn, felt that his life force was personified as Kundavai. Certain events in the past had left him hardened and he had not felt any emotion for several years. Kundavai brought love and happiness back into his life. Every word, action and gesture of Kundavai's rendered the Chakravarthi rapturous. That evening, Kundavai, who was awaiting her father's arrival, was sitting at the nila madam or the moonlight courtyard located on the palace's terrace. It was the twilight of the third day after pournami.

The moon rising amidst the tall and erect palm trees in the west had assumed a blood red hue. On any other day, Kundavai would have completely soaked herself in this beautiful natural occurrence. But nothing held her attention this night. She was preoccupied – thinking of the prince who was led along the street, chained to a horse. At last, Narasimha Varmar arrived. Kundavai ran towards him and wrapped her delicate arms around his broad shoulders in a warm welcoming embrace.

'Why are you so late today, appa?' enquired Kundavai. Narasimha Varmar was taken aback observing her uncharacteristic agitation and excitement. 'It isn't that late, my child. I have come at the usual time. Is there anything special today?' he asked. 'There was an incident today, appa! But I will not divulge the details now. Why don't you tell me if there was any atypical occurrence at the court today?' she enquired.

'Yes, there was one. There was a missive from (Sri) Lanka. Apparently, our forces have secured an unequivocal victory in a major war that broke out there. Your brother wanted to know how we ought to respond to the King of Lanka's entreaty for truce.'

'I'm very happy to hear that, appa. In that case wouldn't anna return soon?'

'Not so soon. Your maternal uncle, your mama, in Madurai has not been keeping well. I have asked him to stay with your mama for some time and then return. Do you also want to visit Madurai, my child? You mama is desirous of meeting you.'

'No! I will not leave you and go. Never mind! Did anything else occur at the court today, appa?'

'Yes! At Chola Nadu...'

On hearing the words Chola Nadu, Kundavai became agitated.

The Chakravarthi, upon noticing her mood swing, enquired, 'What happened, Kundavai? Are you unwell?'

'It's nothing, appa. Tell me what transpired at Chola Nadu,' replied Kundavai.

'At a village named Kazhi in Chola Nadu, a young boy bestowed with divine grace has emerged as a great seer. He, apparently, is a prolific composer of hymns in nectarine Tamil on Shiva Peruman. Those afflicted with incurable diseases are healed when they apply the thiruneeru he dispenses on their foreheads. His name is Gnanasambandar.'

'Isn't it a matter of concern that such an adversary should crop up against Yama! Wouldn't Yama Loka become uninhabited if that boy were to continue dispensing thiruneeru and cure the ailing? More so that you too have ceased waging wars!' retorted Kundavai.

'It's all because of you! How can I wage wars if you were to cling on to me incessantly? Once I get you married to someone...'

'Then he will be imprisoned for life! We'll ignore that subject, appa! What else occurred in the court today?' enquired Kundavai.

'Yes. Something else transpired today. Do you recollect meeting the emissary from Uraiyur when we had visited Kadal Mallai? You had insisted that the Chola prince ought to be given a stringent punishment on reading the epistle. He was imprisoned and brought to Kanchi today...'

'Appa! Did the soldiers seat him on a horse and shackle him with chains while fetching him here?' asked Kundavai.

'Yes! How did you come to know of it?' responded the Chakravarthi.

'I saw him on the streets while going to the temple this afternoon.'

Now, Narasimha Varmar understood why Kundavai was more agitated than usual.

'It may have been him. It's not important. My child! I want to listen to you sing Appar Peruman's pathigam (a verse with ten lines)!' remarked the Chakravarthi.

'Appa, where will the prince be retained tonight?' asked Kundavai.

'Where else? He will be kept in the prison.'

'Aiyyo!'

'What is it, my child? Why are you scared?' asked Narasimha Varmar as he looked around feigning surprise.

Kundavai made him sit and said, 'It's nothing, appa! I was concerned that the prince may escape from the prison.'

'Is that all? Your concerns are unfounded. The Pallava administration has not yet become so lax. The spears of a dozen Pallava guards will pierce Vikraman the instant he tries to escape!'

Kundavai shivered on hearing these harsh words. 'Appa! Will you heed me?' asked Kundavai.

'Will you spare me if I fail to do so?' retorted the Chakravarthi.

'That prince doesn't appear to be wicked. Appa! Treacherous accomplices must have misguided him to revolt against you.'

'You are right. I too heard something to this effect. Apparently a sivanadiyar visits Vikraman and his mother often. News has reached me that it is this masquerader who has led Vikraman astray.'

'Didn't I tell you? My hunch was correct! What transpired at Uraiyur? Was a major battle fought? Were many lives lost?'

'No battle took place; not even a skirmish occurred. This gullible boy was deceived and got ensnared. He has a chithappa by the name of Marappa Bhupathi. He lured this boy by promising to mobilize a large army. Not only did he fail to appear at the site of the incident, but he also tipped off our general, Achuta Varmar. The Pallava warriors were prepared. A few people who were not native to Uraiyur were chased away when they tried to enter the city. Vikraman was finally accompanied by an elderly blacksmith, a boatman and another four to five people. The elderly man lost his life at the site. Everyone else was imprisoned. Vikraman alone was brought here in accordance with my command.'

Kundavai exclaimed, 'Poor man!'

'Why are you feeling sorry for him, my child? Do you feel sorry that his treacherous initiative was not successful?'

'Oh no! It's pitiable that the prince was deceived thus. But appa, how did you come to know of the turn of events beforehand?'

'Aren't you aware that I possess magical powers? Now, won't you sing Appar Peruman's pathigams?' asked the Chakravarthi in an attempt to deflect the conversation.

'Appa, I have an idea. If you were to forgive this prince and free him just this once...'

'What are you saying, Kundavai? You have demonstrated the fickle nature that is so characteristic of women. A few days ago, you had wanted me to mete out a harsh punishment. That's why our elders have decreed that women ought not to be handed the reins of the state...'

'What a blunder! There would be no wars if women were to rule. I will be able to convince that prince to cease revolting if I meet him just once and speak to him. Will you give me a chance, appa?'

'You may be able to do it, Kundavai. I never said that changing his mind is beyond you. Several women before your time have transformed intelligent men into nincompoops, determined men into lunatics and brave men into cowards. Conversely, women have also transformed ordinary men into scholars, strong minded and valorous people. The female gender does possess this ability. But you ought to have demonstrated your prowess a little earlier. Freeing Vikraman today will embolden a man in every town to revolt. Then, what will become of this kingdom?'

The Chakravarthi's eloquence stole words from Kundavai and she was dumbstruck.

'Appa! How do you propose to punish him?' she enquired.

'I haven't decided as yet, Kundavai. An enquiry will be conducted at the court tomorrow and then I will decree a punishment I deem just. The Pallava dynasty has never wavered from the path of justice thus far; neither will it happen henceforth,' concluded the Chakravarthi.

10. At the Harbour

Kundavai spent most of that night sleepless. She was disturbed by what she saw during the day. The proud but crestfallen face of the Chola prince flitted through her mind. That night she would be often overcome by sleep only to be jolted awake by nightmares! So frightening were her dreams!

Lo and behold! The Chola prince is buried in sand, up to his neck. A mad elephant is moving swiftly towards him. Fear and pity fill Kundavai's heart. In a few moments, the elephant's pillar-like legs were set to trample the handsome youth. A distraught Kundavai runs and stands in the way of the advancing elephant. The behemoth, not pausing in its stride, skilfully lifts her with its trunk and places her on its back before resuming its progress. A horrified Kundavai looks on at the Chola prince who is standing buried in sand. Even the gravity of the situation does not rob him of his nonchalance and insolence.

She shrieked and woke up. Even on realizing that it was just a dream, Kundavai was unable to overcome her fear and continued to shiver.

A little later, as she drifted off to sleep again, she had another gruesome nightmare – There is a row of stakes. The Chola prince is brought to be impaled on a stake. Kundavai rushes there. She prays to Durgai Amman that the stakes must catch fire. Next moment the stakes are indeed burning. Kundavai looks towards the spot where the prince is standing with boundless joy. Alas! Twelve Pallava warriors have surrounded him with their spears pointing at him. The very next moment the spears are about to pierce the prince. Kundavai shrieks, 'Aiyyo!' and falls down. On opening her eyes, she found herself on the ground next to her bed.

Kundavai decided that she could not go to sleep and let the nightmares haunt her. She gained courage by reminding herself that under her father's just rule barbaric retributions such as the accused being trampled by elephants and being impaled on stakes did not happen. The night finally came to an end. Soon it was time for the Chakravarthi to leave for the court. Kundavai ached to speak to him once again about the Chola prince.

This was nearly impossible as the Chakravarthi was surrounded by his retinue. He took leave of her and walked ahead. Kundavai felt that her heart would explode if she failed to say something to him. She said, 'Appa! Do remember what I told you.' Narasimha Varmar turned around and looked at her quizzically, 'What are you referring to, Kundavai? Oh! You had asked me to mete out a harsh punishment to the Chola prince, hadn't you? I remember!' He then walked away without looking back. Gripped by indescribable anger and sorrow, she rushed to her bed chamber, fell on her bed and wept inconsolably for some time. She was quite convinced that she had ensured the harshest punishment for the prince. The thought that the prince would hate her when he came to know of her role made her grieve even more. She yearned to do something meaningful. Shortly thereafter she summoned a palace official and commanded, 'Udaya Varmar! Make arrangements to intimate me immediately of the outcome of the Chakravarthi's interrogation of the Chola prince. There must not be even a moment's delay.'

'As you command,' replied the official and sent someone to the court.

Kundavai did not engage in her routine activities. She did not go to the garden to gather flowers, nor did she visit temples. She gritted her teeth and waited for the person to return from the court. Finally, the man returned. He gave her a detailed account of the interrogation and the outcome.

Apparently the Chakravarthi had been very merciful. He had stated, 'If you were to agree to be a vassal to the Pallava kingdom and to pay tribute, I will forgive you and crown you the king of the Chola kingdom.' The Chola prince was obdurate in rejecting the offer. He did not stop at that. He had challenged the Chakravarthi to engage in a sword duel with him! The Chakravarthi then pronounced his judgment. He decreed that he was not awarding the death penalty to Vikraman considering the latter's young age and that he was banishing him from the country instead. The Chakravarthi pronounced that Vikraman will be beheaded if he were to attempt to return to Chola Nadu and commanded that Vikraman be put on a ship immediately and sent to the islands.

The man who had returned from the court informed Kundavai that Vikraman was immediately escorted to the harbour at Mamallapuram, in accordance to the Chakravarthi's decree. Kundavai was somewhat mollified to learn that Vikraman had not been awarded the death penalty. But the thought that he was being forced aboard a ship and that she might never ever see him again caused her much anguish. She was eager to see the young prince once before he sailed away. This fervent passion gripped her body, mind and soul. Her whole body throbbed with the desire to behold the prince at that very moment. A faint hope glimmered in a corner of her heart that she would be able to convince him to change his mind and rule as her father's vassal, if she were to meet him in person. Kundavai wished to meet her father urgently. She was disappointed when she heard that the Chakravarthi had ridden away to an unknown destination on

horseback as soon as Vikraman's trial was over.

The Princess was lost in her thoughts for some time. She then summoned the palace official and instructed him, 'Udaya Varmar! I need to head to the Mallai harbour immediately! I cannot find my mother's navaratna necklace. I may have left it at the palace in Mamallapuram. I must go there and search for it.' Udaya Varmar replied hesitantly, 'May I make arrangements for you to leave once the Chakravarthi returns?' He was taken aback by Kundavai's furious reaction. No one had dared flout Kundavai's commands thus far and although Kundavai's decision to rush to Mamallapuram unescorted was surprising, he made the necessary arrangements.

Kundavai, seated in a palanquin, was soon on the way to Mamallapuram accompanied by her retinue. She uncharacteristically hurried the palanquin bearers. On reaching Mamallapuram, she came to know that the ship carrying Vikraman had unfurled its mast and was about to leave the harbour. A heart-rending sight met Kundavai's eyes when her palanquin reached the seashore. A ship with the lion flag hoisted and its mast unfurled was sailing away. The prince, whom she had seen the previous day, stood on its deck shackled by ropes. He had held his palms together as if paying respect to someone on the shore.

Kundavai looked in the direction he was looking at, curious to know who it was that inspired so much devotion and gratitude. A majestic looking sivanadiyar sporting matted locks stood on the shore, his right hand aloft, blessing Vikraman. Kundavai turned towards Vikraman again. It appeared as though he looked at her for a moment. Before she could ascertain if this was reality or a reverie, Vikraman turned to face the sivanadiyar again.

The princess recollected her father mentioning the previous day that it was a sivanadiyar who had misguided Vikraman. There was no doubt that the man standing on the seashore was indeed that wicked ascetic! Kundavai, with the intention of apprehending the monk red-handed, commanded that the palanquin move towards him. But the very next instant, the sivanadiyar had vanished mysteriously amidst the labourers in the harbour! Kundavai was unable to trace him despite searching everywhere. By then, the ship carrying Vikraman had sailed away.

11. Ponnan's Suspicion

It was just another of those early mornings, when the rising sun cast its golden rays on the Ponni river adding resplendence to the undulating flow. As Ponnan's boat tore across the river towards the Vasantha Maligai, the dispersed water glittered like precious gems. Valli stood on the bank watching her husband row the boat whose only passenger was the sivanadiyar with matted hair.

'Finally, how many people had congregated under the Ilavarasan's banner?' enquired the sivanadiyar.

'Don't make me relive that ignominy, swami! If only the Ilavarasan had not ordered me at the last moment to convey a message to the Maharani…'

'I see! What would you have done, Ponna? Would you have annihilated the Pallava forces single-handedly?'

'Do not mock me, swami, though the situation warrants me becoming the butt of your ridicule. One may wonder how I am still alive even after suffering such a humiliating defeat. But swami, actually, I am still alive only because of the Maharani's wish…'

'Is it just the Maharani's wish, Ponna? Doesn't Valli's affection for you matter as well?'

'Valli is not so self-centred, swami! She is not amongst those who would safeguard their own lives at all costs. We should not forget that she is Veerabhadra Achari's granddaughter. Aha! There are no words to describe that old man's gallantry!'

'How did Veerabhadra Achari get involved in this skirmish, Ponna?'

'The old man had no intention to engage in combat; he merely wanted to watch the proceedings from afar. But he was gripped by fury seeing the Ilavarasan fight single-handedly. We had expected thousands of people to stand shoulder to shoulder with the Ilavarasan and confront the Pallava forces. Only five people excluding me turned up on that fateful day. They were mere peasants from the nearby villages. When they were surrounded by the slogan-shouting Pallava soldiers, they dropped their swords and stood stupefied.

'On observing the goings-on, Veerabhadra Achari let out a fierce roar and ran towards the Ilavarasan in a flash. He picked up one of the swords that lay on the ground and started swirling it around. The echo of his roar, "Vetri Vel! Veera Vel! Long live Vikrama Chola Maharaja!" resonated in all four directions. The very next instant, the Pallava soldiers surrounded us. Aha! The scene that followed! I wonder how the old man's arms acquired that much strength! Maybe because he had worked in an iron furnace all his life. He swirled the sword left and right. The Pallava soldiers fell to the ground. He had despatched seven to eight warriors to Yama Loka before being killed himself. Apparently, the general Achuta Varmar was watching the proceedings from a distance. He was rendered speechless by the old man's heroism. So, he commanded that the old man be cremated with all martial honours.'

'What is so surprising about that, Ponna? Even I, who have renounced the worldly life, feel inspired on hearing about Veerabhadra Achari's valorous death. It is apt to say that a nation's inherent character is still intact, no matter how debilitated it may have become, when it produces such a courageous man. I am now convinced that Chola Nadu will regain its glory,' remarked the sivanadiyar. He paused and then asked, 'What happened after that?'

'The Ilavarasar and I stood rooted to our spots. When he fell to the ground, we rushed towards him. The Pallava soldiers immediately surrounded the Ilavarasar. I then wielded my sword like one possessed. When the Ilavarasar commanded me to stop, I looked towards him. The Ilavarasar was bound in chains. He said, "It is futile to fight anymore, Ponna! You must do this for my sake. Relate all what transpired here to the Maharani. Inform her that I will never act in a manner that sullies my father's reputation under any circumstance."

'I was enraged. I screamed, "Maharaja! Do you expect me to leave when you have been captured by our foes?" as I wielded the sword. I was knocked on my head by a heavy object. I immediately lost my consciousness. When I opened my eyes, I realized that I was in the prison.'

'Oho! So, you were also imprisoned? Then how were you freed?'

'We were all set free the very next day. It seems that Mamalla

Chakravarthi had decreed that everyone except the Ilavarasar be set free,' remarked Ponnan.

'Isn't the Chakravarthi a very compassionate man, Ponna? Why does your Ilavarasar have to be so obstinate? The Chakravarthi was left with no option but to banish him,' said the sivanadiyar.

'Do you want me to say that Narasimha Chakravarthi is a very virtuous soul and Parthiba Maharaja and Ilavarasar Vikraman are wicked!' shot back Ponnan with sarcasm. After some time, he spoke wistfully, 'I have not seen the Chakravarthi. But I am keen to see him. Is he likely to come to Uraiyur, swami?'

'There is talk of the Chakravarthi's visit to Uraiyur soon. Ponna, you suddenly seemed to have developed immense devotion towards the Chakravarthi! You were distraught that you did not die at the battlefield. See what a change has come over you. You came to know of the Chakravarthi's true character only because you're alive. You are now so devoted to him!'

'You are right! Both my spear and I are devoted to the Chakravarthi!' So saying, Ponnan grasped the spear that lay in the boat with one hand. 'This spear is extremely loyal to him. It cannot wait to pierce the Chakravarthi's heart,' remarked Ponnan as he pointed the spear towards the sivanadiyar's chest. Sporting a half smile the sivanadiyar responded, 'Ponna! Maybe you are under the impression that I am the Chakravarthi.'

Ponnan dropped his spear. 'Swami! I consider the Chakravarthi my sworn enemy no matter how virtuous, valorous and divine he may be! The day I meet him in person, I will...'

The sivanadiyar, desirous of deflecting the conversation, said, 'Wasn't Marappa Bhupathi with all of you on that day, Ponna?'

'Why do you bring up the subject of that traitor? He had not only goaded the Ilavarasar but had also informed Achuta Varmar of the plot. Why would that turncoat have accompanied us? But, swami, all except Valli were taken in by his perfidious words. She kept saying, "Bhupathi is wicked and deceitful; he is not trustworthy." Her words came true,' lamented Ponnan.

'Valli is extremely sharp, Ponna. There is no doubt that she is fit to be a general's wife...'

'What did you say, swami?'

'I said that she possesses all the qualities that befit a general's wife.'

'One man had previously uttered the very words you did just now.'

'Is that so? Who is it?'

'It was Marappa Bhupathi. He had said so when he was the general of the Chola army.'

'Oho!'

'Do you know what I wonder sometimes? I'll tell you something if you promise that you will not lose your temper.'

'You may tell me anything, Ponna. I am an ascetic who has attained complete control over the five senses and overcome lust and anger.'

'I wonder if you are also one of Marappa Bhupathi's men masquerading and misleading us at his bidding.'

The sivanadiyar burst out laughing and then asked, 'What are Valli's views on this subject?'

'Valli is very devoted to you. She chided me saying, "You will be led astray by treacherous men and suspect the virtuous." She has the upper hand after Marappa Bhupathi's treachery was exposed. She taunts me often.'

'Didn't I tell you that Valli is an intelligent woman, Ponna? You must always follow her advice. What I meant when I said that Valli is fit to be a general's wife is that – unlike what Marappa Bhupathi had implied – you too have what it takes to be a general!'

'Indeed, who knows? When Vikrama Maharaja ascends the throne of Chola Nadu, I may become a general.'

'Both are possible.'

'Ah! The Chakravarthi has denied a place for our Ilavarasar in this vast Bharata Kandam and has sent him away across the seas! His heart is made of stone! It would have been better if he had killed…'

'You're wrong, Ponna. As long as you are alive, you can hope that your goals will be achieved. Why don't you ask the Maharani? She will be content that her son is still alive… Look! Isn't that the

Maharani?' exclaimed a surprised sivanadiyar as he spotted the Maharani on the banks.

The boat was then sailing along the banks of the island on which the Vasantha Maligai was located. Arulmozhi Devi and a lady-in-waiting were standing at the quay. Arulmozhi Devi was looking at the sivanadiyar with devotion-filled eyes and her palms were held together in reverence. Ponnan tendered a heartfelt apology saying, 'Swami! Please forgive me for blabbering.'

12. The Rani's Distress

On reaching the bank, Ponnan anchored the boat and the sivanadiyar got off. No sooner did he step on the bank, Arulmozhi who was waiting there, prostrated before him seeking his blessings. Her eyes were glistening with tears. The sivanadiyar was visibly moved when she enquired in an anguished voice, 'Swami! Where is Vikraman?' Ponnan looked away since he was troubled by her grief-stricken face. Even the birds flew away as if they too were unable to bear her plight! 'Arulmozhi! Why this unbecoming behaviour on your part? Have you forgotten what your husband told you before leaving for the battlefield? Shouldn't you be a brave mother? How can you lose your resolve? Let us go inside the palace and converse once you compose yourself.' They walked through the picturesque mango orchard towards the Vasantha Maligai. The palace that once was full of gaiety looked lacklustre and desolate. The sivanadiyar occupied the tiger skin covered high seat in the atrium of the palace.

Arulmozhi sat on the floor. Seeing her distressed, the sivanadiyar said, 'Amma, you should not lose courage.'

'Alas! How can I lose heart when I have become stone-hearted already! It is my body which suffers now. Ache fills my body and bones fearing what I am about to hear about my child, Vikraman! Swami, you assured me of his safety! Were you able to keep up your word?'

'I certainly have, Arulmozhi. I promised you that I would save Vikraman's life. I have indeed saved his life. I had promised his father that I will ensure Vikraman becomes a brave man; I have fulfilled that promise too. Amma! You would have felt so proud had you been present at the court of the Pallava Chakravarthi on the day of the trial. 'Overwhelmed more is the mother on her son attaining stature than when she gave birth to him.' These words of Poyyamozhi Peruman (another name for Thiruvalluvar; meaning the great soul whose words are always true) cannot be more applicable to anyone else than you!

'The Chakravarthi went to great lengths to counsel Vikraman. He offered, "If you agree to be a vassal of the Pallava kingdom and pay tribute, I will forgive your treachery and instate you to the throne of Chola Nadu!" Vikraman was unshaken in his resolve. He challenged the Chakravarthi to a duel, "If you are indeed the brave warrior you are renowned to be, you must win me in a sword fight. You may demand that I pay tribute after vanquishing me." His eyes emitted sparks of fury. Arulmozhi, I was fortunate to witness that scene which you could not! I am sure it is because of his valour that the prince wasn't given the death penalty and was instead banished.'

Arulmozhi, whose eyes had widened with fervour, brimmed with tears as she remarked, 'Isn't it obvious that I am a wretched woman? I continue to be alive after losing my husband at the battlefield and my son being banished to a faraway country. Swami, is it true that the Pallava Chakravarthi is likely to visit Uraiyur? If he does, I will fall at his feet and beseech him, "Please send me to the country to which Vikraman was banished..."'

'How can you speak thus, Arulmozhi! Do you propose to fall at the feet of your husband's sworn enemy and plead with him? Do you think it's worthy of the wife of Parthiba Maharaja, who has now become a martyr?'

'True. He will not be pleased. Neither will I seek alms from his foe! I uttered those words as a mother in a rush of emotion. Ah! My husband had built castles in the air. He was desirous of the Chola kingdom extending from Kanyakumari to the Himalayas. However, there is no place in this vast country for his son...'

'Didn't Parthiba Maharaja have one more aspiration? Didn't he wish to hoist the tiger flag in the nations that lie across the ocean? Do recollect his paintings in the cloistered chamber of the Chitra Mandapam.'

'Alas! Should his dreams be realized thus? Has Vikraman led an army across the seas to conquer far-flung nations? At which barbaric island would they have offloaded him? He must be experiencing much hardship, wandering across forests and mountains. Why do you try to deceive me, swami?'

'I will never ever deceive you, amma. What will I achieve by misleading you? I believe that your son will lack nothing. Haven't people been banished and sent to the forests in the past? Didn't Rama and the Pandavas meet with similar fates? The hardships that Vikraman faces overseas will serve to enhance his valour. When he returns to his motherland...'

'Oh, no! He need not ever return, swami! Hasn't the Chakravarthi decreed that Vikraman will be beheaded if he were to set foot in his motherland? It would suffice if he were alive in a distant nation!' lamented Arulmozhi.

'It will be impossible for him not to return, Arulmozhi! He is bound to return one day. His love for his mother and his motherland will draw him here. An ardour that is deeper than his love for you and his motherland has now possessed him. You are unlikely to be aware of this...' remarked the sivanadiyar and paused.

'What are you saying, swami!'

'A power that is stronger than his love for his mother and his patriotism will force him to return. It is the magnetic charm of a maiden's dark eyes. Amma! Though I am now an ascetic free of all desires, I have experienced the joys and sorrows of falling in love before I renounced the world…'

'What are you saying, swami? I don't quite understand. How is it possible for Vikraman to fall in love?' enquired an amazed Arulmozhi.

The bemused sivanadiyar replied, 'Every mother harbours such misconceptions about her son. She is shocked when she ultimately faces the reality. You ought to be aware of this, amma. Vikraman met a maiden on the streets of Kanchi. That meeting occurred when he was on horseback, shackled by chains. That maiden has also lost her heart to Vikraman. This is something I heard of and conjectured. But I personally witnessed an amazing incident which strengthened my surmise.

'That girl rushed from Kanchi and reached the seashore, when the ship Vikraman was made to board was about to set sail. Then, not just their eyes but even their souls met! Vikraman will never be able to forget that maiden's wide eyes that were filled with love and tenderness. That girl's visage will haunt him day and night, when he is awake and asleep. Vikraman will never be able to erase her from his thoughts any time. He will return to his motherland one day consumed by his desire to see her.'

Arulmozhi, who sat shell-shocked thus far, asked softly, 'Oh! The only treasure I was left with in this world was my son's love for me. Even that is at risk now! Who is that maiden, swami?'

'The Pallava Chakravarthi's daughter, Kundavai.'

'Aha! The daughter of my husband's sworn enemy. I don't know what has beset me. My head is swirling,' moaned Arulmozhi. The next instant she swooned and fell to the ground.

13. The Boon the Sivanadiyar Sought

The ladies-in-waiting, who were at a distance, rushed towards Arulmozhi on seeing her falling down. They surrounded her to help her regain her senses. But the sivanadiyar gestured them to move away and sprinkled water from his kamandalam on her face. Like a miracle, Arulmozhi opened her eyes immediately and looked towards the sivanadiyar. In a feeble voice she asked him what transpired. 'Nothing happened to you, amma. I was just talking about your son and assured you that he would certainly return safely,' said the sivanadiyar.

'No, you conveyed something very distressing!'

'I had mentioned that your son had chanced to see the Chakravarthi's daughter. I thought that will make you happy…'

'Yes! Now, I remember. But is this happy news? My son is besotted with the daughter of the greatest foe of Chola Nadu, the vile adversary responsible for my husband's death, the man who is responsible for my desolation today. I cannot believe that Vikraman is indeed my son…'

'Be patient, Arulmozhi. Do not curse people in haste!' said the sivanadiyar with some trepidation. Despite his sharp intellect, he did not anticipate such a sharp and antagonistic reaction from her. 'Listen to me, amma! Your son is unaware that the maiden is the daughter of Narasimha Varman, the target of your intense ire. The duo never approached one another, nor have they conversed. They have only looked at each other from a distance! Why do you despair as though they are already married?' stated the elderly man.

'Thank God! Your words comfort me. I wondered if this was yet another ruse of the Pallava Chakravarthi. Swami, I would rather prefer that Vikraman lives in a faraway land, hungry and thirsty, than being enamoured by the daughter of our sworn enemy!'

'Recollect the desire buried in the depths of your heart, Arulmozhi. Did you never ever wish that your son marries the Chakravarthi's daughter?'

'I did wish so in the past, swami. I do not mind revealing this to you. I did harbour such a crazy desire before the Vennaru Battle. I used to think that the marriage will resolve the enmity between the Pallavas and the Cholas. However, the very instant my Lord lost his life on the battlefield, I erased that desire from my heart. After all that has transpired, the news of my son's death will make me happier than that of him marrying the Chakravarthi's daughter!'

'Arulmozhi! You have not met that child, Kundavai. Hence you speak with so much hatred...'

'Have you seen her, swami?'

'I have seen her. I've interacted with her at close quarters. Kundavai is extremely devoted and loyal to me, amma. After having realized the joy of enlightenment, I became completely detached from worldly desires. But my affection for that child does not wane. You will feel similarly if you were to spend a couple of days with her...'

'Not necessary! I do not wish to see or mingle with anyone. I look forward to the day when I will depart from this world and be reunited with my husband...'

'Arulmozhi! You had once sought a boon from me. I kept my word by saving your son's life. I also fulfilled the promise I had made to your husband at the time of his death. Don't you agree with me?'

'Yes, I do.'

'In return, I am about to seek a boon. You must grant it without any hesitation.'

Arulmozhi exclaimed, 'Shiva! Shiva!' and stood up with her palms conjoined. 'Swami! It sounds blasphemous! How can you seek a boon from me? You ought to command me!'

'Fine, then I will command you. You must not flout my orders.'

'I will never ever defy your decree.'

'Heed me in that case! The Chakravarthi's daughter, Kundavai, will come to you one day. She lost her mother when she was young and grew up unaware of a mother's love. This is the reason for me showering so much affection on her. You must not to reject her. Accept her as your own daughter. This will help the healing of your heart's wounds,' said the ascetic. His gentle tone and words softened Arulmozhi.

'I will try to abide by your command, swami! But how can I be affectionate to the daughter of our clan's adversary...'

'Is it fair to hold the crimes committed by the father against the daughter? There is something else I wish to share with you. Listen to me. Kundavai was of immense help in my efforts to save your son's life. You are unaware of her efforts to ensure that Vikraman was not awarded the death sentence. She, who had never argued with her father even once thus far, interceded fervently on Vikraman's behalf with the Chakravarthi...'

'Is that so, swami? I am now keen to meet that child. But why would she come in search of an unfortunate woman like me?'

'That's not true, amma. You are not unfortunate. How can you, who begot a brave son like Vikraman, be unfortunate? Kundavai will come seeking your audience very soon!' concluded the sivanadiyar.

14. 'The Fault Lies in his Age!'

It was the time when Tamizhagam was witnessing the renaissance of both Saivism and Vaishnavism. The bhakti movement flourished. Inspired by the hymns of the saints, people started visiting temples. Many savants were constantly on pilgrimages. This enlightenment resulted in newer mellifluous compositions in nectarine Tamil. Thirunavukkarasar, also known as Appar, was peerless among those who wrote verses in praise of Shiva. He had gained eminence during Mahendra Varmar's reign. But now he was old and not very mobile. Despite his infirmity, he had just then returned from a pilgrimage. Hearing of his return, Kundavai went to his monastery in Kanchi seeking an audience. The wise saint welcomed her with all affection and bestowed his blessings on her.

Appar's exhaustion was palpable. Looking at his condition, Kundavai enquired, 'Swami! Why do you have to travel in such delicate health? Is there any temple in Tamil Nadu that you have not visited? Which temple did you visit this time?' Appar replied, 'My child, I visited only Thillai (present day Chidambaram, Tamil Nadu). No matter how many times one visits the Lord who dances on the golden stage, there is always an urge to visit him again. Words cannot describe the bliss of seeing His "Ananda Natanam" (joyful dance)! One may be born again and again to experience that ecstasy!' Tears of joy flowed from his half-closed eyes as he sang the following verse:

The eyebrows arched like bows
The lips shining like the red fruit
Sporting a suppressed smile
The matted locks dusted with specs of snow;
The milk white holy ash-smeared body
That mimicked the lustre of corals
Finally, the golden foot raised in dance...
Just to witness this divine scene
It is worth to be born a mortal again and again
In this world!

Thus singing for some time, Appar Swami fell silent as if in a trance. Usually, Kundavai would have been consumed by such a display of ecstatic devotion and would have shed tears of joy. But on that day she didn't as her mind was elsewhere!

When Appar regained his self, Kundavai asked, 'Swami! Apparently a sivanadiyar has emerged in Chola Nadu. He is meddling with state affairs. Do you know him?' The elderly man, who was still ecstatic, heard her incorrectly and replied, 'My child, are you asking about the sivanadiyar who has recently risen to prominence in Chola Nadu? Aha! Meeting him was the primary motivation for my embarking on a pilgrimage. When he heard that I was on my way to meet him, he came in search of me. We met at Thillai. Aha! The name "Gnanasambandan" is so apt for that boy! How did that child, who is barely out of infancy, acquire so much wisdom and eloquence? I am convinced that he has been reared by the Gods themselves. How else can he compose such divine verses even before reaching adolescence?'

Kundavai exercised much restraint but finally interjected, 'Swami! I was enquiring about another person. The sivanadiyar

I was asking about is no child. He is an adult, who sports matted locks and drapes himself in tiger skin.'

'My child, I do not know who you are referring to! There are several sivanadiyars who sport matted locks and drape themselves in tiger skins. In this monastery itself, there are a hundred such people. Do let me know if he has any other unique identification.' stated Navukkarasar.

'The sivanadiyar I was referring to often interferes in matters of the state. Apparently, he is instigating people to revolt against my father…'

'What are you saying, amma? That's surprising! I do not know of such a sivanadiyar. Your father protects Saivism and Vaishnavism like his two eyes! Why should sivanadiyars involve themselves in matters of the state under Narasimha Varma Chakravarthi's reign? Why instigate dissent against your father? That's ridiculous! A person engaging in such acts is unlikely to be a Saivite or Vaishnavite. He must be an impostor!'

Realizing that not much will come out of the conversation, Kundavai took her leave. As she was returning to the palace in her palanquin, she thought: 'Age seems to cause much deterioration even in the best of humans. They talk incessantly but do not answer your question clearly. The fault lies in his age!'

15. Sea Voyage

The ship, with Ilavarasan Vikraman on board, accelerated on its eastward course. The Mamallapuram coastline, temple towers and tree tops disappeared from sight. The tiny waves covered with white froth that lapped the seashore were no longer visible. The ship was sailing in the vivid blue sea, swayed by waves that laboriously scaled great heights and touched cavernous depths exuding an incessant mournful sound. The sight that Vikraman witnessed around him mirrored the state of his mind. He experienced deep in his heart a sense of absolute calm akin to what prevailed at the depths of the seas and, at the same time, several thoughts rose like waves in his mind, assailing him.

Vikraman recollected Parthiba Maharaja sharing with him his vision of Chola Nadu's future greatness. He also recollected his desire since childhood to embark on an overseas voyage. He was bemused at the ironic manner in which his wish had come true. The difference between embarking on an overseas invasion, leading the Chola forces in ships atop which tiger flags fluttered majestically and being shackled in chains and banished from the country in a Pallava vessel atop which the lion flag was hoisted was stark! As Vikraman stood immersed in such thoughts, the captain of the ship, accompanied by a few men, approached him. The captain instructed the men to undo the chains that restrained the prince.

Vikraman asked, 'What is this?'

'The Chakravarthi's orders,' replied the captain.

'Where are you taking me?'

'To an island which will take twelve days to reach. We have orders to offload you close to that island.'

Vikraman probed further, 'Who are the inhabitants of that island?'

'We don't know. You may freely wander around this ship till we reach the island. But we will chain you again if you try to escape.'

Vikraman walked around the ship for some time. Nothing came of his attempts to converse with the sailors. They were all tongue-tied. The prince returned to the ship's upper deck and surveyed the sky and the sea; he was again lost in thought. This time, his mind was preoccupied with his mother, Arulmozhi. What will she be doing now? What was she thinking? Will she be disappointed that his efforts came to naught? Will she be proud of his unyielding stance and brave response to the Pallava Chakravarthi? Will their separation cause her anguish? Wouldn't the sivanadiyar have visited Uraiyur to console her?

Vikraman was reminded of the sivanadiyar. Didn't the elderly man somehow reach the seashore just before the ship's departure and bless me? He bears immense affection for me. Even as Vikraman was thinking of the sivanadiyar, he was reminded of another person – a maiden. How did the damsel he had seen in Kanchi the previous day arrive at the Mamallapuram seashore?

Who could she have been? Aha! Her wide eyes were…Why did tears glisten in her eyes? Did she pity him? Why should she feel compassion for a stranger? Why did she look at him with so much sympathy? Vikraman thought about that maiden for a long time. He did not observe the sun setting and darkness enveloping the ship. He was taken aback to see the reflection of the stars in the sea when he happened to glance down. He was a trifle embarrassed ruminating about a damsel of unknown antecedents.

Vikraman then thought of Ponnan and Valli. They loved him dearly and must be discussing him now. Or they may be talking about Valli's grandfather. That elderly man was fearless. If only all the menfolk of Chola Nadu were like him…One jaamam had passed since sunset. The rising moon was transforming the blue sea into a red-gold expanse. It was not the full moon but the gibbous moon that resembled a large golden bowl emerging from the sea. It was probably this golden bowl that bore the nectar when the ocean was churned eons ago. Even today, it emits divine light that spreads across the universe. The moon that rose from the sea reminded Vikraman of that maiden's countenance yet again.

Her complexion was akin to the golden hue of the rising moon. It was then that Vikraman realized for the first time how beautiful she was. The black locks that framed her face enhanced her beauty manifold. Yes, that maiden was indeed endowed with peerless beauty! It was rare to encounter such divine beauty even in paintings and sculptures. Who could she be?

Twelve days had passed. Vikraman, who often contemplated about Kundavai, did not realize the passage of time. He was stunned at the sight he beheld on the sunrise of the thirteenth day. The sun, as opposed to rising from the sea like an iridescent ball, rose from behind verdant trees radiating light rays. Even as he was witnessing this wondrous sight, the ship's captain approached him and enquired, 'Ilavarasey! We have orders to offload you close to that island. Do you know how to swim?'

'At what distance from the shore will you offload me?'

'Not very far. We will also provide you with a log of wood.'

'What if I were to refuse to disembark?'

'We have orders to fasten you to the log of wood and lower you into the sea. What is your preference?'

'I will disembark,' stated Vikraman.

As the ship neared the coast, Vikraman was lowered into the sea along with a log of wood. He swam towards the shore, holding on to the log. When he felt tired, he lay on the log and floated. As he neared the shore, he realized that what appeared to be a colony of ants from the ship was in reality a horde of people. Who are these people? Why have they congregated at the seashore? What language did they speak? Why did the Chakravarthi command that he be offloaded at this island? Waves of such thoughts flooded Vikraman's mind.

16. Shenbaga Theevu

The prince was in for a pleasant surprise as he neared the shore. He heard the melody of musical instruments rising to a crescendo drowning the noise of the sea waves. The conches, horns, drums and trumpets, being played in unison, echoed in all directions. But what gave Vikraman goosebumps was the voice of the women chanting, 'Vetri Vel! Veera Vel!' Vikraman till then was pondering on the nature of the island, its inhabitants, their language and their customs and practices. The glorious Tamil refrain of Chola Nadu filled him with elation and amazement!

'Which magical island is this? Why are the Tamil refrains of Chola Nadu heard here? Why have so many people congregated on the shore?' A volley of thoughts struck Vikraman. His heart started beating faster. Suddenly, he started shivering. The log of wood, which supported him in the water, slipped from his grasp.

He felt dizzy and his vision blurred. It was then that a giant wave struck Vikraman hard. He felt as though the ocean was attacking him with full fury. He felt breathless and thought that his end was nearing. Just then, the prince was reminded of the promise he had made to his father, Parthiba Maharaja. Further, Arulmozhi Devi's gentle visage, the sivanadiyar's statuesque face and finally the wide-eyed maiden's countenance flashed in his mind. He perceived consciousness slipping out of him. On regaining his senses, he realized that he was lying on the shore. The not too distant sound of the waves echoed in his ears. He could feel something being applied on his forehead and from the familiar smell he guessed it must be the thiruneeru. As he slowly opened his eyes, he could see people thronging near him!

The sounds of people cheering and musical instruments that he had heard as he was approaching the shore had died down. An unnatural calm prevailed instead. A cuckoo cooing mellifluously from a distant mango grove accentuated the eerie stillness around him. He recollected being hit by a wave and losing consciousness. That was obviously the reason behind the crowd's anxious silence. With great effort, Vikraman shook himself and sprang to his feet. Immediately the multitude broke into rapturous cheering. Amidst the joyous din, an elderly man who looked worried, announced, 'Make way! Make way! Gajaraja is coming, the royal elephant is coming!'

This elderly man was the one who had submitted a petition to Narasimha Chakravarthi seeking a chieftain on behalf of the inhabitants of Shenbaga Theevu at Mamallapuram on Vijayadasami. On hearing him call out, the onlookers hurriedly stepped aside. A regally caparisoned elephant stood at some distance. A mahout guided it towards Vikraman. The elephant held a beautifully strung flower garland balanced at the curved tip of its upturned trunk. Vikraman, like one mesmerized, stood tall with his arms crossed.

When the elephant neared the prince, he lowered his head almost involuntarily. The elephant gently placed the garland around his neck. Words cannot describe the crowd's rapturous response. Vikraman too felt elated on hearing the onlookers cheer, 'Vetri Vel! Veera Vel!', 'Long live Vikrama Chola Maharaja!' and 'Long live the King of Shenbaga Theevu!'

The events that occurred after he reached the shore baffled

Vikraman. He was keen to speak to someone who could enlighten him. Before he could do that, the prince, amidst uproarious cheering, was helped atop the ambari on the royal elephant. He was taken inland in a majestic procession. Vikraman thought, 'No, this cannot be real. I must be dreaming. This must be a fantasy.' However, the coconut groves, mango orchards, fields and canals that he passed by reminded him of Chola Nadu. Soon they reached a village that looked like any village in Tamizhagam. At the entrance to the village was a temple that resembled the ones in Tamizhagam, dedicated to the village deity.

Moving further, they soon entered a city that lay a short distance away from the village. Its squares, streets and houses were fashioned after those in Uraiyur, though smaller than Uraiyur. It did not seem to be densely populated and there were fewer mansions and temple towers. Men, women and children, beautifully attired, stood outside their houses eagerly watching this procession. They appeared to be of Tamil ancestry. The island's inhabitants looked upon Vikraman with boundless enthusiasm and showed their joy by cheering him.

All of a sudden, Vikraman became suspicious. Was this a charade staged by the Pallava Chakravarthi? Was it possible that the ship which he boarded sailed for several days and finally offloaded him on the coast of Chola Nadu? Was this uproarious procession a ruse to deceive him and coerce him into accepting the Pallava Chakravarthi's suzerainty? These thoughts made Vikraman furious. By then the elephant came to a halt outside what appeared to be the largest palace in that city.

The palace attendants helped Vikraman climb down from the ambari. While the crowds that accompanied Vikraman stood outside, the elderly man who had previously ushered the elephant escorted him into the palace. The elderly man stated, 'Maharaja! This palace has traditionally served as the royal residence to the rulers of Shenbaga Nadu. The subjects submit that you live in this palace.'

'What did you say the name of this country is?'

'It is Shenbaga Nadu, Maharaja.'

'What is this city called?'

'This is Kumarapuri, the capital of Shenbaga Nadu.'

'Are you sure this is Kumarapuri and not Mayapuri?'

'It is indeed Kumarapuri, Arasey!'

'May I request you to reveal your identity?'

'I am your humble servant, Siddharthan. I used to be the Prime Minister of the now deceased Vishnuvardhana Maharaja. If you so desire…'

'Did you say you were a minister or a magician?'

'I'm a minister, Maharaja!'

'I thought you were a magician. If you were not a magician, how did you know who I was and that I would be offloaded at this island in the morning?'

'That's a long story, Maharaja! I'll relate it to you at leisure. For now…'

'For now, it would suffice if you tell me if this is a palace or a prison.'

'Prison! There are no prisons in this country! Prisons, treachery and death penalties exist only in Bharata Kandam, Maharaja!'

'Is that so? How far is this island from Bharata Kandam?'

'It usually takes twelve days of sea voyage from here to Bharata Kandam. The journey may take longer if it rains or a cyclone erupts.'

'Are you speaking the truth?'

'Your servant speaks nothing but the truth.'

'If so, please explain how you, who live so far away from Tamizhagam, speak Tamil.'

'Maharaja! People of Tamil ancestry reside not just in Shenbaga Theevu but also in the islands to the east. Tamil is spoken in all these islands. The Tamils of Chola Nadu migrated to this verdant island during the times of your ancestor, Karikala

Chola. A son of Karikala Chola established this city and christened it Kumarapuri.

'Those days a general ruled this country on behalf of the Chakravarthi. His descendants ruled this country till ten years ago. The last king of that dynasty, Vishnuvardhanar, died without any heir. This country has been bereft of a sovereign since then. The neighbouring islanders often attack and plunder our cities and villages... natives speaking in alien tongues, barbarians and those belonging to the flat-faced race inhabit the islands surrounding ours. We, the denizens of a nation without a monarch, are unable to vanquish them. We are indeed fortunate that you, a scion of the Chola dynasty, have reached our shores by the grace of Lord Muruga at this juncture.'

Vikraman listened to the elderly man with rapt attention especially as he mentioned Karikala Chola's name. His doubts and distrust dissipated. Siddharthan's tone and facial expression instilled trust in Vikraman. 'You say this nation has been inhabited by Tamils since the times of Karikala Chola, of whom my father often spoke so highly. I have reached this country by an unbelievable twist of fate.' This thought caused Vikraman's hair to stand on its end and his eyes turned misty.

He continued, 'Aiyya! I trust you implicitly. You may brief me on matters of the state later. But I wish to clarify one issue upfront. I will agree to ascend the throne of this nation on the condition that I will not be a vassal. I will only be the monarch of an independent country. The denizens of this country must join me in promising to give up their lives to safeguard this country's independence. Surrendering to an adversary, vile or virtuous, is out of question. Let me know if you acquiesce to this condition.'

'Maharaja, we too have heard of Parthiba Maharaja's valorous death at the battlefield. The bravery of Chola Nadu courses through our veins. The subjects of this nation are willing to lay down their body, soul and possessions to defend their sovereignty. We lacked a courageous leader. Now that you have arrived, we lack nothing!' The sound of the temple bells was heard. The old man, Siddharthan, concluded, 'Maharaja, I will take your leave now. I request you to bathe, eat and relax. We will visit the temple dedicated to Lord Muruga in the evening. We also need to deliberate about the coronation ceremony.'

17. Kundavai's Pledge

The Chakravarthi and Princess Kundavai were seated in the open courtyard located in the upper reach of the Kanchi palace. The stars in the firmament twinkled brightly on the eve of the new moon. The beam of the Mamallapuram lighthouse shone brilliantly far away in the east. The dulcet mixture of sounds of horns, bells, lutes and devotees singing were heard from the numerous Shiva and Vishnu temples. The fragrance of champa, dew flowers and night jasmine wafted in with the cool breeze from the palace gardens.

The Chakravarthi enquired, 'You look out of sorts, my child. Are you unwell?'

'It is my heart and not my body that is sick, appa.'

'You know, my dear, the heart is a very wicked entity. Elders have likened the heart to an elephant that runs amok. We have to teach our mind to rule over our heart.'

'Appa . . .!'

'What is it, my child?'

'How did you know that I had visited the Samana (Jain) monk?'

'Hmm! How can I rule this expansive Pallava kingdom if I am

unaware of even my own daughter's whereabouts?'

'Appa, I am thinking of embracing Samanam or Buddhism.'

'Why is that, my child? What shortcomings have you noticed in the Saiva and Vaishnava faiths?'

'I have come to detest living in this material world. I regret being born!'

'I see! Matters have come to such a pass. Didn't Appar Peruman impress upon you the beauty of human existence when you met him? It is to behold the Lord who performed the Ananda Natanam (joyful dance) at Thillai…'

'Please stop this discourse, appa! Devotional fervour has rendered that elderly man insane. I fail to understand why the Lord has to engage in Ananda Natanam after creating such a "wonderful" world.'

The Chakravarthi laughed heartily on hearing this. The princess looked away in annoyance.

'Why do you think I laughed, Kundavai?'

'Perhaps you too have become insane…'

'No, my child, not at all…I have not gone mad. My reasons for laughing are different. Years ago, I, like you, had become disdainful of this world. I felt bitter about living! Can you fathom why?'

'Could it be because you begot me…?'

The Chakravarthi smiled slightly and replied, 'Not at all, my child! My zest for living was rekindled after your birth. I was disenchanted with living for a few years preceding your birth due to the anger I bore towards my father.'

Now Kundavai could not help smiling. Observing this, Narasimha Varmar remarked, 'Your disenchantment with the world is probably because you too are cross with me.'

Kundavai wiped the tears that suddenly appeared in the corner of her eyes, lowered her head and replied, 'Appa! Why should I be angry with you? I am sad that injustice has been done under your just rule.'

'Is that all, Kundavai? Why do you worry? Don't I possess the power to rectify the injustice I may have caused? If I come to know that a wrong has been committed, I will not rest till I make amends,' stated the Chakravarthi.

'Do you really mean it, appa? Will you reduce the punishment if you come to know that the Chola prince was not responsible for his action?'

'Definitely, my child!'

Hearing this, Kundavai vowed to herself, 'I will change my name if I fail to nab that masquerading sivanadiyar and drag him by his beard to the Chakravarthi's court!'

'Kundavai, you seem to be lost in your own thoughts. I am going to Uraiyur in a couple of days. Do you want to accompany me?' asked the Chakravarthi.

'I will come, appa. But you must not object to what I propose to do at Uraiyur.'

'Will you divulge what you propose to do or is it also a secret?'

'It's not a secret, appa! I am going to meet Arulmozhi Rani.'

'Fine by me, but Arulmozhi Rani must consent to meet you.'

'Why would she refuse to meet me?'

'You are the daughter of the man who banished her son from this country. Wouldn't she be angry with you?'

'Why should she be angry with me? I did not misguide or goad her son to rebel against the Chakravarthi. Is it rational for her to be angry with me?'

Hearing this, the Chakravarthi thought, 'It is futile to expect women to follow any precise logic.'

18. Ponnan's Ignominy

Domestic quarrels are not unheard of. But the one at Ponnan's house turned out to be quite serious! Thunder, lightning and cyclone raged within Ponnan's dwelling for three days.

'I have accepted my mistake perhaps a thousand times! Why do you continue to berate me?' remonstrated Ponnan.

'You may apologize now, but did you take leave of your senses when it happened?' thundered Valli.

'It is still not the end of the world, Valli! My spear thirsts for the Chakravarthi's blood!'

'Even now you don't understand...Of what use is a spear to you? God has endowed you with hands to row a boat and to fold them in front of everyone. An obsequious man like you is totally incapable of wielding a spear.'

This incessant squabble between the loving couple had its origins in an incident that occurred when Narasimha Chakravarthi, Kundavai and their retinue traversed the highway abutting the Kaveri River, a few days ago. The royal retinue stopped briefly at the quay near the couple's hut. The Chakravarthi pointed out to Kundavai the Vasantha Maligai with its golden turret nestled among the trees on the island in the middle of the Kaveri and said something to her.

Just then the Chakravarthi noticed Ponnan and Valli, standing outside their hut. The Chakravarthi gestured to Ponnan to come near. Ponnan eagerly ran towards him, prostrated and stood before him in all humility, with his arms folded. That he had sworn to seek revenge by piercing the Chakravarthi with his spear had totally slipped Ponnan's mind. He was completely mesmerized by the Chakravarthi's statuesque appearance and charismatic personality.

Ponnan felt elated when the Chakravarthi asked, 'Aren't you the one who plies boats at this quay?'

He stammered, 'Yes, Maha... Chakra... Prabhu...'

'Doesn't Arulmozhi Rani reside at that Vasantha Maligai?'

'Yes.'

'Here is my child, Kundavai Devi. She is likely to come here again to meet the Rani. You must row the boat carefully and take her across to the island. Is that understood?'

'As you command, swami!' replied Ponnan.

The Chakravarthi and his retinue then proceeded to Uraiyur. Valli, who was standing outside the hut, had heard snippets of the conversation between the Chakravarthi and Ponnan.

Valli exuded fire and brimstone when Ponnan returned to the hut. When he informed her of what exactly had transpired, she entered into a heated argument with him. Valli accused Ponnan of betraying Vikrama Maharaja on account of his servile responses to the Chakravarthi. She scolded him saying, 'You are a traitor who has betrayed the clan that feeds you!' Their bickering continued for three days.

Ponnan, unable to bear Valli's taunts, headed to the riverbank. He sat on the protruding root of a lush tree that grew by the river and thought of ways to redeem himself in Valli's eyes. The month of Kārthikai was drawing to a close. It had finally stopped raining after a month of incessant downpour. The canals were overflowing. The rains had washed away the dust from the trees and their leaves glistened like emeralds. A cool breeze was blowing across the region. Ponnan's mind was embroiled in a heated turmoil in sharp contrast to the cool environment.

Ten years ago, this very month of Kārthikai was such a joyous one. Parthiba Maharaja, Rani and the Ilavarasar used to visit the Vasantha Maligai often. The Royal Boat was used frequently. The quay was then abuzz with activity. Elephants, horses and ivory palanquins were brought to this very mango orchard for the Royal Family's use. Those times were long gone and now the quay was desolate. Parthiba Maharaja had lost his life on the battlefield. The Ilavarasar was struggling in a faraway island. Arulmozhi Rani was drowned in sorrow. No one visited the Vasantha Maligai and the Royal Boat was hardly used. Wouldn't Vikrama Maharaja have ascended the Chola throne had that devious Marappa Bhupathi not acted treacherously? Then the Pallava Chakravarthi would not have visited Uraiyur. Valli would not have had any reason to speak to him derisively.

When Ponnan was immersed in such thoughts, he heard the sound of horse hooves. He looked around. Marappa Bhupathi was climbing down from his horse by the roadside, close to Ponnan's house.

19. Marappan's Aspiration

Marappa Bhupathi entered Ponnan's hut without announcing his arrival. It was ill-timed and as soon as he set foot on the doorway, he heard Valli harshly criticizing him and Ponnan! 'Is life worth living after losing one's honour? You have betrayed our Maharaja and our country. How different are you from that vile Marappan?' Marappan turned red on hearing this. He stood motionless for some time and then smiled strangely, recollecting something.

Pretending to be amused, he said with a smile, 'Valli! I hear you aiming your verbal darts at me. What happened? What sin has Ponnan committed for you to speak of him and me in the same breath?' Valli, who was engrossed in cooking, had assumed it was Ponnan who was entering their hut. She looked around, startled, on hearing another man's voice. She was taken aback on seeing Marappan at her doorstep. Quickly regaining her composure, she replied, 'It is beyond me to aim darts at you, aiyya. Maybe someone courageous is there somewhere to do just that.'

As Valli muttered the latter half of the sentence softly, Marappan could not hear what she said. Before he could ask her,

Marappan observed Ponnan walking towards the house from the riverbank. He called out, 'Ponna! I have an important matter to discuss with you. Come with me.' Both of them sat under a tree on the riverbank.

Marappan stated, 'Ponna, you have rendered a great service to me. One day, I will definitely reward you.'

'How have I served you, aiyya? I don't seem to recollect.'

'You unconsciously did me a good turn.'

'Oh oh! Please do not mention this to Valli! She will not spare me!' exclaimed Ponnan.

'That's it, Ponna! That's precisely it. You have rendered me a great service by marrying Valli! I was tempted to marry her years ago. Imagine what she would have put me through had I married her!'

'That's true, yejaman (master)! You, who are so docile, will have found the pugnacious Valli totally incompatible. Doesn't the entire world know that the very mention of a combat will cause you to shiver with fever?' taunted Ponnan.

'What did you say?' asked Marappan as he removed his sword from the scabbard.

'Oh! So you have brought your sword along. Is that a real sword? I'll call Valli. She has been insisting for days that the sword you carry is a fake one made of wood!' mocked Ponnan as he stood up.

'Don't do that, Ponna. Sit down. You must never involve women in tasks meant for us men. They will complicate matters. We had put in great effort to coronate Vikraman as the King of Chola Nadu. Were we successful? Didn't our efforts come to naught as we had included Arulmozhi Rani in our deliberations?'

'Is that so? How did the Maharani sabotage the rebellion? Was she the one who goaded the Ilavarasar and also informed Achuta Varmar in stealth? What was the reason for her animosity towards her son?'

'That's not so, Ponna! The Rani trusted a sivanadiyar

of unknown antecedents and divulged everything to him. I cautioned her several times not to trust that masquerader. She never heeded me. That fake ascetic is, in reality, a spy for the Pallava Chakravarthi! He spilt the beans!' Ponnan himself had harboured some doubts about the sivanadiyar and now he became even more suspicious. He also felt somewhat embarrassed for having suspected Marappan unnecessarily.

'I will not spare the traitor even if he happens to be a sivanadiyar...,' pronounced Ponnan as he gnashed his teeth. He grabbed Marappan's sword that lay on the ground, swirled it around and struck the tree hard. His vigorous stroke caused

the sword to embed firmly in the tree. Marappan shivered for a moment. He nevertheless regained his poise before Ponnan turned around to face him.

'Let bygones be bygones, Ponna! The Ilavarasar is not going to return. We have to take care of our affairs.'

'What is there to take care of? All is lost!'

'All is not lost till both of us are alive. But we ought to change our strategy. What cannot be achieved through combat may be achieved through compromise. You're intelligent, Ponna. I heard that the Chakravarthi, while passing by this way, summoned you and spoke to you. You too paid your obeisance to him. That's the correct strategy. We will be able to save Chola Nadu if you assist me a little. We can hand over the kingdom to Vikraman, if he were to return one day. We would never be able to regain control of the kingdom if its administration were to be handed over to someone else.'

Ponnan was initially put off by Marappan's words. But he wanted to believe that the erstwhile general was speaking the truth when he broached the subject of returning the kingdom to Vikraman. 'How may I be of assistance?' asked Ponnan.

'You don't have to do much. The Chakravarthi's daughter, Kundavai Devi, is likely to visit Arulmozhi Rani. I know you will be the one who will row her across the river. Speak of me favourably to her when an opportunity arises. Aren't you aware of what Valli's grandfather foretold, Ponna? The events are panning out in a manner that indicate that his predictions may come true. Otherwise, why would Kundavai Devi visit this place?' concluded Marappan.

Ponnan recollected Arulmozhi Rani's desire of getting Vikraman and Kundavai married. When Marappan spoke thus, Ponnan understood the real thrust of the general's plans. He felt furious but remained outwardly calm. 'Why not? I will talk about you to Kundavai Devi at an opportune moment,' said Ponnan.

'I will never ever forget the help you will have rendered,

Ponna. The Chakravarthi has summoned me. I am meeting him tomorrow. He is likely to appoint me a general. It will not take long for me to assume total control of Chola Nadu. I will take care of you then,' promised Marappan as he got on to his horse and galloped away.

20. At the Chakravarthi's Court

Ponnan in all exuberance ran to his house as soon as Marappa Bhupathi disappeared from his sight. He knew precisely what to do to deflect Valli's anger. When he recounted to her the details of his conversation with Marappan, of course coloured with his imagination, Valli's reaction was as he expected it to be. The furious Valli presently shifted her anger towards Marappan.

'Oho! So, he wants you to be Manmathan's (Cupid's) messenger to win over the Chakravarthi's daughter! Had I been in your position, I would have burnt him alive. A meek man like you can only give him your ears!'

'You think I kept quiet. What do you know? I was unable to control my anger, Valli! I was about to decapitate him using his own sword. The tree that stood between us prevented me from doing so.'

'True! You're only capable of wagging your tongue as you are totally inept at wielding the sword!'

'Come with me! You can see for yourself that I'm speaking the truth!' Saying so, Ponnan held Valli by her hand and dragged her to the tree under which he had sat a little while ago.

Valli's face blossomed on seeing the sword's mark on the tree.

She said, 'You ought not to have aimed the sword at this tender tree. Marappan ought to have been your target!'

'Never mind! The time will come. I will not spare him then!'

Ponnan and Valli then discussed at length what their future course of action ought to be. They decided that they should somehow inform the Chakravarthi of Marappa Bhupathi's vile nature. But they were unsure of the means of contacting the Chakravarthi.

'Didn't you bow and prostrate before the Chakravarthi the other day! Why don't you visit Uraiyur and inform him? But how will you meet the Chakravarthi? Wouldn't the guards restrain you?'

While they were engrossed in this discussion, they heard horses coming to a halt outside their hut. Valli and Ponnan stepped out of the hut wondering who the visitors could be. They were taken aback on seeing five to six Pallava guards.

Their chief remarked, 'Boatman! The Chakravarthi has commanded us to bring you along immediately to Uraiyur. Will you respectfully submit to his command or should I handcuff you?'

Ponnan looked at Valli with consternation.

Valli boldly replied to the chief guard, 'It is not the Chola Nadu but the Pallava Nadu that seems to be deficient in respect!'

'Oho! You must be the voluble Valli? The Chakravarthi ordered us to bring you along too!'

'Aha! I will certainly come. I wish to meet your Chakravarthi and ask him to carry "some courtesy" back to Pallava Nadu when he leaves Uraiyur!' shot back Valli.

Ponnan and Valli were overcome by anger and sorrow when they observed that Uraiyur was beautifully decorated to commemorate the Chakravarthi's visit. The last time they had seen Uraiyur in such a festive appearance was when Parthiba Maharaja left for the battlefield.

'The denizens of Chola Nadu seemed to have completely

forgotten those times! They have decorated the city to welcome Narasimha Chakravarthi – the man responsible for Parthiba Maharaja's death! What a disgrace! What has become of Chola Nadu? How would Arulmozhi Rani feel if she were to witness this scene?'

Ponnan and Valli, immersed in their discussion, headed to the new palace that had been built for the Chakravarthi. They were stunned by the palace's grandeur and the sculptures within. Their rage intensified on observing the pomp displayed by an alien in the Chola capital. They were made to wait in one of the chambers of the palace. A resonant male voice dominated the proceedings in the adjoining chamber. They could also hear a maiden's mellifluous voice punctuated by laughter and a feeble male voice. Ponnan was startled as the feeble male voice sounded like Marappan's.

Ponnan and Valli surmised that they had been summoned for an enquiry on their role in the rebellion against the Chakravarthi when they embarked on their journey to Uraiyur. They conferred that Ponnan ought to reply boldly to the queries posed by the Chakravarthi, thereby erasing the ignominy of prostrating before the Chakravarthi. They were convinced that their conjecture was correct on hearing Marappa Bhupathi's feeble voice. As Valli was whispering something into Ponnan's ear, the resonant male voice in the adjacent chamber commanded, 'Summon the boatman!'

Ponnan and Valli were ushered to the adjoining chamber. They observed the Chakravarthi sitting majestically on a jewel studded throne, the princess standing next to him and Marappan in front of them with his head lowered and trembling. When they were made to stand in front of the Chakravarthi, Ponnan and Valli were unable to bring themselves to look at him in the face. The Chakravarthi's charisma blinded them and rendered them docile.

Mamalla Chakravarthi thundered, 'Is he the boatman? Didn't we see him at the quay the other day? Didn't he pretend to be extremely meek? What will become of the Pallava kingdom if mere boatmen begin to rebel?' When the Chakravarthi spoke thus, Ponnan and Valli lost all courage. Their hearts started pounding hard. The sharp contrast between the Chakravarthi's pleasant demeanour at the quay and his commanding deportment at the Court rendered them speechless.

The Chakravarthi continued, 'Boatman! Reply to my question now. Why are you looking down? Look at me and state the truth! Who was primarily responsible for instigating Vikraman to rebel against me?' Ponnan unwaveringly replied, 'Prabhu! It is the man standing in front of you – Marappa Bhupathi.'

21. Valli's Curse

Marappan felt the sting of a thousand scorpions on hearing Ponnan's accusation. He shot a fiery glance at Ponnan and lowered his head immediately. He was startled on hearing the roaring voice of the Chakravarthi, 'Bhupathi! How will you explain this?' He was so enraged that tears glistened in his eyes!

'Prabhu! What he is saying is completely untrue. I did not instigate the Ilavarasan. I merely pretended to be on his side for a while so that I could get to know of their treacherous plans. My role in the rebellion was just that. I informed your general, Achuta Varma Pallavar of their plans as they unfolded…'

As Marappan spoke, a female voice could be heard muttering, 'Sinner! Traitor!'

The Chakravarthi asked in a reprimanding tone, 'Who was that?' and looked around.

Although it was Valli who had spoken beneath her breath, she assumed a naive expression when the Chakravarthi looked in her direction. Marappan mustered courage and continued talking, 'Prabhu, I swear your servant did not incite Vikraman. I also promise that I'm aware who egged him on. I'll divulge his identity on your command.'

'You may speak fearlessly,' remarked the Chakravarthi.

'A sivanadiyar sporting matted locks used to frequently visit Arulmozhi Rani and Vikraman. He is a masquerader, not a genuine sanyasi. He is the one who goaded Vikraman to embark on this heinous venture.'

Kundavai, who was thus far watching the proceedings silently, interjected, 'How are you so sure? Have you seen that fake sanyasi?'

'Indeed, Devi! I have seen him with my own eyes. They used to frequently meet at the hut of this boatman, who now feigns innocence, to hatch their plot. I tried to nab that fake sanyasi and reveal his true identity. Ponnan and Valli thwarted my efforts.'

'I'll chop your tongue off if you speak of me,' mumbled Valli in a low voice.

The Chakravarthi looked at her and smilingly remarked, 'Lady, your lips often move, yet I'm unable to hear you speak. You may speak your mind fearlessly!'

Valli immediately bowed before the Chakravarthi and stated, 'Prabhu, he is lying. The charge that the sivanadiyar incited the Ilavarasan is absolute perfidy. The ascetic is a great man. He used to visit often and offer our Maharani words of solace — that's the reason for her being alive till now. Although the sivanadiyar tried to desist the Ilavarasar from engaging in a rebellion, he was unable to change the Ilavarasar's mind. Those sinners who falsely accuse the sivanadiyar will go to hell…'

'Quiet, lady! Enough of your swearing!' Having cut Valli short, he smilingly asked Kundavai, 'Did you hear that, my child?'

'I did; this woman too has fallen under that sanyasi's spell! I don't believe any of them is speaking the undiluted truth, appa! All their statements appear motivated,' said Kundavai.

The Chakravarthi then turned to Marappa Bhupathi and pronounced in a rather harsh tone, 'Bhupathi! The suspicions about you have not been cleared. I forgive you this time. It is premature for you to desire a General's post. You must demonstrate your suitability for that role going forward. You must also ensure that there are no further accusations against you. You may leave now!'

A very subdued Marappan exited the Court.

At this juncture, a guard entered, bowed to the Chakravarthi and submitted a message. As soon as the Chakravarthi received the message and read it, he said, 'Boatman! You and your wife may leave now. I will speak to you later. Ask your wife to be careful with the sivanadiyar. She seems to be totally mesmerized by him.' Valli on hearing the Chakravarthi's words wore a coy look, which morphed into a smile immediately. She lowered her head and followed Ponnan but was looking at the Chakravarthi from the corner of her eyes till she was out of the Court!

The Chakravarthi kept looking in the direction they left and said, 'I have seen several women, But Valli...' Kundavai interrupted him asking, 'Never mind, appa. What message did that guard deliver?'

'Weren't we just speaking of the fake sivanadiyar? A genuine sivanadiyar is now visiting. We have to receive him at the city gate.'

'Who is the "genuine sivanadiyar" appa? Is Appar Peruman visiting? I thought ill of him. I must seek an audience with him again and ask for his forgiveness,' said Kundavai.

'His stature will not be diminished because a child like you thought ill of him. He is a great soul completely, perpetually and blissfully immersed in his devotion to Lord Shiva. Don't worry, my child. It is Paranjyothi Adigal and not Appar Swami who is visiting now.'

'Wasn't he your erstwhile general who accompanied you to Vatapi and helped you vanquish Pulikesi?'

'He did not help me, Kundavai! It was Paranjyothi who routed Pulikesi. He decimated the Chalukya army, whose numerous soldiers resembled white ants swarming out of an anthill. That great warrior now drapes an unstitched cloth around his waist, smears thiruneeru on his forehead, dons a chain of rudraksha beads and is on a pilgrimage. He has even changed his name. He now calls himself Siruthondar, a humble servant.'

'Why did he relinquish the general's post? Was he very old?' asked Kundavai.

'No, he is not all that old. I'll tell you why later. He is likely to arrive any time now and his wife is also accompanying him on the pilgrimage. Why don't you come with me? We'll receive them together.'

'I'll certainly come, appa! I've been keen to meet him for long,' said Kundavai.

22. Siruthondar

There lay to the west of Uraiyur, a short distance away from the Kaveri, a beautiful lotus pond. As it was dusk, the petals of the lotus flowers that floated on the pond were converged. The sun, which lent a golden hue to the sky, swirled like a gilded disc as it swiftly dipped into the horizon. The Chakravarthi and his beloved daughter had reached the mandapam adjoining the lotus pond. A few spear-wielding guards stood unobtrusively at the rear of the mandapam. The royal elephant and horses stood a short distance away. The Chakravarthi was eagerly looking westwards at the road adjoining the Kaveri. Kundavai walked down the stairs leading to the pond and stood at the lowest step. She felt joyous for some time observing the beautiful lush green lotus leaves, closed flowers and buds. She admired the water droplets glistening on the lotus leaves like pearls and the swaying of the leaves in the gentle breeze that caused the water droplets to playfully glide on the leaves' surface.

Kundavai chanced to observe her image in the clear waters of the pond. The beauty of her long arms that appeared to be made of sandalwood toned ivory and lotus-like feet appeared accentuated in her reflection in the crystal-clear waters. The princess stood still for some time gazing at her own image. She looked like an ivory statue crafted by an extremely skilled sculptor, adorned with luxurious attire and jewellery. The statue came to life when Kundavai heaved a deep sigh.

Many people had extolled her beauty. Her grandmothers and companions had praised her. Painters and sculptors were dazzled by her magnificence. Kundavai had never heeded these compliments. But, now, she realized they spoke the truth. She thought, 'My companions neither flattered nor mocked me; their comments about my beauty are indeed true. But...of what use is my beauty?' She then contemplated, 'Aha! Doesn't that prince hail from Uraiyur? If only he were standing by my side now...' She then felt an indescribable sorrow that triggered more thoughts. 'Why do I have to adorn myself thus? I will forego ornaments from tomorrow. Of what use are these? It is not as if I appear more beautiful by wearing these! I am content with my looks. I will remove and discard my ornaments right away!'

The princess was about to remove the ornaments that adorned her forehead when her father called out, 'Kundavai, come here!' Startled out of her thoughts, she shot a glance in her father's direction.

'Look, Kundavai! The palanquin is coming down the road! My dear friend, the Pallava General is coming! The great warrior who vanquished the Chalukyas and slew Pulikesi is approaching us! We are so fortunate to have visited Uraiyur now...' rejoiced the Chakravarthi like a child welcoming family members. Kundavai had never seen him as animated as now.

The palanquin reached the lotus pond shortly thereafter. The bearers quickly lowered the palanquin on seeing the Chakravarthi at the mandapam. A tonsured, elderly man sporting thiruneeru and rudraksha beads stepped out of the palanquin, as did an elderly woman. The elderly man exclaimed, 'Arasey!' as he walked quickly to the mandapam. The Chakravarthi too called out, 'Senathipathi!' as he rushed out of the mandapam. The two men stood transfixed for some time staring at each other with conjoined palms, both misty-eyed. They then stepped closer simultaneously and embraced each other. Tears finally started flowing down their cheeks.

Kundavai, meanwhile, walked towards the elderly woman. When she tried to prostrate, the elderly lady pre-empted the princess, hugged and blessed her saying, 'My child! By the grace of the Lord who dons the crescent moon, may you be blessed with all fortune. May you wed the man your heart desires and lead a long and happy married life!'

Hearing this benediction, Kundavai's hair stood on end. The two men who were locked in embrace shedding tears of joy stepped away after some time and gazed at each other. 'We are indeed fortunate to have visited Uraiyur now. Otherwise we would not have been able to meet you. You have forgotten me; you never visit Kanchi!' said the Chakravarthi

'Arasey! How can I ever forget you? I remembered you at every temple I visited in the southern country. That you had not accompanied me on this pilgrimage saddened me. I thought of you at the sanctum of the Lord who resides atop the Palani Mountain (Muruga, the son of Shiva and Parvati). The boon I sought at his sanctum was immediately granted. I saw you on reaching Uraiyur…'

'Senathipathi!'

'Prabhu, please do not address me thus!'

'Paranjyothi!'

'That was my name during my previous birth. I do not wish to hear it now.'

'Heed me, respected sivanadiyar!'

'I'm not worthy of such honour, Prabhu! Several great devotees of Lord Shiva live in this realm now. I am a "Siruthondar" who serves them.'

'Heed me, respected Siruthondar. What I wish to tell you...'

'Do tell me, Arasey.'

'There are two tasks I have not yet accomplished on earth. Once I accomplish them, I will, like you, renounce this world and embark on a pilgrimage. But I will not tonsure my head like you. I will sport matted locks that will make people wonder if I am Vasishta, Vishwamitra or Agastya!' So saying, the Chakravarthi burst out laughing. Siruthondar joined in the laughter.

The laughter of the two men mingled with the chirping of the homebound birds at dusk and echoed in all four directions.

23. In the Dead of the Night

The city of Uraiyur was soaked in the silence of the midnight hours – to be precise a jaamam and a half past dusk. The earthen lamps atop the stone pillars were dim, about to be extinguished. The Kaveri was also bathed in darkness from Uraiyur to Srirangam. The overcast sky added to the darkness on that fourth night of shuklapaksham (the fortnight of waxing moon). There was slight drizzle too. A boat cruising from the east along the western bank of Kaveri could be heard amidst the darkness. The bare outlines of a person seated in the boat and another walking along the bank with a rope were visible.

The person tugging the boat along the riverbank was none other than Ponnan. Valli was seated in the boat holding a small wicker basket; an earthen lamp was flickering within it. Valli carefully covered the wicker basket with the loose end of her sari to ensure that the flame of the lamp was not put out. It was no mean task to navigate the boat westwards against the flow of the river in the dead of the night. Bathing ghats, mandapams and a dense overgrowth of trees obstructed the boat's course. Nevertheless, Ponnan displayed no fatigue in manoeuvring around these obstacles.

A tall figure was trailing the boat by some distance. This figure tarried whenever the boat came to a halt and resumed walking when the boat was in motion. That was none other than Marappa Bhupathi. Walking along the riverbank, shadowing Marappa Bhupathi was a sivanadiyar sporting matted locks. It was the same sivanadiyar who had granted Parthiban a boon on the battlefield and who frequented Ponnan's dwelling.

It was almost midnight when Ponnan brought the boat to a halt and hissed, 'Valli! Get down! We've reached.' At that very moment, temple bells rang marking the end of the midnight prayers at the Srirangam temple. Shattering the silence of the midnight, the resonant Om, Om sounds from the temple bells rose to the skies and echoed in all directions. Ponnan and Valli shivered.

'This is a good omen, Valli! We will accomplish our task successfully! Get down quickly!' Valli carefully held the wicker basket with the lamp as she got off the boat. Ponnan tethered the boat to the aerial root of a tree. The duo then waded up to the riverbank. A long wall lay ahead of them. The door leading to the building within was locked. Ponnan removed the bunch of keys he had fastened to his waist and unlocked the door with one key. The couple pushed open the door and stepped inside. They were greeted by the fragrance of the shenbaga (champak) flowers.

'Aren't the shenbaga flowers fragrant, Valli? You haven't visited this palace before, have you?' quipped Ponnan.

'Don't speak loudly!' warned Valli.

Ponnan closed the door shut and locked it from inside.

'Don't be scared! Follow me!'

'I only want you to keep your voice down.'

The two some walked through the shenbaga garden. Shortly thereafter, Marappan reached the locked door. He bolted the door from outside. He then walked down to the river, unfastened the rope that tied Ponnan's boat to the aerial root and pushed the boat, causing it to drift along the river, and quickly walked away along the wall. The boat cruised along the riverbank for some time. The sivanadiyar stopped the boat and fastened it to the base of a nearby tree. He walked ahead and reached the door Marappan had bolted. He unlatched the door from outside and returned to the tree to which the boat was tethered and sat behind it.

A group of people holding torches aloft were at the opposite bank of the river. Soon, those people boarded multiple boats and reached the middle of the river. The boats reached a place that lay to the east of the tree behind which the sivanadiyar was hiding. Amongst those who got down from the boats were Siruthondar, his wife and Kundavai Devi. Achuta Varmar, who ruled Uraiyur on behalf of the Chakravarthi, walked ahead of the group. The retinue followed them. Chakravarthi Narasimha Varmar was not seen amongst the devotees who had visited the Srirangam temple to participate in the midnight prayers. As the group that had illuminated the banks of the Kaveri with their torches was disembarking from the boats, the sivanadiyar hid himself well behind the tree and stood immobile. Even the sound of his breathing could not be heard. It was only after the group had entered the city and had disappeared from sight, did a darkness more intense than what had prevailed earlier descend on the Kaveri.

The sivanadiyar emerged from behind the tree and sat beside the boat. Even in the pitch darkness, his sharp gaze unwaveringly dwelt on the closed door and his ears were alert in anticipation of the sound of the door being opened.

24. Marappan's Apprehension

Why did Marappa Bhupathi shadow Ponnan and Valli? Revisiting the events of that evening will provide the answer. An extremely dismayed Marappan had left the royal court. He had not expected all the services he had rendered to the kingdom to come to naught. Seven years had passed since Parthiba Maharaja's death at the battlefield. Marappan had expected to be rewarded with the Uraiyur throne for abstaining from that fateful battle. His desire had not been fulfilled. He did not betray any trace of anger or revulsion. Neither did he display any sign of diminished loyalty to the Pallava kingdom. He had optimistically hoped for years that his sincere service to the kingdom would bear fruit.

Further, Marappan had tipped-off the general, Achuta Varmar on Vikraman's plot. The rebellion was nipped in the bud only because of his warning. He was confident that he would be suitably rewarded after that incident. His limited aspiration was to be a tribute-paying vassal to the Pallava Chakravarthi. Even if he was not immediately made a vassal, he expected to be appointed a general as before. Contrary to his expectations, the Chakravarthi grew suspicious of him. He, a contender to the

Chola throne, was humiliated in the presence of a mere boatman and his wife – the thought enraged him. He felt disenchanted with his life and the world at large. He aimlessly wandered around on horseback.

The horse being an intelligent beast understood its master's state of mind and perambulated languidly. After loitering around Uraiyur's thoroughfares, the steed finally reached the banks of the Kaveri. Then the quadruped ambled eastwards down the road adjoining the river. That being the fourth day of shuklapaksham, the crescent moon appeared in the western sky once the sun set. The stars appeared one by one, twinkling. Soon, innumerable stars akin to sparkling diamonds illuminated the firmament.

Marappan, lost in his thoughts, was blind to the wondrous sight unfolding in the skies. After having travelled for around half a kaada in a daze, he jolted back to self-consciousness. He looked around to ascertain where he was heading. By then, the crescent moon had descended towards the western horizon. Marappan guided his horse to turn around and head towards Uraiyur. Soon after he rode into Uraiyur, he encountered a group of people carrying numerous torches, playing musical instruments and blowing conches. Observing the lion flag fluttering amidst the contingent, he surmised that the Chakravarthi accompanied by his retinue was heading to the Srirangam temple. He immediately got off his horse and meekly stood by the side of the road.

As the group walked past, Marappan observed that while the Chakravarthi was not present, the general Achuta Varmar and a tonsured sivanadiyar were amongst the contingent. The sanyasi was charismatic and of sturdy build. A thought flashed like lightning in Marappan's mind, 'Was he the fake sanyasi who used to sport matted locks?'

This was when Achuta Varmar happened to glance in Marappan's direction. He gestured to Bhupathi to come towards him and said, 'Adigal! Do you recognize him? He is Parthiba Maharaja's sibling, Marappa Bhupathi!'

Siruthondar glanced at Marappan from head to toe and remarked, 'Is that so? I have seen him long ago, during Mahendra Chakravarthi's reign. I'm unable to recognize him now.'

Achuta Varmar continued, 'It was Bhupathi who had unravelled Vikraman's plot. Nevertheless, the Chakravarthi is not favourably disposed towards him.'

Siruthondar did not reply to Achuta Varmar. He looked at Marappan again from top to toe and walked ahead. After the duo walked on, a palanquin surrounded by the ladies-in-waiting made its way. Marappan hurriedly stepped away from the road thinking that the Chakravarthi's daughter might be seated in the palanquin. But, to his surprise, the palanquin came to a stop. He heard a dulcet female voice calling out, 'Bhupathi!' Marappan looked around to face the radiant Kundavai Devi and an elderly woman, who appeared to be an ardent devotee of Lord Shiva. Marappan was filled with surprise and joy on realizing that it was Kundavai Devi who had called him.

Marappan walked towards the palanquin reticently. Though he wished to look at Kundavai in the face, bashfulness caused him to look down.

'Bhupathi! Do not be crestfallen that my father treated you harshly today. I believe what you said. You ought to somehow nab the fake sivanadiyar. I will then support you!' When Kundavai spoke thus in a sympathetic tone, Marappan felt ecstatic. He felt as though he was instantly transported from the nether world to the heavens.

Marappan raised his head a bit and said, 'Ammani! Your word is my command! I shall not rest till I apprehend the fake sivanadiyar.'

'I am happy to hear that. Do inform me as soon as you capture him,' so saying, Kundavai commanded the palanquin bearers to move ahead. The palanquin and the retinue departed, but Marappan stood rooted to his spot for some time. After reassuring himself that what had just transpired was not a dream, he got on to his horse. He recollected the tonsured godman who had accompanied Achuta Varmar.

Marappan had heard of a general named Paranjyoti, who had led the Pallavas to victory in the Vatapi war. He was a good friend of Parthiba Maharaja's. Marappan wondered if he was the one who had masqueraded as the sivanadiyar sporting matted locks from time to time. He was determined to unravel the truth. He believed this may be achieved by befriending Ponnan and Valli. It was then that Marappan remembered that despite traversing a long distance down the road adjoining the Kaveri that led to the quay, he had not bumped into the couple during his onward and return journey to Uraiyur. So, Marappan concluded that they were likely to be in Uraiyur and residing at Valli's grandfather's house. Marappan swiftly rode his horse to his palace, handed over his horse to the guard at the entrance and started walking. He forgot about his dinner. Thoughts of hunger and thirst completely evaded him.

Marappan started walking towards Uraiyur's Kammala Street in his eagerness to meet Ponnan and Valli that very night. More than a jaamam had passed since sunset. Very few people were out on the streets and commotion had subsided. The streets were dotted with mendicants and those returning from temples and from watching street plays. He could hear the actor who had donned the role of Vishwamitra hollering at a distance, 'Come, my son! Harishchandra Maharaja!' Marappan walked swiftly and unobtrusively along the streets. As he neared the Kammala Street, he halted for an instant as though he had seen a ghost. He had witnessed a figure in the light cast by the fading earthen lamp. It was that of the sivanadiyar. The earthen lamp died away the very next moment.

Marappan ran towards the spot where the figure was standing. He was looking forward to nabbing that wicked masquerader and dragging him to Ilavarasi Kundavai that night itself. But he found no one when he reached the lamp post and looked around. The lamp post was at the junction of four streets. Marappan was unable to guess the street down which the sivanadiyar must have walked away. It occurred to Marappan that if the figure he had seen was indeed the sivanadiyar, it was quite likely that he had come there to meet Ponnan and Valli. The sivanadiyar might have headed to Veerabhadra Achari's house. He wondered what plot the trio were hatching.

This treachery was occurring at the time of Narasimha Chakravarthi's visit to Uraiyur! Marappan was keen to nab the trio red-handed so that the Chakravarthi would stop suspecting him for no reason. Another surprise awaited Marappan as he walked towards Veerabhadra Achari's house. Two people opened the main door and stepped out of the house. Marappan hid himself behind a pillar at the porch of a neighbouring house and watched closely. The duo that emerged were Ponnan and Valli. Valli was carrying a wicker basket with a lamp that she had covered with the loose end of her sari. They both walked down the alley adjacent to Veerabhadra Achari's house, northwards. Marappan contemplated, 'There is mystery afoot; they are engaged in treachery. The sivanadiyar is involved. This couple is headed to the place the sivanadiyar has already reached.'

Intense agitation and enthusiasm had transformed Marappan into a new man. He quietly followed Ponnan and Valli from a distance, while ensuring they do not disappear from his sight. Ponnan and Valli walked down the alley and reached the banks of the Kaveri. Valli sat in a boat that was tethered to the base of a tree. She set the basket carefully down and covered it. As described previously, Ponnan pulled the boat along with the rope. On reaching the palace, he fastened the boat to a tree's aerial root and stepped into the palace gardens accompanied by Valli. Marappan was aware that the edifice was the ancient Chola palace previously occupied by Parthiba Maharaja, which was now unoccupied and locked as per the Chakravarthi's command.

Marappan thus conjectured that Ponnan and Valli were

entering the palace through the rear entrance to perform a devious task and that the sivanadiyar was likely to have preceded the couple into the palace. Yet another horrific and dangerous suspicion struck Marappan. He wondered, 'Is the news of Parthiba Maharaja dying at the battlefield false? Did he escape from the battlefield, disguise himself as the sivanadiyar and indulge in heinous acts?'

Marappan was confident that all mysteries would be solved that night. He latched the door from outside and rushed to fetch his men for assistance before Ponnan left the palace.

25. A Friend in Need

Ponnan, who was unaware that two people were following him, was enthusiastically traversing the palace gardens. He frequently passed comments like, 'Valli! Maharaja and Maharani used to spend their evenings under that mango tree. Did you notice the lotus pond in that corner? It was there that the Ilavarasar learnt to swim.' Every time he spoke, Valli cautioned him, 'Speak softly!' Their conversation caused a few birds that were sleeping on the trees to wake up and to flap their wings. Ponnan then banged the staff he was carrying to the ground and called out, 'Oosh!'

When Valli quipped, 'You are very courageous with sleeping birds. You will flee the instant you see an armed adversary,' Ponnan fell silent for some time. On reaching the rear of the palace, Ponnan asked, 'Valli, do you want to step in and look around the palace? Or do we complete the task at hand and return?'

Valli replied, 'The oil in the earthen lamp is almost over. Let's complete the errand at hand quickly and return. Where is the temple?' Ponnan replied, 'In that case, come here.' He led Valli eastwards.

The small, beautiful temple located in the eastern part of the palace complex had three entrances. The main entrance led into the palace. The rear entrance of the temple was in the palace gardens. Water from the Kaveri to perform abishegams (ritual ablution for the deities) and flowers to adorn the deities were fetched through this entrance.

There was also a small entrance in the eastern wall through which the priests entered the temple directly from outside the palace complex.

The couple reached the rear entrance of the temple. Ponnan unlocked the temple's backdoor and stepped in, followed by Valli. In the dim light cast by the earthen lamp, the duo beheld the idols installed in the temple. They were transfixed for some time. Despite prayers and rituals not being conducted at that temple for long, the deities exuded a divine aura. It was Ponnan who came back to his senses first. He muttered, 'Valli! We cannot tarry here for long,' as he walked towards the idol of Mahavishnu. He then took a beautifully carved, rectangular wooden casket that was placed at the idol's feet.

'Valli, this casket contains the Chola dynasty's invaluable treasures. Thank God! This casket escaped the attention of Narasimha Chakravarthi. He would have carried it away to Kanchi had he come to know of it.' So saying, he stepped out of the temple, followed by Valli.

'Oh my God! The lamp is extinguished,' exclaimed Valli.

'Never mind! The lamp was fortunately lit till we accomplished our mission. How will we leave the palace? Finding our way through the palace gardens will be difficult in the dark. Let's leave through the door in the eastern wall. Come with me; let's see if we are able to open the door,' said Ponnan as he quickly walked towards the eastern wall of the palace complex. Just as the couple reached the door, they were startled to hear the following conversation faintly from the outside.

'Do you trust Marappa Bhupathi to stand here with your

sword aloft? Is it even remotely possible for a thief to enter the palace?'

'How can I not believe Marappa Bhupathi when he claims to have seen the miscreant enter with his own eyes?'

'Is this likely to be the burglar's escape route? Is there no other exit?'

'The robber is unlikely to escape through the palace entrance. He has to choose between this entrance and the one that runs

through the palace gardens, which directly leads to the Kaveri. But then... look there!'

'What is happening there? I see several men carrying torches.'

'Marappa Bhupathi is coming here after having mobilized his men.'

Ponnan felt enervated on overhearing this exchange. His imagination ran wild. He visualized Marappan apprehending him red-handed with the casket and producing him at the

Chakravarthi's court. He also pictured the Chakravarthi asking him, 'You pretended to be extremely upright. Are you a common thief?' He immediately grasped Valli's hand and ran down the garden path to the exit that led to the Kaveri. The couple ran into trees and stumbled over shrubs and creepers as they rushed towards the palace's rear entrance. They stood by the door for some time and cautiously checked for sounds outside. It was silent outside; they opened the door slowly and stepped out. They rushed down the flight of stairs leading to the Kaveri only to realize that their boat was missing! They could see illuminated torches and hear the commotion arising from a group of men running in their direction from a distance.

The couple stood dazed not knowing what to do for some time. Then Ponnan remarked, 'Valli, the boat must have floated away in the river and have got stuck elsewhere. Come, let's search for it.' The duo ran eastwards by the river. They heard the group of men heading towards them call out, 'Look! They are running!' Ponnan and Valli ran even faster. They were taken aback to see their boat fastened to the base of a tree a short distance away. But the time was not nigh for them to stand immobilized with surprise. By then the group carrying torches had also neared the banks of the Kaveri. Ponnan panicked wondering, 'Oh God! The casket ought not to fall into their hands!' At that very instant, a figure stepped out from behind the tree to which the boat was tethered! On realizing that it was the sivanadiyar, Valli shrieked with astonishment and joy, 'Swami! Is that you?'

The sivanadiyar gestured to her to keep quiet and remarked, 'Ponna! There is no time to speak. Hand the casket over to me. I will safeguard it and return it to you. Otherwise, you will get caught.'

Valli prodded Ponnan saying, 'Give it to him!'

Ponnan hesitantly handed over the casket to the sivanadiyar.

The sivanadiyar remarked, 'Valli! You once helped me slip away from Marappan. I have, in return, helped both of you to escape from that very Marappan today!' The very next moment the sivanadiyar miraculously disappeared into the shadow of the tree.

Ponnan hurriedly unfastened the boat and the couple sat in the boat. By then Marappan and his men had reached the banks of the Kaveri and were running towards the duo.

26. Hullabaloo in the Hut

The next day, Ponnan and Valli had much to reminisce, to laugh about and to wonder. Marappan had reached the boat along with his men, many of whom were holding torches, just as Ponnan was about to start rowing the boat, and created quite a commotion. Assuming a rather pompous air, he had commanded, 'Stop the boat!', 'Nab the two and tie them to a tree!', 'Don't spare them!' and 'Inspect the boat!' Ponnan and Valli had maintained their composure. By the time Marappan's men got around to inspect the boat, the couple had gotten off the boat and stood on the riverbank. Marappan was disappointed and furious on realizing that the attempt was futile as the boat was empty.

'Ponna! Where is it?' he demanded.

'Where is what, general?' shot back Ponnan.

'That which you brought along.'

'If I had indeed brought something, how can it not be here?' replied Ponnan.

Marappan threatened the couple, but it was of no avail. Marappan commanded his men to comb the river and its banks. The search yielded nothing.

Valli intermittently whispered into Ponnan's ears and burst

out laughing. This further enraged Marappan. 'Where are you stealthily rowing away in the dead of the night? Whose boat is this?' he demanded.

'We were leaving now so that we could reach the quay by dawn. This is my grandfather's boat. We're taking it to the quay,' replied Valli.

'You broke into the palace and stole something. You have hidden your loot. If you do not confess, I will imprison you immediately,' threatened Marappan.

'In which prison will you incarcerate us?' asked Ponnan.

'Why do you speak to him? Our case will be adjudicated at the Chakravarthi's court tomorrow,' remarked Valli.

Marappan's face fell on hearing this and he was lost in thought for some time. He then instructed his men to leave and reasoned with Ponnan, 'Ponna, you and I have known each other for long. Your wife's impertinence has been the sole cause of the occasional disagreement between us...'

'You wield an oar and are married to a boor...' observed Valli.

'Quiet, Valli! Don't interrupt when two men are conversing,' interjected Ponnan.

'Oho! So the two of you are men? I'm unable to perceive this in the dark. This may be apparent if this place were better lit,' murmured Valli.

'Ponna! Don't exclude Valli thus. She ought to be aware of what I'm about to say. Both of you must help me accomplish an important task. I will never forget your support. You too may need my assistance someday. Even a twig may come handy...'

'How can you compare yourself to a twig, general?' remarked Ponnan.

'Harm will befall those who use this twig,' murmured Valli.

'How can I be of service to you, general? A poor boatman...'

Valli again interjected, 'Who will believe you if you claim to be impoverished? The "pon" (gold) obtained by smelting you will fetch a kingdom.'

Marappan too laughed hearing these words. 'True, Ponna! Your name contradicts your claim. I want to discuss another matter with you. Do let me know where the fake sivanadiyar is. I have committed to the Chakravarthi's daughter to capture him. Kundavai Devi is furious with you and Valli. If you were to help me, I will intercede on your behalf and assuage her anger...'

'General! We ply boats for a livelihood. How will the Ilavarasi's anger affect us...?' retorted Ponnan.

'Won't you divulge where the sivanadiyar is?'

'How can I when I'm unaware of his whereabouts?'

'That fake ascetic is in Uraiyur today. Can you truthfully deny this?'

'How can I? The man of God possesses magical powers. One can never ascertain where he is at any given point of time,' remarked Valli.

'Do you swear you don't know where he is now?'

Ponnan and Valli replied truthfully in unison, 'We do'. They were indeed unaware of the sivanadiyar's whereabouts.

'Never mind, Ponna! I swear I will apprehend the masquerader red-handed one day, pull away his matted locks and reveal his true identity! I will not spare the two of you then!' growled Marappan as he left.

Valli recollected the events of the previous night, laughed and remarked, 'Aha! Marappan will swoon if he actually pulls away the sivanadiyar's matted locks...'

'Valli, who is the sivanadiyar? You keep threatening to reveal his true identity,' asked Ponnan.

'I will tell you who the sivanadiyar is if you tell me what the wooden casket contains.'

'I am concerned about that! If I'm unable to recover the casket...Aiyyo! How will I face the Maharani?'

'Do tell me what that wondrous casket contains.'

'It is indeed a wondrous casket, Valli! It holds the hoary treasures of the Chola dynasty. Karikala Chakravarthi's sword and the palm leaves inscribed by Valluvar Peruman (Thiruvalluvar) himself with the Tamil Veda (Thirukkural) were in the casket. Parthiba Maharaja had handed over that casket to the Maharani before heading to the battlefield asking her to bequeath it to the Ilavarasar when he comes of age and becomes the sovereign of an independent nation.'

'Why did the Maharani instruct you to retrieve the casket that lay in the castle for so many years? Did she intend to send it to the Ilavarasar?'

'How can the casket be sent to the Ilavarasar? We are unaware of his whereabouts. Poor man! I wonder what tribulations he is undergoing at a faraway island... That's not the reason. The Maharani commanded me to retrieve the casket from the palace on hearing of the Pallava Chakravarthi's visit to Uraiyur.

Aren't you aware of the Pallava dynasty's custom? They appropriate fine artefacts. They will spirit away sculptors and painters. The only objects they are unable to seize are paintings on the walls of buildings. That's the reason why Parthiba Maharaja restricted himself to creating a Chitra Mandapam at Uraiyur!'

'Oh my God! Is that so? I was unaware of this!'

'Hence my reluctance to hand over the casket to the sivanadiyar. You insisted that I give it to him!'

'What did I do? What else could we have done in that precarious situation? Something tells me that the casket will be returned to us safely.'

'It will be good if the casket is returned to us. If not, I will be unworthy of facing the Maharani ever again! But what are your suspicions about the sivanadiyar, Valli?'

Valli whispered something into Ponnan's ear. He was taken aback. It was then the sounds of horse hooves and voices of palanquin bearers were heard outside. The surprised couple stepped out of the hut.

27. A Flood of Tears

On stepping out of their hut Ponnan and Valli noticed that the quay, which was forsaken since Parthiba Maharaja's death, was abuzz with activity. They also observed the royal retinue approaching the quay from Uraiyur down the highway adjoining the Kaveri.

The contingent comprised infantry, cavalry, beautifully caparisoned horses and ivory palanquins fitted with pearl-embedded canopies meant for women of the royal household. Ponnan and Valli were taken aback seeing the royal retinue halt at the quay. Yet another surprise awaited them. They saw a fleet of beautifully decorated boats sailing from the direction of Uraiyur like a bevy of swans. On seeing the lion flag fluttering amidst the boats, Ponnan realized that the Chakravarthi and his entourage were visiting.

As Ponnan was wondering if the boats were headed to the quay, the vessels changed course! They started sailing laterally towards Vasantha Theevu. Ponnan then pondered, 'Oh! Why is the Chakravarthi headed to Vasantha Theevu? Is he likely to meet our Maharani?' He immediately enquired from the guards who were at the grove surrounding the quay. His conjecture was correct. The Chakravarthi, Kundavai Devi, Siruthondar and his wife were headed to Vasantha Theevu to visit Arulmozhi Devi. Ponnan wished he were at Vasantha Theevu then and privy to the events unfolding at the palace.

However, when he shared his desire with Valli, she snapped, 'What! How can you go to Vasantha Theevu when the Chakravarthi is visiting the island and he has not commanded you to accompany him? Why the hurry to find out what is happening at Vasantha Theevu?' Ponnan reluctantly tarried at the opposite bank. After a muhurtham had passed, the quay at Vasantha Theevu started humming with activity. Several people arrived at the quay and sat in the boats, which then started sailing towards the opposite bank.

Ponnan and Valli observed the approaching boats with much eagerness. As the boats neared the riverbank, the couple were able to identify the passengers. The Chakravarthi and a tonsured sivanadiyar were in the boat atop which the lion flag fluttered majestically. Surprise! Arulmozhi Devi was amongst the three female passengers seated in another boat. When the boats reached the riverbank and the passengers disembarked, Ponnan and Valli approached Arulmozhi Devi ignoring everyone else and prostrated before her. Once they stood up, they gazed at her face in surprise.

Arulmozhi Devi spoke to them in a choked voice, 'Ponna! Valli! I am unable to live here in solitude. I am going on a pilgrimage. There is no need to be concerned about me. Do continue living at this quay. If he were to return someday...' Hearing this, tears welled in Ponnan's and Valli's eyes. Arulmozhi Devi too turned misty-eyed. She felt a lump in her throat and was unable to continue speaking. She clasped the hand of Siruthondar's wife who stood beside her and walked ahead. That day at the quay, the tears shed by many people augmented the water flowing in the Kaveri. The Chakravarthi and Siruthondar turned teary as they took leave of each other. When Siruthondar's wife and

Arulmozhi Devi bid farewell to Kundavai, the three women wept inconsolably.

Those travelling eastwards were the first to leave the quay. Siruthondar sat by himself in a palanquin, while his wife and Arulmozhi Devi sat in another palanquin. The palanquin bearers lifted the palanquins and started walking surrounded by the ladies-in-waiting with horsemen leading and bringing up the rear of the entourage. After the palanquins had moved some distance away, Ponnan recollected something and ran towards Arulmozhi Devi's palanquin. The Devi instructed the bearers to halt and asked, 'What happened, Ponna? Why are you so agitated?'

Ponnan blurted, 'Devi!' and then remained tongue-tied.

The Rani remarked, 'You may speak your mind in this ammaiyar's (a respectful way of addressing middle-aged and elderly women) presence.'

'Devi! Didn't you mention about the casket?'

'What? Have you found it?' asked the Rani eagerly.

Ponnan stuttered, 'Yes! No! I will find it soon. That casket...'

Arulmozhi Devi was lost in thought for some time. 'Ponna! It is your responsibility to safeguard that casket. If he were to come here during my absence...' The Rani started sobbing unable to speak further.

'As you command, amma! I will safeguard the casket and hand it over to the Ilavarasan,' stated Ponnan as he wept. The palanquin moved on. As Ponnan was returning to his hut, he saw Kundavai Devi standing beside her palanquin and weeping. The Chakravarthi was consoling her. Ponnan heard Kundavai moan, 'I thought I had found a mother, appa! I'm not that fortunate!' Then Kundavai sat in the palanquin, the Chakravarthi mounted his steed, and they headed towards Uraiyur.

Ponnan entered his hut to find Valli weeping and complaining, 'Aiyyo! Had I known earlier, I would have offered to accompany the Maharani. What will I do here?'

Ponnan mustered courage and countered, 'Spoken like a woman! Your brave talks were a pretence after all!'

That instant the couple heard the sound of horse hooves outside their hut. They rushed out. The Chakravarthi alone had returned on horseback. He enquired, 'Ponna! Wouldn't you continue residing here at the quay? You're not planning to travel, are you?'

'I will be here, Prabhu. I'm not headed anywhere,' replied Ponnan.

'Look there! I am leaving the palace boat here. Kundavai Devi may be desirous of visiting this place and residing at the Vasantha Maligai. You must ply the boat then…'

'At your service, Prabhu!'

'One more thing. A friend of mine – a sivanadiyar – handed over a casket to me asking me to pass it on to you. It is in the boat. Do retrieve it,' So saying he glanced at Valli. She, who was gazing at him steadfast till then, promptly looked down with a shy smile. The next moment, the Chakravarthi's horse sped away like wind.

Part III

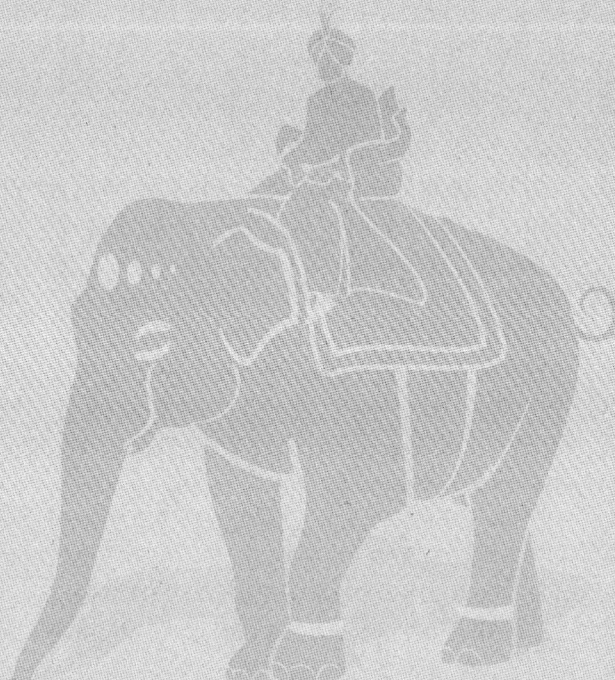

1. Ratna Vyapari

(A trader of precious gems)

A ship with its white masts unfurled was gliding westwards like a swan across the tranquil, blue sea at sunrise. Nature had spread her beautiful canvas in the eastern horizon as if to welcome the sun. The people aboard the ship, most of whom appeared to be traders, were very excited. They were lugging bundles of merchandise and preparing to disembark. Some of them congregated at a corner of the upper deck and were looking westwards eagerly.

Amongst them was a youthful trader of about twenty years of age. While his attire and the bundles of merchandise that lay next to him indicated that he was a trader, he had a regal bearing. If he were indeed a trader, he was no ordinary trader. He must have been extremely wealthy. The passengers aboard the ship glanced in the direction of the young trader often. They eyed him with deference and concern.

The young trader looked steadfastly to the west, ignoring everyone on board. He appeared extremely eager and joyous. Was he returning home after a long sojourn overseas? Was he keen to set sight on his motherland again? Yes! Indeed! Soon, the passengers caught sight of land, which resembled a dark

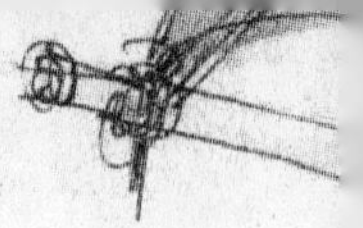

ridge, a short distance away. The young man stood transfixed for some time and his smile was akin to a lotus blossoming at sunrise. Shortly, what appeared to be a ridge morphed into trees, hillocks and temple towers. His face reflected the exhilaration

that consumed his heart. By then the sun had risen and started its journey for the day.

The youth, who was looking towards the land till then, turned around. As most of those aboard were observing him, they congregated around him respectfully when he gestured to them.

'Do you remember my instructions?' asked the young man.

'Yes, Maha…,' a trader started to reply and immediately fell silent.

'Is this the manner in which you abide by my commands?' asked the young man angrily.

'Please forgive me, swami!'

'Do you promise to conform to my command?'

'We will, swami!'

'You will not try to contact me while I'm in my motherland. Is that understood?'

'Yes, swami!'

'If we happen to meet by chance, you will not give away the fact that you know me from before.'

'As you command, swami!'

'All of you must return to this harbour by the next amavasai, the new moon.'

'We will!'

'How will you enquire about me if for some reason, I do not return to the harbour by the appointed date?'

'We will enquire about the ratna vyapari Devasenar.'

'There must be no slip-ups.'

'We will be mindful, swami!'

As must be evident by now, the young trader was the son of Parthiba Chola Maharaja and the ruler of Shenbaga Theevu, Vikraman. Three years had elapsed since Vikraman was offloaded at the island. It had, under Vikraman's reign, achieved impressive development on all fronts and attained immense fame. Adversaries had invaded Shenbaga Theevu just once after Vikraman ascended its throne. No one dared attack the isle thereafter. Shenbaga Theevu's army, on the other hand, under Vikraman's leadership, did attack the neighbouring islands and hoist the tiger flag. Tidings of Vikraman's valorous deeds and virtues began to spread to far-flung nations. Denizens of several islands, desiring good governance and protection, submitted to Vikraman's rule on their own accord.

The prince of Chola Nadu had neither forgotten his mother nor his motherland during these three years. He was also unable to stop thinking of the moon-like countenance of the young maiden he had encountered on the streets of the Pallava capital. The denizens of Shenbaga Theevu, who considered it their good fortune to be bestowed with a just ruler like Vikraman, were keen that his dynasty be sustained. They broached the subject of marriage a few times. They had often sought Vikraman's consent to head to Bharata Kandam and seal an alliance with a maiden from a pre-eminent royal family. Vikraman had turned down their entreaties and expressed his utter distaste for marriage. Was he so mesmerized by the dark eyes of the Kanchi maiden that he was unable to consider marriage with anyone else?

With the passage of time, Vikraman became acutely aware of his solitude. Even when amidst a throng he felt the absence of a companion. He felt a vacuum growing in his heart despite his military successes, fame, power and the adulation of his subjects. He often thought, 'If only that wide-eyed maiden were with me now!' He felt a curious joy in that torment and unconsciously heaved deep sighs. The maiden who had stolen his heart appeared in his mind from time to time, rendering him breathless.

An incident occurred a couple of months ago that caused Vikraman to put these bitter-sweet dreams at the back of his mind. Arulmozhi Rani had appeared in Vikraman's dreams. She was not clad in a queen's attire and ornaments and was instead draped in white apparel and sported thiruneeru and rudraksha like an ascetic steeped in Shiva bhakti. She had appeared to be more luminous than ever before. The Queen Mother was chanting the name of Shiva and looked at Vikraman compassionately. After some time, she said, 'My child! I take leave of you!'

Vikraman, who was perplexed and taken aback, enquired in his dream, 'I have barely met you after so long, amma. Where are you headed to now?'

Arulmozhi Rani did not reply to his question and instead remarked, 'My child! I have given my word. You must fulfil my promise. I am visiting you primarily to convey this.'

'What does this promise entail, amma? To whom did you give your word?'

'You ought to marry the Chakravarthi's daughter, Kundavai!'

A shocked Vikraman blurted, 'What are you saying, amma! Why should I marry the Chakravarthi's daughter? To whom did you make this promise?'

'I gave my word to the sivanadiyar, my child! You ought to uphold my word like Lord Rama, who kept his father's promise.' Having uttered these words, Arulmozhi Devi approached Vikraman and blessed him by placing her palm on his forehead. Vikraman immediately opened his eyes and sat up. He was relieved that it was a mere dream and was confident that it was just a figment of his imagination. Conversations from the past and recollections must have fused and manifested as a dream. After all that had transpired, why would his mother command him to marry the Chakravarthi's daughter? Why would she give her word to the sivanadiyar to this effect?

This dream did help Vikraman to cease thinking of the maiden in Kanchi that often. He became extremely keen to meet his mother. He wondered where and how she was in his absence. Vikraman felt an uncontrollable urge to return to his motherland. He decided to bring his mother back with him to Shenbaga Theevu and also take possession of the Chola dynasty's proud possessions – the heirloom sword and the Thirukkural. Vikraman communicated his decision to his ministers and influential denizens. He was impervious to their objections. They felt somewhat assuaged when he playfully alluded that he may return with a queen. So, preparations were made for Vikraman's departure to Bharata Kandam and a merchant ship was readied for this purpose. Vikraman travelled in that ship disguised as a ratna vyapari. A few traders from Shenbaga Theevu and guards disguised as traders accompanied him.

There was some discussion regarding the harbour at which the ship ought to be docked. While the rest of the passengers felt that the ship ought to be docked at Nagapattinam as Vikraman was headed to Uraiyur, he commanded that the ship be moored at Mamallapuram. He had heard of the city's sculptures since his childhood and was eager to view these sculptures before heading to Uraiyur. When the Pallava guards had imprisoned him and led him to the Mamallapuram harbour, he rued leaving the city without seeing the sculptures and now looked forward to fulfilling his long-standing wish.

There was another important reason for Vikraman deciding to moor the ship at Mamallapuram. He was desirous of inviting the foremost sculptors and painters there to Shenbaga Theevu, wishing to transform the island nation into a centre for exquisite sculptures over time. There might have been yet another reason for Vikraman wishing to disembark at Mamallapuram. It was quite possible that he was subconsciously hoping to see the maiden he had encountered at Kanchi and subsequently at the Mamallapuram seashore. Is it ever possible for anyone to unravel the mysteries concealed in the human heart?

2. Encounter

The annual Arts Festival was under way at Mamallapuram. The Chakravarthi was not presiding over the celebrations that year. Some people alluded that it was because he was in the throes of sorrow. A few others insisted that the Chakravarthi had left Pallava Nadu some time ago, that he had handed over the reins of the kingdom to his son after the latter had returned from Lanka, and that he was travelling across the country incognito.

But the residents of Mamallapuram showed no signs of diminished enthusiasm in conducting the festival as Ilavarasan Mahendran and Ilavarasi Kundavai were there to grace the celebrations.

The ratna vyapari loitered around, taking in the various sights, the exquisite sculptures culled out of rocks, the music, dance and drama performances. His face exuded uncharacteristic delight as his eyes scanned the place with unbridled eagerness. It appeared that his artistic thirst was not quenched despite spending much time at the festival. Was he ecstatic or envious or both when he viewed the wondrous sculptures, life-like paintings and listened to the soul-stirring music? He was accompanied by a dwarf, who appeared to be a porter. The dwarf was carrying his bundles. The trader conversed with the midget in gestures as the latter was apparently deaf and mute.

The young trader's behaviour was indeed suspicious! As he walked around viewing the sculptures and paintings, he would tarry for some time at certain places. If any sculptor or painter happened to be by himself, he would pat the man on his back and ask, 'I need to discuss an important matter with you. May we head to a quieter place?' The artist, enthralled by the trader's majestic appearance and handsome countenance, would comply. The trader would then wax eloquent about the island he resided in and its affluence. He further elaborated that the descendants of the Tamils who had immigrated to this island during the times of Karikala Chola resided in this island and that they knew no want except for temples and sculptures akin to the ones in Tamizhagam.

'Would you like to work in that country? If you do, you will be extremely wealthy by the time you return to Tamizhagam. There is no poverty in that land. There is an abundance of precious gems there!' he would say, showing the artist a handful of precious gems from the bundle he was carrying. The artist who had most likely come under the spell of the young man's words would agree on seeing the gems. The trader would then hand over a large-sized gem to the artist and instruct him, 'A ship with the tiger flag will arrive at the harbour the next new moon. You will be permitted to board the ship if you show the crew this gem.'

The ratna vyapari was engaged in recruiting artists during all the three days of the arts festival. On the third day, which was Vijayadasami, while walking down the road, he witnessed an unexpected sight. Was it truly unexpected or an occurrence he was anticipating? He looked around on hearing some commotion behind him. A palanquin surrounded by guards was moving in the same direction as he was. Yes, indeed! He realized in an instant that the damsel who resided in his heart was seated in the palanquin. The last three years had caused a slight change in the damsel's countenance. Then her face shone with a golden glow like the full moon rising in the blue seas. Now, her face had assumed a pale golden tone like the moon setting in the west during daybreak. Her exuberance had now been replaced with fatigue. Her eyes that had sparkled with mischief were now filled with sorrow. These changes did not make her beauty wane but enhanced it.

The trader felt breathless and tears welled in his eyes. He had often planned how he ought to behave should such an opportunity arise, but he found himself unable to act as per his plans. He stood by the side of the street, avoided looking at the palanquin, and instead looked in another direction. As the palanquin crossed him, he felt a pair of wide, dark eyes dwelling on him. Though he was gripped by an intense urge to look in the direction of the palanquin, he gritted his teeth and continued looking in another direction. Only after the palanquin had crossed him and travelled some distance away did he look in its direction. He observed that

the maiden seated in the palanquin was gazing at him without batting an eyelid. The trader looked down.

The palanquin came to a halt. One of the guards accompanying the palanquin approached the ratna vyapari and said, 'Sire! The Devi is desirous of enquiring about an important matter. Do come with me.' The trader was assailed by innumerable thoughts during the few moments he took to reach the palanquin. 'Who could this maiden be? Why is she summoning me? Has she

recognized me? If so, she must have remembered me through these years! She is certainly of noble birth. Could she be the Chakravarthi's daughter? Oh God! If that were the case …'

The young man, on reaching the palanquin, came face to face with the maiden. She shot a sharp glance at him. Is this why women's eyes were compared to swords and spears in literature? Indeed! Kundavai's gaze pierced through him as though she wished to discover the secrets buried in the depths of his heart. She beheld him thus for some time and then said, 'Aiyya! Who are you? It appears that you are not native to our country.'

'True, Devi. I reside at Shenbaga Theevu across the seas. I'm visiting here to trade in precious gems. My name is Devasenan,' blurted the ratna vyapari as if repeating a text he had memorized. Kundavai ought to have been taken aback by his agitation. She once again surveyed him silently and asked, 'What was the name of the island you mentioned? Shenbaga Theevu–Shenbaga Theevu – Shenbaga Theevu – I recollect hearing about it somewhere. Who is the ruler of that island?'

The trader did not fail to observe that Kundavai's face glowed as she spoke thus. He thought, 'She still remembers that man who was banished from Tamizhagam! But who is she? She, who has such a regal bearing and is endowed with such beauty, is probably…' The very suspicion of her antecedents unnerved the trader.

Kundavai then asked, 'Didn't you mention that you were a ratna vyapari?'

'Yes, thaye (a respectful way of addressing a woman; also means mother)! The bundles this dwarf is carrying contain gems of peerless quality. I am happy to show them to you now, if you so desire.'

'Not now! Crowds will throng the street. Do visit the palace in the evening,' she instructed.

On hearing the word "palace" the young trader grimaced. Kundavai appeared not to have noticed his reaction. Speaking as if she was reminded of something she had forgotten, she remarked, 'Yes! You must definitely visit the palace in the evening. The Chakravarthi's daughter, Kundavai Devi, is extremely fond of gems. She will certainly buy some from you. She may probably purchase your entire merchandise.'

The young man heaved a deep sigh as though his mind was rid of a heavy burden and replied, 'I do not wish to sell all my merchandise at one place. I wish to visit many other places in this country. It would suffice if you purchased the gems you require.'

'You would have to visit the palace to sell gems to me. Will you definitely come?'

'I will. But whom should I say summoned me to the palace?'

'You will be brought to me if you informed the guards that Kundavai Devi's companion, Madhavi, called you.'

'I hope I don't face any obstruction.'

'You will face none! You are loitering around carrying these bundles of gems. Aren't you scared of robbers?'

'That's a good question! Should one be scared of thieves under Narasimha Pallava Chakravarthi's reign?' retorted the young trader, with a twinkle in his eyes.

Kundavai smiled and said, 'I am happy to note that our Chakravarthi's fame has spread thus to nations beyond the seas. Hope you will definitely visit the palace in the evening.'

'I will,' affirmed the trader.

Kundavai then ordered the palanquin to move ahead. The ratna vyapari stood rooted to that spot staring at the palanquin till it disappeared amidst the multitude.

Hearing a harsh voice remark, 'Why are you staring in one direction for so long? Your eyeballs may pop out!' the young trader turned around with a start as though he had stepped on embers. It was Marappa Bhupathi, seated on a black stallion, eyeing him condescendingly.

3. Marappan's Smile

All the love and respect Vikraman garnered at Shenbaga Theevu could not compensate the vacuum he felt. He could never forget his native land and its people. Often, he remembered his mother Arulmozhi, the Sivanadiyar, Ponnan, Valli and the maiden from Kanchi. Alas! He could not avoid thinking of Marappan too though the recollection was upsetting. The ignominy wrought by the latter's treachery remained fresh in Vikraman's mind. He came to know of Marappan's deceitful nature on the day he had intended to hoist the Tiger flag atop the Chirapalli hill. When Vikraman was being taken to Kanchi after his imprisonment, he deduced from the guards' conversation that not only had Marappan reneged on his promise by not participating in the revolt, but he had also tipped off the Pallava general.

It was quite natural Vikraman felt bitter whenever the thought of Marappan crossed his mind. That such a man was born in the illustrious Chola dynasty caused him much anguish. So, the revulsion Vikraman felt on encountering Marappan unexpectedly was indescribable. Observing the trader's stunned expression, Marappan asked, 'Why do you seem so shaken up? I heard you mentioning robbers. Did you think that I was a thief?' and laughed tauntingly. By then, Vikraman had somewhat regained his composure and remarked, 'I do not reside here. But I have heard that there are no robberies in Narasimha Chakravarthi's reign. Hence, you are unlikely to be a thief.'

'Despite being a foreigner, you are haughty. Which country do you come from? What is your name? Why have you come to this country?' probed Bhupathi.

'I will tell you if you must know. My name is Devasenan. I have come here to sell precious gems.'

'Oh! So, you have come here to sell gems. Why should a ratna vyapari beckon every sculptor and speak to him secretively? Are you aware of the punishment Narasimha Chakravarthi will mete out to those who entice sculptors from Pallava Nadu?'

'I don't. Didn't I mention that I was a foreigner? May I know who you are and why are you interrogating me?'

Marappa Bhupathi burst out laughing and then retorted, 'Do you wish to know who I am? I am the brother of Parthiba Maharaja, who embraced martyrdom at the battle fought on the banks of Vennaru. I am currently the premier general of Chola Nadu.'

So saying, Marappan closely observed the young man to ascertain his reaction. As he remained stone-faced, Marappan asked, 'Even if my fame has not reached your shores, you must have heard of the bravest of brave warriors, Parthiba Maharaja. Which obscure country do you hail from?'

The young trader seemed lost in thought for some time. He then looked up to Marappan and stated, 'Yes! I have certainly heard of Parthiba Maharaja's valorous deeds. I am a subject of Shenbaga Theevu, which is now ruled by Parthiba Maharaja's son, Vikraman. Hence I warn you not to speak ill of or mock Parthiba Maharaja within my earshot!'

Marappan now appeared to be slightly surprised. Nevertheless, he regained his composure and retorted, 'Oh! You are such a loyal subject. I am blessed to have met you, aiyya! I am so reluctant to part ways with you. What did you say your name was?'

'Devasenan.'

'Devasenan. Aha! What a divine name! Those who claim name and fame are illusory in this world, are wrong. People will surely buy gems from you on hearing your name. Didn't Ilavarasi Kundavai Devi summon you to the palace to buy gems from you?'

'Ilavarasi Kundavai Devi? Who are you referring to?' asked the jewel trader with genuine surprise.

'The Devi who just passed by in the palanquin.'

'Isn't she Kundavai Devi's companion, Madhavi?'

'Oh! Is that how she lied to you? She is a worthy daughter of her father. It is clear to me that you are not a subject of this country. Alternatively, you may have been banished from here . . .' Marappan spoke the last sentence to himself.

Marappan then stared at Vikraman intently and enquired, 'Didn't you mention that Vikraman ruled your country? Is he aware of the accident his mother, Arulmozhi Devi, met with?'

Vikraman's reaction did not disappoint Marappan. The trader, who had worn an impassive look all along, appeared alarmed as he shrieked, 'What! What happened to Arulmozhi Devi?'

Marappan smiled broadly. It was then they heard the multitude to the rear of them cheer with great gusto.

'Long live the decimator of Vatapi, Narasimha Pallavendrar!'

'Jaya Vijayi Bhava!' echoed several voices in unison.

Several people whispered, 'The Chakravarthi is coming, the Chakravarthi is coming!'

4. Waylaid

The Chakravarthi was visiting Mamallapuram after long and sans prior intimation. People thronged around the royal procession, gazing at their majestic ruler seated on an elephant and cheered with boundless enthusiasm. Marappa Bhupathi, on hearing the crowds cheer, swiftly rode away. Vikraman made way and stood by the side of the road. His heart was beating fast. He was determined not to look at the Chakravarthi. Gritting his teeth, he looked in another direction. But as the royal mount walked past him, his resolve faltered. Despite being a sworn foe of the Chola dynasty, Narasimha Chakravarthi was a valorous warrior lauded by the whole world. Vikraman involuntarily looked at the Chakravarthi. Coincidentally, the Chakravarthi happened to glance in his direction. For a brief moment, the Chakravarthi's gaze dwelt on him. Yet, there was no change in his expression nor was there was an iota of recognition in his eyes.

The royal elephant walked ahead. Vikraman, having escaped a grave danger, heaved a deep sigh of relief. He continued standing at that spot for some time, till the crowds dispersed, lost in thought. He was in great turmoil. He shuddered on recollecting his chance encounter with Marappa Bhupathi. His uncle was now the general of Chola Nadu! He had been rewarded for his treachery! He wondered why Marappa Bhupathi spoke to him in a probing manner. Had he been recognized? Was that maiden indeed the Chakravarthi's daughter? If it were so, why did she provide him with a false name and insist that he visit the palace? Devasenan felt that danger surrounded him and that his continuing to remain at Mamallapuram would lead to disastrous consequences. Marappa Bhupathi's mischievous allusion to Arulmozhi Devi troubled him immensely. He decided to head to Uraiyur and look up his mother immediately. He would attend to other chores later.

Vikraman had initially intended to purchase a horse at

Mamallapuram and ride to Uraiyur. He changed his mind, being concerned that his purchasing a horse might lead to unintended consequences. Vikraman realized that it would be difficult to dodge Marappan if they were to meet again. The Chakravarthi's visit had fortunately ended his uneasy encounter with Marappan. Vikraman recollected that he had panicked on Marappan's referring to Arulmozhi Devi. Did Marappan speak deceptively as he was suspicious of Vikraman? Vikraman believed that his uncle would have undoubtedly recognized him had the Chakravarthi arrived even a moment later. Vikraman shuddered thinking of the possible outcome had this happened but he realized that Marappan's presence at the port city worked to his advantage. He decided to visit his mother at Uraiyur while Marappan was still at Mamallapuram. He would purchase a horse en route to Uraiyur.

Vikraman rushed to the inn where he was staying, cautiously looking around to ascertain if he was being shadowed. He hid himself amongst the crowds on hearing the sound of horses. On reaching the inn, he gathered his merchandise and personal effects, took the dwarf-porter along to carry his bundles and left for Uraiyur. Being preoccupied, Vikraman failed to observe the dwarf communicating with someone outside through gestures while entering the inn. It must have been a jaamam to sunset when Vikraman and the midget left Mamallapuram. By the time the duo exited the city and reached the highway, the evening sun had assumed a golden hue. Those days, highways linked Mamallapuram to Kanchi and Kanchi to Uraiyur. People on horseback, elephants and in palanquins frequently travelled down the Mamallapuram–Kanchi highway, resulting in that thoroughfare being abuzz. Villages flanked the highway and so did temples, monasteries, inns, pandals that distributed water to travellers, shops and schools. This gave foreigners the impression that a single, large city encompassed Mamallapuram, Kanchi and the highway linking the two cities.

There existed by-roads that forked from the highway. One such by-road branched off the highway close to Mamallapuram, ran through dense forests and joined the highway leading to Uraiyur that lay a short distance to the south of Kanchi. Travellers walked three kaada less when they used this by-road. Nevertheless, people eschewed the forest road, particularly at night. Even the most fearless of people did not use this road at night due to fear of wild beasts and the Bhadrakali (a ferocious incarnation of Goddess Parvathi) temple, where saktars and *kabalikas*[4] were rumoured to perform human sacrifices contravening the Chakravarthi's command.

Vikraman, who was ignorant of the beasts and sacrifices, reached the intersection of the highway and the by-road at sunset. He was initially reluctant when the dwarf indicated through gestures that they walk down this road but mustered courage. His desire to reach Uraiyur early and meet his mother helped in strengthening his resolve. Moreover, Vikraman had observed four men sitting at a short distance down the by-road, chatting, when he had reached the intersection. The instant he entered this road, the four men stood up casually and walked away briskly. Vikraman too started walking fast thinking that he would be able to catch up with those four men and would have company during his journey. However, as the dwarf now walked slower than usual, Vikraman was unable to catch up with them.

As he walked down the by-road, Vikraman observed the forest had become denser on both sides. The onset of twilight resulted in the skies becoming progressively darker. Soon it was completely dark except for the stars in the clear sky providing sufficient light for travellers to find their way. The sight of countless stars twinkling in the skies viewed from the road flanked by dense trees gave the impression that the angels in the forests were displaying their magical prowess by illuminating the skies with lamps. As time passed, the brave Vikraman started becoming anxious. The intermittent noises heard in the forest, sounds made by wild beasts and the bone-chilling hooting of owls heightened his anxiety. He wanted to ask the dwarf how much further they had to go and where they could stay at night, but the darkness made it impossible for the duo to communicate through gestures.

When more than a jaamam passed since nightfall, Vikraman was unwilling to proceed further. He instinctively felt that danger awaited him in that dark forest. The thought of retracing his steps to the highway occurred to him and as time passed, this thought gained credence. He tapped the dwarf's shoulders to stop him. As soon as they paused, he heard the sound of horse hooves at a distance. He was taken aback to see that the dwarf was paying close attention to that noise. How could he have heard that faint sound if he were indeed deaf? Vikraman immediately drew out the sword fastened to his waist and camouflaged by his robe. The sword, which was sharp and lubricated with ghee, glistened in the dead of the night. He grabbed the dwarf by his unruly hair, raised his sword and threatened, 'Hey you! State the truth! Are you truly deaf? Didn't you hear that noise now? If you don't state the truth, you will fall by my sword this very instant, at this very spot!'

The dwarf laughed loudly in a tone that caused Vikraman's blood to freeze. He extricated himself from Vikramans's grip, taking advantage of the latter's frozen stance. Leaping ten feet ahead, the midget cupped his mouth with his palms and let out an eerie growl. Those who heard from afar that repulsive noise, which resembled neither a human voice nor an animal cry, were likely to lose their nerve thinking that it was a ghost or ghoul. Vikraman shivered. As the dwarf ran off into the forest, he quickly regained his poise and leapt forward in pursuit of the dwarf, determined to kill him. That very instant, four men who were hiding behind the trees came running to the forest road. Vikraman regained his courage on seeing them armed with knives. The darkness, solitude and the midget's ghastly roar had prompted Vikraman to believe that he had been transported to a world inhabited by ghosts; he lost his nerve. On seeing armed men, Vikraman was reassured that he still was in a world inhabited by humans.

Vikraman's fear vanished and he started swirling his sword. The four men attacked the young ruler in unison. Vikraman swirled his sword around ferociously as he combatted them. One man fell to the ground, grievously injured, by the first sweep of Vikraman's sword. Another man lost grip of his knife when it was struck by Vikraman's sword. The knife struck the dwarf, who was standing at a distance. The dwarf shrieked as he fell to the ground. The two others, on realizing Vikraman's peerless prowess in sword fight, fought with him from a distance and were cautious not to come within the trajectory of his sword. They kept looking around as they fought and it was evident that they were expecting someone. Vikraman was not surprised when he heard the sound of a horse approaching them. In the dim light cast by the stars, they observed a warrior seated on a horse, holding his sword aloft. One of the men implored, 'Master! Master!' Vikraman thought his end was imminent. Although he was exhausted by the combat, he was confident of handling these two men but he wondered how he could confront the man on horseback.

Vikraman was sure he would die without seeing his mother and rued his stars. He also remembered the maiden in the palanquin who had looked at him with kindness and had spoken to him. The image of the Chakravarthi seated on the royal mount flashed in his mind's eye. He pondered whether Narasimha Maha Chakravarthi's administration was so lax and if he was indeed being waylaid. Vikraman wielded his sword with greater ferocity. One of his two remaining attackers fell. At the same time, the warrior on horseback aimed his sword on the last of Vikraman's attackers, who fell to the ground lifeless.

Vikraman was stunned beyond words. There was no reason to doubt that the warrior had erroneously aimed his sword at one of the remaining attackers as it was evident that Vikraman was wearing a robe while his attackers were bare chested. As he wondered who this warrior was, the man jumped off his horse and enquired, 'Aiyya! Who are you? Why were you travelling alone in the dark?'

5. The Spymaster

Vikraman felt grateful to the warrior who came to his rescue at the appropriate time and replied, 'Sire! I am a trader and was travelling down this shortcut to Uraiyur. Fortunately, you saved me from the imminent mishap en route.'

'Are you indeed a trader? Can the hands that grip the weighing scales wield the sword so deftly? That's incredible, aiyya. What kind of trade do you engage in?'

'I am a ratna vyapari. I am also trained in sword fight…'

'How astute of you! You, a ratna vyapari, venturing down this forest road, that too at night…'

'I was deceived by Narasimha Chakravarthi's reputation. I have heard people in far-flung countries laud him saying that there is no thievery in his reign…'

'Oh! So, you are a foreigner! I thought so. Which country do you come from, aiyya?'

'I belong to Shenbaga Theevu.'

'Did you say Shenbaga Theevu? I too have heard that precious gems abound in that country. You, who came here to sell gems, ought to have first gone to Kanchi. Why the urgency to visit Uraiyur?'

'I will answer your query, aiyya. But first, may I know who you are?'

'How does my identity matter to you?'

'Shouldn't I know the identity of the person who saved my life?'

'It wasn't I who saved your life. You were able to defend yourself. You, who were able to vanquish three men, would have easily overcome the last one standing. Nevertheless, I will divulge my identity. Didn't you mention that all you had heard about the Kanchi Chakravarthi was untrue? I am one of that Chakravarthi's spies – the head of the espionage force. I received a tip-off that you were travelling all alone down this forest road. I came here anticipating a mishap...'

'Is that so? That's impressive. Does the Chakravarthi's espionage force function so competently? In that case, I was wrong...'

'Aiyya! The administration here may not be as efficient as it is in Shenbaga Theevu. But we do prevent the occurrence of killings and thefts to the best of our ability. In fact, I ought to produce you in the Chakravarthi's court for travelling down a deserted road at night and taking away the lives of four men.'

In the dim light cast by the stars, the warrior observed Vikraman grasping the handle of his sword.

'No, aiyya, don't. I have no intention of producing you at the Chakravarthi's court. You are a foreigner who strayed down this road ignorant of the impending perils. In the absence of people like you, who voluntarily put themselves in danger, people like me will be idle. There will be no need for a head of the espionage force. Well, the task I set out for has been accomplished. In fact, I need not have come at all. You are competent enough to take care of yourself independently. I will take your leave,' concluded the warrior.

Vikraman was perplexed. He believed that he had not appropriately conveyed his gratitude to that warrior. Vikraman was desirous of befriending that warrior and buying his horse so that he could travel to Uraiyur. He was also concerned about his lodging for that night.

'That's not so. I might have lost my life had you not come to my rescue then. Moreover, I need your assistance with regard to another matter,' stated Vikraman.

'It's not my habit to turn down a person who seeks my help. I also do not assist people who do not seek my succour.'

'I have an urgent task to attend to at Uraiyur. Only you can help me at the current juncture. If you could…'

'I know what you are about to ask for. My horse. But if you were to ride my horse through this forest at night, both of you are likely to become a prey to the forest beasts. I am not concerned about you but I am unwilling to allow my horse to become a prey to wild animals.'

'What do you suggest we do?'

'There is a sculptor's house a short distance from here. You may accompany me. We will spend the night there and leave at dawn.'

Vikraman thought for a moment and replied, 'As you say, aiyya.'

The duo gathered the bundles scattered on the ground and fastened them to the horse's back. The warrior then guided the horse into the forest, followed by Vikraman.

6. The Sculptor's Abode

A narrow lane meandered through the dense forest. Even during the day, this lane remained overcast and one can imagine how dark it must have been in the dead of the night. The stars that were intermittently visible in the forest path were imperceptible in this lane. The brave Vikraman's heart thumped as he followed a complete stranger through the extremely narrow path. The overgrowth of trees, shrubs and creepers that flanked the lane frequently brushed against him and bone-chilling cries of owls and bats were heard in the vicinity. The horse neighed in reaction to a growl heard from afar. The chief of the espionage force patted it reassuringly.

The horse led the way followed by the spymaster with Vikraman after him. Vikraman stumbled over an aerial root of a tree and fell down. The spymaster grasped his hand and helped him to his feet. Vikraman felt boundless wonder and thought, 'Ah! What a vice-like grip that was! His hands are so strong! He is no ordinary man. He must be a peerless warrior. The Chakravarthi indeed chooses the apposite person for every task.' Just as Vikraman wondered how much further their destination was, the darkness receded and the sky became visible. The faint outline of a building that lay ahead was perceptible.

'We have reached our destination. We will halt for the night at this house and you may leave at dawn,' remarked the spymaster.

'As you say. But whose house is this? Who is residing amidst such a dense forest? Why?' enquired a puzzled Vikraman.

'The person who built this house is no more. This place was not such a dense forest when he was alive. That's a long story. I'll relate it if you are unable to sleep at night,' replied the spymaster. He then went to the house and knocked at the door. On nearing the house, Vikraman realized that it was no ordinary house. It appeared to be a painting gallery or a sculpture studio. An old lady opened the door with a stone lantern held high. She shot a surprised glance at the spymaster and her eyebrows arched slightly. The spymaster placed his index finger on his lips and rapidly moved it off. The woman seemed to understand the gesture and the surprised expression on her face disappeared. She said, 'Welcome, aiyya!' and flung the door wide open.

The two men stepped into the house and so did the horse, as if it belonged to that house. It walked through the front hall and inner courtyard of the house and came to a halt at the door that led to the backyard. The elderly woman opened the door and the horse voluntarily walked through. The spymaster told Vikraman, 'This horse is indeed sharp! When I had visited this place earlier, I had tethered it in the backyard. This time it headed to the stable on its own. I will go and tend to it. Meanwhile, you may view the sculptures in this house.' He was followed by the elderly woman holding the stone lantern.

An illuminated lamp had been placed in an alcove in the wall. Vikraman looked around the house. Exquisitely carved sculptures lay scattered around the place. The walls were covered with paintings in several hues. These must have been sketched several years ago but notwithstanding their age, the life-like quality of the paintings remained undiminished.

The sculptures and paintings mostly depicted a maiden

endowed with divine beauty in various dance postures. The beauty and aesthetic quality of the art pieces left Vikraman speechless. The paintings and sculptures he had seen at Uraiyur's Chitra Mandapam and Mamallapuram's art festival paled in comparison to those that were cloistered in this desolate building. He was eager to ascertain the identity of the great artist who had created these masterpieces. The spymaster had meanwhile fed the horse and had re-entered the house. Vikraman blurted out to him, 'Aiyya! These sculptures are indeed breathtaking. Which great sculptor carved these? Is the maiden of divine beauty depicted in the sculptures real or a figment of the sculptor's imagination? Why should these wonderful sculptures lie hidden in the middle of a forest? Shouldn't everyone have an opportunity to appreciate these sculptures? Please tell me what transpired here.'

'Didn't I tell you that it is a long story? I will relate the story to you if you are desirous of spending the rest of the night bereft of sleep. I am famished. The paatti (grandmother) is bringing puffed rice and jaggery. Let's eat first,' replied the spymaster.

'You have not yet mentioned your name to me,' remarked Vikraman.

'My name is Veerasenan. What is yours?'

A surprised Vikraman replied, 'I am Devasenan.'

'Well, our names are well-matched. So, you may speak freely to me. Why are you so eager to rush to Uraiyur? If your intention was to sell precious gems, shouldn't you have gone to Kanchi first?'

Vikraman, while feeling grateful and affectionate towards the spymaster, was still wary and anxious. He was concerned that the spymaster may be able to unravel his true identity and decided to tread carefully.

'My mother lives in Uraiyur. I was rushing there in my eagerness to meet her.'

'But didn't you mention that you hailed from Shenbaga Theevu?'

'I'm a native of Uraiyur. I migrated to Shenbaga Theevu a few years ago to build a fortune. Once Uraiyur ceded to the Pallava Empire, it ceased to be as prosperous as before. How can one sell precious gems in a city bereft of a royal family?'

Vikraman had expected Veerasenan to mention something about Arulmozhi Devi after he had broached the subject of royalty. But he was disappointed. Veerasenan remained mum till he finished eating. Once the duo had finished eating, Vikraman once again pressed Veerasenan to relate the story of the sculptures.

Vikraman was puzzled when the spymaster asked, 'Aiyya Devasenar, do you believe in death?'

'What kind of a question is this? What do you mean by asking me if I believe in death…?'

'Do you really believe that people die? In other words, when we say that someone has lost his or her life, has that life indeed

been extinguished? Or is it that the mortal body dies while the life continues to inhabit this world? Do the dead think of us, visit us and observe our deeds?'

Vikraman was somehow reminded of his father and the promise he had made to Parthiba Maharaja. He wondered if his father was still in this world watching his actions.

'There are times my thoughts resonate with yours. But there appears to be no one to lay my doubts to rest.'

'I somehow believe that death is illusory. I believe it is foolish to grieve over a loved one's demise. Thirty years ago, the sculptor Aayanar and his daughter, Sivakami, used to reside in this house. This house used to resonate with the sounds of anklets and chisels. Sivakami was an exquisite dancer. Aayanar used to paint portraits and carve sculptures replicating her various dance postures…'

'Oh! So, the maiden endowed with divine beauty was Sivakami!'

'Yes. I used to visit this house often then. It was during the reign of Mahendra Chakravarthi…His son must have been of your age then. I used to accompany him – Narasimha Varmar. We could hear the sound of anklets even when we were at a distance from this house. I'm unable to believe that Aayanar and Sivakami are no longer in this house. There! If I listen carefully, I can still hear the sounds of anklets and chisels…'

Vikraman's eagerness knew no bounds. He requested Veerasenan to tell him about Aayanar and Sivakami. Veerasenan complied. He described Aayanar's peerless skills as a sculptor, his daughter's wondrous beauty and her prowess in dancing. He mentioned in the passing of the deep love that had blossomed between Narasimha Chakravarthi and Sivakami when the former was the crown prince. When the demonic Pulikesi had invaded Kanchi from the north, the lovers were separated. Pulikesi abducted and imprisoned Sivakami, who undertook an oath[5]. Narasimha Varmar had exercised herculean efforts to free Sivakami and to fulfil her oath. Ultimately, Sivakami had realized that her love could never be consummated and was heartbroken.

Vikraman shed tears several times as he heard the tale. His regard for Narasimha Chakravarthi grew multi-fold. He even developed a sense of devotion towards the Chakravarthi. He recollected his promise to Parthiba Maharaja and reminded himself that Narasimha Chakravarthi was a sworn enemy of his dynasty. It was almost dawn by the time Veerasenan completed the story. The two men were able to sleep for just a nazhigai. Vikraman, who woke up to the sounds of birds chirping, wondered whether the events of the previous night were a dream. He looked around and confirmed that what had transpired was real.

Vikraman heard the spymaster call out from outside the house, 'Aiyya, Devasenar! The horse is rested and ready to leave. It, after all, was not awake all night like us! You may complete your morning ablutions and leave…'

Vikraman partook the simple breakfast offered by the elderly woman and took leave of Veerasenan saying, 'Aiyya! I am deeply indebted to you. I will never be able to repay you for having saved my life. But I am unwilling to take your horse for free. I request you to accept these precious gems in exchange for the horse.' He handed over a fistful of gems to Veerasenan.

'You have misunderstood. I'm not gifting my beloved horse to you. I am only lending this horse to you. Once you complete your errands at Uraiyur, you should leave the horse at this house on your way back,' remarked the spymaster.

'I will do as you say. However, I would like to gift these precious gems to you as a symbol of my gratitude,' stated Vikraman.

Veerasenan acquiesced and accepted the gems. As soon as Vikraman mounted the horse, the spymaster patted the horse and said, 'Aiyya! This horse has been to Uraiyur often. It is familiar with the route and will take you to Uraiyur of its own accord. You need not stop to enquire about the route.' The horse started trotting down the forest path. Vikraman kept looking back until the sculptor's house and the spymaster disappeared from his sight. He was rather impressed on observing the spymaster's well-built and charismatic appearance in daylight.

7. Scattered Gems

Once Vikraman reached the forest road and disappeared from sight, the spymaster re-entered the sculptor's house. He stood there for some time, with his arms folded across his chest, looking at the divine sculptures. He turned misty-eyed and remarked to the elderly woman, 'Amma! If this boy were to return, do allow him to stay here. But please do not divulge anything about me. I will be back here in another five to six days.'

'As you say, swami,' replied the elderly woman.

The spymaster then headed to the backyard of the house. There stood another horse of the same breed as the one on which Vikraman rode away. The warrior mounted the horse quite deftly and left the house. He did not ride down the route Vikraman had headed and instead retraced his steps through the forest lane to the spot where Vikraman was almost waylaid.

As the spymaster examined that area closely, he appeared surprised. The longer he looked around, the more perplexed he became. The corpses of the four men who had been brought down by the ratna vyapari as well as their swords had vanished! The spymaster had expected to see a ghastly sight and had imagined that he would be a witness to the skeletal remains of the men devoured by wild beasts. But there was no trace of the remains. Had the wild beasts gobbled even the skeletons? Even so, they wouldn't have taken the men's clothes and swords too. The spymaster surmised that another person must have visited the spot after he had left with Vikraman and something else must have happened there.

He jumped off the horse and looked around even more carefully. Suddenly an object caught his eye. He was not only surprised but also puzzled. That object was a skull! It could not have been the skull of one of the four men who were killed there the previous night. The skull in question was very old. The spymaster concluded, 'The person who had visited this spot after we left must have been a kabalika. A kabalika or a group of them must have moved the corpses away!'

The spymaster observed a few precious gems lying scattered on the ground. When the dwarf had dropped the trader's bundles down, a bundle must have opened up, causing the gems to spill. The spymaster bent down with the intention of gathering the gems. It was then that he heard the sound of horses' hooves a short distance away. It appeared from the clattering that four to five horses were approaching the spot. The spymaster rushed to his horse, mounted it and rode into the nearby forest. He left his horse at a distance, returned to the spot and hid behind a tree. He had an unobstructed view of the approaching contingent from his hiding spot.

Six warriors on horseback came to a halt at the spot of Vikraman's encounter. On seeing the man who appeared to be their leader, the spymaster's eyebrows furrowed and then arched. His face displayed surprise, revulsion and anger simultaneously. The leader was none other than Marappa Bhupathi. As Bhupathi brought his horse to a halt, the other warriors followed suit. Then Marappan dismounted his horse and like the spymaster, surveyed the area closely. It was the skull that caught his attention too initially.

Marappa Bhupathi then observed the signs of the swordfight that had occurred the previous night. Blood stains and the trails of bodies being dragged away were evident. He gathered the scattered gems with much gusto. He laughed aloud as he looked at the gems in his palms. 'What a stroke of good fortune!' he commented to those who had accompanied him. The contingent soon rode away swiftly after discussing among themselves for some time.

The spymaster subsequently walked to his horse, mounted it and retraced the route by which he had come the previous night. The horse, after going around a bend on the forest road, trembled. The spymaster brought the horse to a halt and looked around. Vultures were circling the area behind a small rock that lay a short distance away. The mystery of the missing corpses was solved. Those who had come to this spot after he and the trader had left the previous night must have dragged the carcasses to the area behind the rock. But who could they have been?

The spymaster rode away without tarrying at that spot for long. He soon reached the highway linking Mamallapuram and Kanchi. Coincidentally, the royal retinue was heading to Kanchi from Mamallapuram on that highway. The palanquin bearing Kundavai Devi was amidst the retinue. Seated on a majestic white steed that was walking beside the palanquin was Narasimha Chakravarthi's son, Mahendran. The spymaster who observed the retinue from a distance, rode away swiftly, ahead of them towards Kanchi.

8. Masquerader

Princess Kundavai and Prince Mahendran observed the chief of the spies racing ahead towards Kanchi without stopping to pay his respects to the royal retinue. Kundavai's palanquin and Mahendran's horse were moving abreast making it possible for them to converse with each other. Mahendran was like Kundavai in appearance for he had her tenderness and good looks, but he also possessed the Chakravarthi's regal and gallant bearing. Since Mahendran had been governing the kingdom on behalf of Narasimha Varmar for almost a year by now, the act of the horse rider ignoring the retinue surprised everyone.

'Anna! Did you observe the warrior riding ahead of us? How majestic he looks! Do you know who he is?' enquired Kundavai.

'I don't know him, thangai (younger sister). He appears to be a royal. He is tall and well-built. Look at his horse! It has galloped far ahead of us so quickly!' replied Mahendran.

'He seems to be heading to Kanchi. Could he be a foreigner? Why else would he have ridden ahead of us without even acknowledging us? Several foreigners disembarked from the ship that arrived at the harbour four days ago; hence we see many unfamiliar people.' remarked Kundavai.

'Kundavai, did the ratna vyapari from Shenbaga Theevu pay you a visit?' asked Mahendran.

Kundavai's disappointment was palpable in her reply.

'He is bound to visit the Kanchi palace,' stated Mahendran.

Kundavai did not respond to this statement. She believed that the trader would never visit the palace if her hunch was correct. Images of the Chola prince she had seen at a street in Kanchi three years ago and the trader she met at Mamallapuram the previous day alternately flitted in her mind. If the two were indeed different people, the similarity in their looks was indeed astounding.

Mahendran did not fail to notice Kundavai's silence and her sombre countenance.

He affectionately called out, 'Thangai'.

'What is it, anna?'

'Why do you appear to be out of sorts?'

'I am fine, anna.'

'I have an idea. May I tell you?'

'Do tell me, anna!'

'I am going to tell appa that I am incapable of shouldering the burden of ruling this kingdom and that he ought to do so.'

'Why do you speak thus, anna?'

'My governing this kingdom when he is the Chakravarthi is akin to a cat occupying the throne of a lion! Everyone in this country thinks so.'

'Not at all, anna!'

'Besides, an important task awaits me. I ought to embark on yet another sea voyage.'

'Are you headed to Lanka again?'

'No, I am intending to visit Shenbaga Theevu.'

'What are you saying, anna?'

'I am going to request appa to forgive Vikraman. I will then personally travel to Shenbaga Theevu and bring him here. A year has passed since I returned from Lanka. I have not seen you smile even once since I returned. I will ensure that you are happy again before attending to any other task,' announced Mahendran.

Mahendran's voice was full of emotion as he spoke. Seeing Kundavai turn teary-eyed, he fell silent for some time.

'Appa will not consent to this,' remarked Kundavai.

'It is my responsibility to secure his consent. I had intended to speak to him about this yesterday. But he had not returned last night. I will certainly ask him today.'

'Of what use would your voyage be even if appa were to consent and you sailed to Shenbaga Theevu?'

'Of what use? I will get a brother-in-law.'

'That is unlikely to happen, anna! That arrogant prince is unlikely to agree to marry a maiden of the Pallava dynasty,' quipped Kundavai.

Mahendran burst out laughing. 'Thangai! Have you even looked at yourself in the mirror?' he asked.

'Go away, anna!' replied Kundavai shyly.

'I certainly will go away, thangai, to Shenbaga Theevu. I will capture that Ilavarasan, produce him before you and make him apologize for the sorrow he has caused you. I am not worthy of being Mahendra Chakravarthi's grandson if I fail to accomplish this task!' pronounced Mahendran.

Kundavai and Mahendran, on returning to the Kanchi palace, headed to their respective quarters. Kundavai on entering her chamber in the anthapuram, the women's quarter in the palace, was shell-shocked to see a stranger sitting on the seat meant for the Chakravarthi! It took her a moment to realize that it was the warrior who had overtaken their retinue at the junction of the forest road and the highway. This surprised and angered her.

'Who are you, aiyya? How dare you enter the anthapuram?' she demanded.

'Devi, I am the chief of the Pallava kingdom's espionage force. I came here to interrogate you about a tip-off,' replied the stranger.

The instant he replied, Kundavai's anger transformed into gaiety.

'Appa! What kind of a joke is this?' she queried as she ran to him, embraced him and pulled away his false moustache. Narasimha Chakravarthi emerged from the façade of the spymaster.

'It was your voice that gave you away, appa. You are otherwise unrecognizable. How did you become so adept at assuming disguises, appa?' questioned Kundavai.

'My child, this is the most valuable of the skills my father, Mahendra Chakravarthi, imparted to me,' replied the Chakravarthi.

9. Why the Robbery?

Kundavai looked at the Chakravarthi in amazement. Her naturally wide, kohl-lined eyes widened further in surprise as she enquired, 'Why do you say that, appa? It is the stage artists who don disguises. Why should kings be adept at masquerading?'

'My child, the person governing a kingdom ought to be well-versed in several arts; particularly in the art of disguising himself. Only then will he be able to ascertain the denizens' sentiments from time to time. The occurrence of crimes within the nation may be averted...'

Kundavai interjected asking, 'Which crime do you plan to forestall by assuming this disguise? Do you believe that I am about to transgress in some way?' She smiled revealing her teeth that resembled jasmine buds.

'You are, without doubt, guilty of a major offence, Kundavai. Four men met with their deaths last night because of you!' pronounced the Chakravarthi. Kundavai was stunned.

'What are you saying, appa? I am completely in the dark!'

'Yes, you are indeed ignorant. Didn't you summon a ratna vyapari who had come from overseas to the palace?'

'Yes, I did. Is that a crime?'

'Did you conceal your identity and tell him that you were Kundavai Devi's companion?'

'True. But what of it?'

'The mishap occurred on account of that. Someone subsequently informed the ratna vyapari that you were the Chakravarthi's daughter. He became concerned wondering if some danger lurked in your invitation and headed to Uraiyur through the forest road that night itself…'

'To Uraiyur?' asked Kundavai in a tone that betrayed shock. 'Appa, I am wondering why the trader has to go to Uraiyur instead of coming to Kanchi. There is no one at the palace in Uraiyur.'

'Apparently, this trader's mother lives in Uraiyur. He went to Uraiyur to meet her …'

Kundavai was about to say something. At the last moment she bit her tongue and kept quiet. Her suspicion that the ratna vyapari might have been Vikraman was confirmed. She wondered if her father also harboured the same doubt. She decided not to say anything untoward and to arouse his suspicion. The Chakravarthi asked, 'What are you ruminating about, my child?'

'Nothing, appa! Just some old memories. I recollected our previous trip to Uraiyur…Never mind that, appa! Tell me what happened to that trader thereafter,' she asked.

'As he was travelling down the forest road in the night, four men armed with swords attacked him suddenly. But that trader was not the one to be trifled with. He single-handedly killed three of his attackers. The fourth man fell to this sword!' So saying, the Chakravarthi pointed to his sword.

An extremely surprised and eager Kundavai asked, 'How did you manage to reach the spot then?'

'How else will I be able to govern this expansive kingdom, my child?'

'Don't blow your own trumpet! What ever happened of the claim that there is no theft in Narasimha Chakravarthi's kingdom? If robbers were emboldened to attack a merchant from overseas at a spot so close to Kanchi and Mamallapuram...'

'Like you, I too initially thought that the attackers must have been robbers. But they were not robbers after all.'

'But who else could have acted so audaciously?'

'My child, they were engaged in a crime whose severity exceeds that of theft and highway robbery!'

'What is it, appa?'

'Did you observe the trader closely?'

'Yes, I did.'

'What did you think of him?'

Kundavai haltingly said, 'Nothing!'

The Chakravarthi questioned, 'How did you fail to observe that he appeared to be a royal?' Kundavai panicked wondering if he had recognized Vikraman.

The Chakravarthi, without waiting for her to reply, remarked, 'People of royal lineage are most preferred by those who perform human sacrifices!'

Kundavai shrieked, 'Aiyyo!' She then queried, 'Appa, does this barbaric practice still continue in our country?'

'Indeed, my child! I am trying to exterminate this barbaric ritual but I am yet to meet with success. If I eradicate this superstitious practice at one place, it crops up elsewhere.'

'So, that naïve trader faced this peril...What would have befallen him had you not reached that spot in the nick of time?'

'He is not all that naïve, Kundavai. He too is a thief. Hence he was trapped in such a situation.'

Kundavai felt incapable of breathing for a moment and questioned, 'Is that so, appa? Were all the gems he was carrying his loot?'

'No, Kundavai. He did not steal the precious gems. He was engaged in an underhand activity at Mamallapuram. He was trying to lure some of our sculptors to his country, Shenbaga Theevu. Do you understand the gravity of this crime, my child? Are you aware of the punishment this crime entails?'

'I do, appa!'

'The trader had hired a mute dwarf as his porter to ensure that his activities remain undetected. However, I suspected for long that the dwarf belonged to a gang of kabalikas. I was right. The dwarf misled the young man and had I not reached that spot in the nick of time...' The Chakravarthi's voice trailed off as he became immersed in thought.

'What transpired after that, appa? Where is the ratna vyapari now?'

The Chakravarthi related the events of the previous night and finished by stating that he had lent his horse to the trader so that the latter could ride to Uraiyur. Kundavai paused for some time and then enquired, 'Did he recognize you?'

'He did not. Why do you ask so?'

'I wanted to check how effective your disguise was.' Kundavai continued, 'Appa! I intended to ask you something.'

'What is it, my child?'

'Anna has never been to Uraiyur. Both of us are thinking of visiting Uraiyur.'

'Aha! Do go there by all means. I recollect something as the subject of Uraiyur has come up. I saw Marappa Bhupathi at Mamallapuram yesterday. Why was he there? Are you aware of his visit?'

'I do. Anna and I had summoned Marappa Bhupathi...'

A surprised Chakravarthi interjected asking, 'Why?'

'Achuta Varmar had informed us that he was feeling debilitated and that he was unable to attend to matters of the state. So anna had summoned Marappa Bhupathi and had reinstated him as the general of Chola Nadu.'

The Chakravarthi merely said, 'Oh!' and was again lost in thought. Kundavai, realizing that attempting to converse with him was futile, started playing a doleful melody on the yazh, her fretless harp.

10. The Flooded Forest Stream

Some readers may find reference to human sacrifices in the previous chapter strange and repulsive. But those who have studied the history of those times in Tamizhagam will know it is factual and real. However unpleasant or revolting it may be, it is necessary to be aware of the practices of that period to understand the current narrative.

Saivism and Vaishnavism flourished in Tamizhagam during the reigns of Mahendra Pallavar and Narasimha Chakravarthi. Love and empathy for fellow beings were the foundation of these two faiths. By then, Saivism and Vaishnavism had imbibed the laudable aspects of Jainism and Buddhism, which were on the wane. The two faiths also preached devotion and surrender to the Almighty, thereby transforming Tamil Nadu into a divine land. The Saivite gurus like Appar and Sambandar and the Vaishnavite Alwars were instrumental in spreading the bhakti movement across the nation through their divine songs. Exquisitely sculpted temples dedicated to Shiva and Vishnu dotted the land.

While majority of the people followed faiths like Saivism and Vaishnavism that preached universal love, a miniscule segment of the population did clandestinely embrace horrific cults such as

Kabalikam, Saktam and Bhairavam that extolled human sacrifice. The founders of these sects instilled extreme and blind devotion in their followers. It was this blind devotion that impelled the followers of these faiths to flock to the Kali and Durga temples and casually behead themselves. The followers believed that by beheading themselves they would be the recipients of immense good fortune in their subsequent births. The priests at these temples helped entrench such beliefs. Temples dedicated to Kali and Durga were constructed amidst dense forests and

uninhabited mountains.

These horrific faiths made inroads into Tamizhagam along with the army of Pulikesi, who had invaded the country during the reign of Mahendra Pallavar. Severe famine gripped the nation both in the wake of Pulikesi's departure and when Narasimha Pallavar embarked on a campaign to conquer Vatapi. The famines facilitated the spread of the cults that propounded human sacrifice. Narasimha Chakravarthi had undertaken the herculean task of finding ways to annihilate these cults. He understood that the use of force alone could not obliterate superstitions. No punishment was, after all, strong enough to deter people who were prepared to decapitate themselves. He had, therefore, handed over the reins of the kingdom to his elder son and was travelling across the country incognito to ascertain the extent to which these faiths had spread and to find the nerve centres of these cults.

Vikraman, however, was oblivious to the gravity of the peril he had encountered. He thought he had been attacked by a gang of robbers. Several thoughts rose and ebbed, like waves, within

Vikraman once he had taken leave of the spymaster and resumed his journey riding the horse he had borrowed from the latter. The desire to meet his mother was foremost on his mind. Though the spymaster's horse was galloping at the speed of wind, Vikraman's impatience prompted him to wish for the quadruped to further accelerate. The spymaster's majestic appearance flashed frequently in his mind. Vikraman recollected the assistance the spymaster had rendered and felt extremely grateful to him. The suspicion that the astute spymaster must have unravelled his secret occurred intermittently to Vikraman. He wondered if the spymaster lending him the horse was a major ruse to ensnare him.

Vikraman repeatedly recalled the tale of Narasimha Chakravarthi's youthful romance related by the spymaster. He was lost imagining Sivakami dance in the sculptor's house amidst the forest, Aayanar chiselling statues observing Sivakami's dance postures and Narasimha Varmar appreciatively watching the duo. The golden hued countenance of the maiden in the palanquin who had eagerly gazed at him flashed often in his mind. He tried to convince himself that there was no treachery lurking behind her bewitching form but wondered whether she was indeed the Chakravarthi's daughter or a companion to the princess.

Vikraman was riding along lost in such thoughts and stopping at villages that lay en route to enquire if he was proceeding in the right direction. The horse, as mentioned by the spymaster, was travelling of its own accord towards Uraiyur. This caused Vikraman much surprise and joy. His trust in and regard for the spymaster grew. Vikraman decided to break his travel at night and to stay at a village inn, in deference to the spymaster's instructions. But shortly before sunset there was a major impediment to his journey.

The eastern sky turned dark unexpectedly, enveloped by dense clouds. A cool, dusty wind started blowing. It started raining at a distance and the fragrance of petrichor pervaded. Soon there was a deluge accompanied by thunder and lightning. It appeared as though the sky had given way and the water it had stored for long was being showered on earth. Vikraman, who was thoroughly drenched and shivering, sought refuge under a tree for some time. The rains showed no signs of receding. Time passed and nightfall was imminent. Vikraman, realizing the difficulty of navigating through a dark and rainy night, decided to ride ahead and stop at a village or a temple for the night.

Soon, he reached a forest stream. It appeared as though the waters were just ankle deep. As the stream's waters were rapidly swelling, Vikraman thought it prudent to quickly cross the stream and directed the horse into the waters. He rode a short distance into the stream when the water flow accelerated. The horse, unable to trot against the flow of the water, started trotting in the direction of the flow. The flow was swelling by the minute. Even as Vikraman was wondering whether he ought to proceed further or return to the bank, the waters had risen to an extent that required the horse to swim. Realizing that the horse was in danger, Vikraman leapt into the stream.

11. A Familiar Voice

The rising and ebbing waves in the swiftly flowing forest stream tossed Vikraman around. He resolutely gritted his teeth and used all his strength to remain afloat. Swimming along with the flow of the stream, he suddenly remembered the horse and panicked thinking that the flood may have swept the quadruped away. Vikraman looked around and observed the horse a long distance away struggling in the flood to reach the bank close to the place where he had leapt into the stream. He derived solace thinking that at least the horse had escaped; Vikraman's confidence in reaching the bank and surviving was rapidly waning. As Vikraman tried to swim towards the bank nearest to him, the speed of the water flow increased exponentially. The stream rapidly rumbled on at a pace that would have swept elephants and hillocks away. His arms started flagging and he felt despondent.

Vikraman contemplated about the strange ways of fate and his aspirations. The castles he had built in the air had come to naught! His dreams, like his father's, would remain unfulfilled. Parthiba Maharaja was at least fortunate to embrace martyrdom at the battlefield. An untimely death in a flooded stream was awaiting him. Did he rush back to his motherland to encounter such a fate? Alas! He was dying without even seeing his mother. Coming to terms with imminent death would have been easier had he met his mother and told her, 'Amma! I have fulfilled the promise made to my father. I have established an independent kingdom in a nation across the seas.' Vikraman wished to meet the lotus-eyed maiden whom he had met at Mamallapuram again. Notwithstanding her antecedents, he wanted to beseech her, 'Are you willing to be banished from this country along with me?' He could well imagine her disappointment in the event of her expecting to meet the ratna vyapari again. He regretted his inability to return the horse to the majestic spymaster.

Vikraman's arms felt limp and his body weighed heavy as though it were made of iron. He felt incapable of holding out any longer...It was then that he observed a dark object floating towards him. He thought that the floods had felled a large tree. But alas, the floods swept the object away from his reach! Vikraman lost all hope. His eyes closed involuntarily. He suddenly remembered Ponnan. When Vikraman was learning to swim in the Kaveri as a boy, it was Ponnan who used to rescue him during the times fatigue set in and he was about to drown. He yearned for Ponnan to rescue him at the current juncture...Vikraman was unable to believe his eyes. Was it indeed Ponnan? Was this an illusion? Vikraman remembered his mother as he was hit by a huge wave. He lost consciousness.

As Vikraman gradually gained consciousness, he heard a feeble voice calling out, 'Maharaja'. The voice appeared to be coming from the netherworld; he wondered whose voice it was. It was familiar. Indeed! It was the boatman Ponnan's voice. Vikraman wondered if the voice he heard was real, a dream or a fantasy. Vikraman recollected swimming in the flooded forest stream and drowning after his arms had weakened. He thought that he was hearing this voice in the world of the dead. Vikraman, whose eyes were shut thus far, exercised great effort to open

them. He saw Ponnan soaked to the skin with water dripping from his body and shedding tears.

'Ponna! Is it indeed you? Is this real or am I dreaming?' asked Vikraman.

'Maharaja! I was about to pose the same question to you. Is this really you or am I dreaming or fantasizing? Did I indeed rescue Vikrama Maharaja from the floods? I find it incredible that you are alive and are speaking to me! Aha! If only Valli were here now...'

Ponnan was seated on the aerial root of a massive banyan tree on the banks of the stream and had placed Vikraman's head on his lap. The rains had ceased and there was a slight drizzle. A cool zephyr had set in. Darkness was setting in heralding the imminent nightfall. Vikraman briskly sat up and said, 'Ponna! It is me, Vikraman. You will be amazed hearing this. Do you know whom I was thinking of as I was drowning in the floods? I thought of you. It was you who rescued me and lifted me on to your boat several times when my arms failed to hold up and I was on the verge of drowning as I learnt to swim in the Kaveri. I was reminded of those times and wished that you would come to rescue me earlier today. I observed a human on the bank and hoped that it was you. I then told myself that it cannot be you and that I was imagining things as I drowned. This is a miracle, indeed! How did you come here when I needed you the most?'

'I too am taken aback by this happy coincidence, Maharaja. Look at that mandapam,' Ponnan pointed out to it a distance away. 'I sought refuge there when it started raining heavily. I was observing the stream swelling and the water level rising. I saw someone attempting to cross the stream on horseback. Even as I was thinking that how dangerous this was, you had swiftly entered the water. I did not know it was you then. I reached the bank on seeing you leap from the horse and swim to the opposite bank. On seeing your arms flag and you drowning, I dived into the stream. Maharaja, I am ashamed to admit this. I was hesitant for a moment to brave the floods fearing for my life. I am glad that I overcame my reluctance and swam ahead. Aiyyo! What would have happened had I failed to do so?' Ponnan concluded closing his eyes. He shivered.

'Ponna! Why do you think of what might have happened? It was our clan's deity, Lord Muruga, who emboldened you at the right juncture. No! Not at all! It is the deceased Parthiba Maharaja who continues to guide me in spirit and keeps me out of harm's way... Never mind, Ponna! I was babbling pointlessly! Is the Maharani well?' enquired Vikraman eagerly.

On hearing the word 'Maharani', Ponnan closed his eyes with his palms and started sobbing. Vikraman was extremely agonized by Ponnan's reaction.

'Aiyyo, Ponna! Was there a mishap? Has the Maharani passed away?' he exclaimed.

Ponnan blurted, 'No, Maharaja! No! Maharani is alive somewhere. But her whereabouts are not known...'

'How did that happen, Ponna! I had left the Maharani under your care. How could you have been so careless?'

'Maharaja! I have to explain what transpired. It looks as though it may rain again. You are also drenched to the skin. There is a cold wind blowing! Let us go to that mandapam. There is much to tell you and much to hear from you. Nightfall is imminent.'

The duo walked towards the mandapam.

12. Solar Eclipse

Night had set in by the time Vikraman and Ponnan reached the mandapam. In those days it was customary to erect mandapams in sparsely populated areas for the convenience of travellers. Since Mahendra Chakravarthi had commissioned many such mandapams, they came to be known as Mahendra mandapams. After requesting Vikraman to sit in the patio, Ponnan went inside and brought out a set of his dry robes. Vikraman draped himself in those robes.

Ponnan then narrated the strange decisions of Arulmozhi Rani. The news that Vikraman was banished from Dakshina Bharata and forcibly sent overseas made the despondent Arulmozhi Rani lose all interest in living. The hope of and desire to meet her son one day were her motivations to lead life, albeit apathetically. Residing by herself at the Vasantha Maligai, where she had initially lived with her husband and subsequently with her son, caused her much agony. It was at this juncture Parthiba Maharaja's friend and the erstwhile Pallava general, Paranjyothi Adigal, visited Uraiyur accompanied by his wife on a pilgrimage. The couple visited Arulmozhi Rani and offered her words of solace. When the couple resumed their pilgrimage, Arulmozhi

Rani went along with them. They visited all the sacred sites in Tamizhagam with the exception of Kanchi. Having undertaken a pilgrimage for two years, the trio returned to Paranjyothi Adigal's native place, Thiruchengattankudi, the previous year during the month of Thai to bathe at the Kaveri Sangamam (the confluence of two tributaries of the Kaveri and the sea) on new moon day.

The solar eclipse coincided with the auspicious day of Thai amavasai (new moon day). Devotees from across the country thronged the Kaveri Sangamam on this propitious day to bathe in the sea. Ponnan and Valli travelled for days from Uraiyur to the Kaveri Sangamam in the hope of meeting Arulmozhi Rani. Their desire was fulfilled. The couple secured an audience with Arulmozhi Devi at Thiruchengattankudi. All of them – Paranjyothi Adigal, his consort, Thiruvengadu Nangai, Arulmozhi Rani, Ponnan and Valli left at daybreak of the auspicious day for the Kaveri Sangamam. An unimaginably huge crowd had thronged the Sangamam giving the impression that the entire populace on earth had congregated there. It appeared as though the turbulence of the sea reflected the ardour of the assembled devotees. Subsequent to the sea submerging Kaveripoompattinam, the Kaveri river had deposited large quantities of sand in the sea, causing the sea to be shallow for a long distance from the shore. Hence, the innumerable devotees were able to spread themselves in the sea and bathe. People ducked in the water as the waves approached the shore and stood erect once the waves had passed them, thereby enjoying their dip in the sea and accumulating good karma simultaneously. It was amidst this multitude that Ponnan and the others headed to the sea to bathe.

There was also a solar eclipse that day. It set in with the sunlight waning swiftly. The sky became progressively darker and the sea, more turbulent. The sudden transition from a clear sky and bright sunlight to pitch darkness instilled dread in the hearts of the multitude. The inherently devout turned ecstatic recollecting the miracles performed by the Almighty – the creator, defender and annihilator of the cosmos. While Paranjyothi Adigal was in a rapturous state, Arulmozhi Rani was facing the east with her eyes closed in meditation.

Valli had never seen the sea till that day. Her heart was beating fast and she gripped Ponnan's hand tightly, scared that the waves might wash her away. As she pleaded with Ponnan to help her return to the shore, the shocking and completely unanticipated incident occurred. Arulmozhi Rani opened her eyes and shrieked, 'Vikrama, my child! Here I come to join you!' The Rani's scream drowned the din of the waves and reached Ponnan's and Valli's ears. The very next instant she leapt into the sea only to be drowned by a massive wave.

Ponnan and Valli yelled in shock. Paranjyothi Adigal, who was meditating, opened his eyes and asked, 'What happened?'

Ponnan bawled, 'Aiyyo! The Maharani has been washed away by a wave!'

Paranjyothi Adigal immediately instructed his wife and Valli, 'You two ought to immediately return to the shore!'

By then, the solar eclipse had completely set in. The stars were visible in the sky. People were panicking and could be heard screaming, 'Appa!', 'Amma!', 'Magane!' (Son!). The devout euphorically chanted 'Hara Hara!' and 'Sambo!'

Amidst the dark shadow of the eclipse, Paranjyothi Adigal and Ponnan battled their way through the waves in quest of Arulmozhi Rani.

13. Kabala Bhairavar

Vikraman was visibly upset when he heard about the Maharani's state of mind, which goaded her to take the extreme step of leaping into the sea to join him. His being in a faraway land across the sea must have caused her so much anguish that she behaved like one possessed. As Ponnan started narrating in detail about Paranjyothi Adigal's search for the Maharani, an anxious Vikraman urged him to be quick and asked if he was able to find the Maharani.

A distraught Ponnan replied, 'Sadly no, Maharaja! We were unable to find her! I was not fortunate enough to see her after that incident.'

Vikraman grumbled, 'Was it merely to placate me that you had mentioned earlier that the Maharani was alive? Aiyyo! Was it to hear this dismal news that I travelled across the seas to my motherland?'

Ponnan consoled him saying, 'Please heed me, Maharaja! I am striving to locate the place where she is being held. The task has become easier now that you have arrived.'

Ponnan continued relating to Vikraman the events that had unfolded after Arulmozhi Rani leapt into the sea to the best of his knowledge. Paranjyothi Adigal and Ponnan were unable to locate Arulmozhi Rani despite searching for long. Paranjyothi Adigal mentioned in a sorrowful tone, 'Ponna! Samudra Rajan, the king of seas, has swept the Devi away!' Ponnan wept aloud. The duo realized that since much time had elapsed, they might, at best, only retrieve her mortal remains. Recognizing that it was futile to continue searching for her, the two men returned to the shore. By that time, the eclipse was in its waning phase. The darkness was gradually replaced by sunlight and the weather then was similar to that during a monsoon evening.

Paranjyothi's wife and Valli, who were shivering in the cold, called out, 'Please come here quickly!' Once their men neared them, the women stated that in the dim light that pervaded they observed a one-armed man carrying away a woman, who resembled Arulmozhi Rani. The women had clapped their hands and called out to him but he had quickly disappeared amidst the crowd. It took some time for Paranjyothi Adigal and Ponnan to comprehend what the women were saying as they spoke in a very agitated manner. They, who had previously searched for Arulmozhi Rani in the sea, resumed their quest on the shore. But their efforts came to naught. As they were unable to trace both Arulmozhi Rani and the one-armed man in the teeming multitude despite combing the area for long, they turned skeptical of the women's claims. They believed that Thiruvengadu Nangai and Valli were fantasizing, though the women swore that they had indeed observed a one-armed man carry Arulmozhi Rani away.

Ponnan then related to Vikraman the reason for his believing that Arulmozhi Rani was still alive. Valli and he had tarried at Thiruchengattankudi for a few days and had returned to Uraiyur without unravelling the reasons behind Arulmozhi Rani's mysterious disappearance. The sivanadiyar had subsequently visited them at Uraiyur. He was anguished hearing of the Maharani's fate and taken aback on learning about the one-armed man. He insisted that Valli relate to him all she could remember about the one-armed man. He finally stated, 'Ponna! I find Valli's account completely credible. The Rani is doubtlessly alive. It is our responsibility to locate the place in which she has been sequestered.'

The sivanadiyar then enquired, 'Are you aware of the one-armed man's identity?'

When Ponnan replied that he didn't know about him, the sivanadiyar remarked, 'He is Kabala Rudra Bhairavan, the head priest of the Kabalika clan. He is propagating the barbaric practice of human sacrifice in Tamizhagam. I am striving hard to stop this atrocity. He has apparently constructed a Rana Bhadra Kali temple in a secluded location. If we are able to discover the temple's location, we are most likely to find the Rani there.'

Ponnan had trembled on hearing this and screamed, 'Aiyyo! What if he has sacrificed our Maharani…?'

'No Ponna, not at all! Kabala Bhairavan will not have

undertaken such an arduous task for performing a mere sacrifice. He is harbouring an important, furtive motive. So, he would have kept the Maharani alive and safe. It is imperative for us to locate the Rana Bhadra Kali temple,' remarked the sivanadiyar. Ponnan and the sivanadiyar decided to comb Pallava Nadu and Chola Nadu, respectively. Ponnan left Valli at her grandmother's house and travelled across Chola Nadu in search of the Rani. He then

crossed the Kaveri and resumed his search.

Months of peripatetic living and searching high and low for the Maharani had borne fruit four days ago. Ponnan, after walking westwards along the forest stream for three to four kaada, reached the foot of a large mountain that was surrounded by vast, dense forests. Ponnan surmised that the mountain must be the source of the forest stream along which he had walked and that the mountain must be part of the Kolli Mountain range. He had heard that barbaric tribes who inhabited the upper echelons of the mountain periodically visited the periphery to lure people and sacrifice them. As Ponnan scoured the jungles, it occurred to him that the Rana Bhadra Kali temple must be in the vicinity. He started combing the forest for the temple but it was not possible to penetrate deep into the forest from any direction.

Ponnan then started climbing the mountain along the course of the forest stream. He could hear the roar of a waterfall. The climb slowly became uphill and the route was strewn with massive boulders, deep water-filled depressions and a dense growth of thorny bushes. Ponnan continued climbing undaunted by these impediments. He had started his trek at dawn and came to a halt around noon, extremely fatigued, and sat on a rock. Just as he was thinking of retracing his steps before nightfall, he heard someone speak. Hearing a human voice in that eerie forest instilled in Ponnan a sense of panic and also hope and excitement that he was about to accomplish the task he had set out for. As a matter of caution, he hid himself under a nearby rock.

Shortly thereafter, he observed two men coming down towards him. But what kind of men were they? Were they human? Ponnan saw one of them clearly and he had never set his eyes on anyone so horrific. It was the sharp, penetrating glance of the man's bloodshot eyes that made him look so ghastly. His tall frame, big moustache, red hue of his lush, curly locks and the sandal paste smeared on his forehead with a dot of blood red vermillion in the middle accentuated the gruesomeness of his appearance. A black shawl was draped over his shoulders. As he leapt from one rock to another, the shawl slipped away. What Ponnan saw almost made him scream. The tall man's right arm was missing!

'It is this man who, as alleged by Valli and Thiruvengadu Ammai, must have abducted Arulmozhi Rani!', he thought. 'This man must also be the "Kabala Rudra Bhairavan" the sivanadiyar had alluded to!' The man who accompanied Kabala Rudra Bhairavan also surprised Ponnan. That he was a human could be deciphered only when he came near. He was a dwarf; on a frame of a ten-year-old rested the mature countenance of a forty-year old. Notwithstanding his short build, the agility and swiftness with which he moved downhill, following the Kabala Bhairavar, heightened Ponnan's astonishment and alarm. As Ponnan narrated this part of his account, Vikraman's excitement peaked. He asked Ponnan to describe the dwarf in detail. Ponnan complied and then enquired, 'Maharaja! What is the matter? Did you encounter someone resembling the dwarf on the way?'

Vikraman replied, 'I did, Ponna. I will tell you about that later. You may continue with your account.'

'Nothing much transpired after that, Maharaja! I could not hear anything they said due to the deafening sound of a waterfall nearby. I slid from under the rock after confirming that the two men must have walked a long distance downhill towards the forest. Eager to discover their hideout, the Kali temple and also to meet the Maharani, I continued walking along the stream. But I was soon disappointed. Just a short distance away was the waterfall whose sound I could hear earlier. It was as tall as three adult men. There was a turbulent pool of water at its foot. The rocks there were huge and seemed perilously steep. The mountain at the edge of the waterfall had an almost perpendicular rock face. It was humanly impossible to climb up or down the mountain at that point. How had those two men crossed this spot? Someone must have dropped a rope or a ladder from above. Alternatively, there must be a secret passage to the peak of the mountain. I meticulously searched that area, Maharaja, but my efforts came to naught. Thinking that the two men are bound to return, I waited at the foot of the mountain for three days. However, there was no sign of them. I then decided to return and seek the sivanadiyar's counsel. Fortunately, I reached the mandapam at the right time!' concluded Ponnan.

'Yes, you indeed came at the right time Ponna! Had you not rescued me, I would have definitely joined my father by now!' remarked Vikraman.

'I too might have met with the same fate, Maharaja! The source of the forest stream is in that mountain. Had it rained when I was up the mountain, it would not have been possible for me to have met you. I could not have searched for the Maharani either.'

'Do you believe that the Maharani is being held at that mountain, Ponna?' asked Vikraman.

'Indeed, Maharaja! I was not very convinced when the sivanadiyar had said so. But after sighting the one-armed Bhairavan, I'm confident that the Maharani is alive.'

'I too believe so, Ponna! It is unthinkable that my mother would have passed away without seeing me. The Maharani has often appeared in my dreams during the last six months. You had mentioned that on Thai amavasai, she had leapt into the ocean calling out my name. It is from around then she has been visiting me in my dreams and beckoning me. She must be alive. Even now she is calling out for me, Ponna. Amma! Amma!' shrieked Vikraman.

Ponnan immediately shut Vikraman's mouth with his palm and whispered into his ears, 'Maharaja! Patience! Listen carefully! Human voices!'

Two men engaged in conversation could indeed be seen outside that dark mandapam.

14. Kali's Thirst

As the voices became more audible, Ponnan asked Vikraman to remain within the mandapam and peeped out. He could see two men walking towards the mandapam. Just then a jolt of lightning flashed across the sky, illuminating their faces. Ponnan shivered on recognizing them. The duo was none other than Marappa Bhupathi and Kabala Rudra Bhairavan! Ponnan managed to overcome the astonishment on seeing the two men unexpectedly, went to Vikraman and whispered, 'Maharaja!'

Just as Vikraman started asking, 'What is it, Ponna? Why are you trembling thus?' Ponnan closed Vikraman's mouth with his hands and whispered into his ears, 'Pray, do not speak loudly! We are in grave danger. Please be prepared.'

Vikraman felt his waist and murmured, 'Ah! My sword was washed away in the flood!'

Marappa Bhupathi and Kabala Rudra Bhairavan came to a halt at the porch of the mandapam to avoid getting drenched in the rain. Vikraman and Ponnan could hear snippets of their conversation clearly. On identifying Marappa Bhupathi's voice, a startled Vikraman was about to stand up, only to be restrained by Ponnan.

Marappan enquired, 'Maha Prabhu! I beseech you to tell me what Kali Mata (mother) has commanded me to do?'

Kabala Bhairavan's voice caused one's hair to stand on end and wonder if it was the voice of a ghost or a ghoul. He replied, 'Mata is waiting to endow you with far more powerful positions. She expects you to accomplish stupendous tasks. The annai, the mother, is feeling extremely thirsty and is demanding royal blood to quench her thirst.'

'I tried to offer a prince of an ancient clan of impeccable lineage to Kali. My plan somehow went awry...'

'You were the one who thwarted the plan. I had personally come for the Rajakumaran. You interfered and ruined everything.'

'I beg your pardon, Prabhu! But how did you come to know of the Rajakumaran's arrival?'

'Why are you asking me the same question again? It was Kali Mata who informed me through Arulmozhi Rani. The Rani mentioned that the prince had set sail to Tamizhagam and that his ship had neared the coast. I had come for the prince, but you interfered and thwarted my plan.'

'I beg your pardon, Prabhu...'

'Let bygones be bygones. Mata has forgiven you. But she says that only royal blood can satiate her severe thirst. This month's amavasai, the new moon, has passed. We ought to quench the mother's thirst at least during the month of Tula...You ought to somehow trace him and fetch him.'

'If I do fetch him...'

'Your desire will be fulfilled. Bhupathi! Weren't you appointed general as soon as you surrendered to Kali Mata? Going forward...'

'What is likely to happen going forward, swami?'

'You will certainly scale greater heights.'

'What do you mean by greater heights?'

'The Chola throne awaits you. The Mata is waiting to coronate you!'

'Is that all, Prabhu?'

'Annai will bestow an even more powerful role upon you.'

'What could that be?'

'The Pallava throne.'

Marappa Bhupathi exclaimed, 'Ah!'

Silence prevailed for some time.

'But securing such an exalted position is not easy. You ought to pay an appropriate tribute to Mata.'

'What does Mata expect from her humble servant?'

'You must first trace and fetch Parthiban's son.'

'I will do that. What next?

'You must pay a visit to Kali Mata's sanctum on the first day of the Tula month.'

'And then...?'

'You must behead yourself and offer your head to the Mata!'

'Aiyyo!' shrieked Marappan.

'If you do so, you are likely to become the Chakravarthi of the Kanchi kingdom in your next birth. If not...'

'Is there an alternative, Prabhu?'

'You will become the Kanchi Chakravarthi this birth itself if you sacrifice a person who is at least your equal in stature.'

'Who may I sacrifice, swami?'

'That masquerader who smears himself with thiruneeru and dons rudraksha.'

'Prabhu! Will Kali Mata, who yearns for royal blood, feel satiated with a mendicant's blood?' asked Marappan.

'Bhupathi! You are ignorant. Do you know who that masquerader is in reality?'

'Do tell me who he is, Prabhu!' blurted out an amazed Bhupathi.

'Bhupathi! That is a mystery. It's a secret that no one is capable of unravelling. Even the breeze that is blowing past us should not get wind of it. Come closer. I'll whisper it into your ear...'

Vikraman and Ponnan were both incredulous and startled,

listening to this conversation. At this juncture, they listened with rapt attention but heard nothing. Suddenly Marappa Bhupathi burst out laughing.

'Bhupathi! Why are you laughing? Do you doubt the Mata's words?' interrogated Kabala Bhairavar angrily.

'Not at all, Prabhu! Never!' replied Marappan.

'Then, why did you laugh?'

'Another Devi has commanded me to capture the sivanadiyar and produce him before her. Do you know who she is?'

'Who?'

'It is the dear daughter of the Just King of Kings, Narasimha Pallava Chakravarthi, Kundavai Devi!'

'Well, Kali Mata is using several channels to fulfil her desire!' stated Kabala Bhairavar.

Suddenly, the sound of horse hooves, people shouting and cheering were heard at a distance. Ponnan noiselessly came to the entrance of the mandapam and peered out. Five to six

horsemen were riding towards the mandapam holding aloft illuminated torches. Ponnan thought, 'Today, Maharaja and I are indeed trapped!' His heart beat fast as he swiftly ducked inside the mandapam.

Marappa Bhupathi remarked, 'Maha Prabhu! My men are coming in search of me. We ought to leave now.'

'I will disappear immediately. Don't forget the Mata's command…'

'Where do we meet next?'

'At the usual place. Chitraguptan will be waiting for you.'

By then the horsemen had neared the mandapam.

'Keep in mind all that I had mentioned.'

'As you command, Prabhu!'

There was no conversation for some time after this exchange. The silence was shattered by the horsemen cheering, 'Long live the Chola General, Marappa Bhupathi! Long Live!'

When Ponnan and Vikraman looked out of the mandapam they could, in the light cast by the torches, perceive the contingent riding down the highway leading to Uraiyur.

Ponnan heaved a deep sigh as he remarked, 'Maharaja! We have indeed sidestepped a major crisis.'

Vikraman lamented, 'Ponna! The bundles of gem stones I lost in the flood pales in comparison to the loss of my sword. What will I do?'

'Maharaja!'

'What is it, Ponna?'

'I now recollect the Maharani giving me a casket before embarking on the pilgrimage. She had asked me to hand it over to you.'

'What did the casket contain? Tell me quickly, Ponna!'

'It contained your dynasty's ancient sword with gemstones embedded in its grip.'

'Are you stating the truth, Ponna? Aha! I returned to our motherland with the express intention of taking possession of that sword! Before heading to the battlefield, my father had shown me the sword and Thirukkural in the casket and had said, "These are our dynasty's treasures I'm bequeathing to you. Our ancestor, Karikala Chola, who had brought the whole of Bharata Kandam and far-flung nations across the seas under his reign, wielded that sword." Ponna, I hope you have carefully preserved that sword!'

'Indeed, swami!'

'Where is it?'

'I have buried it in Vasantha Theevu.'

'Why did you leave it there?'

'Where else could I have kept it, Maharaja?'

'Never mind, Ponna! We must now head to Vasantha Theevu and retrieve the sword. Do you know what my father said? The words he had uttered nine years ago resonate within me as though they had been said just yesterday. "Vikrama! You ought not to wield Karikala Chola's sword as long as you are a vassal to another king. This is the reason for my not wielding this sword. Do take possession of this sword when you become the independent sovereign of at least a small nation." Ponna, now that I am the autonomous ruler of Shenbaga Theevu, I may use this sword.'

'Maharaja! You are the monarch of not just Shenbaga Theevu but also of Chola Nadu…'

'That day has not yet dawned, Ponna! But it is imminent. There are two tasks we must accomplish immediately. We need to retrieve that iconic sword and Thirukkural. We must also liberate the Maharani from that mob of kabalikas. We need to prioritize these tasks.'

After some deliberation, the duo decided to first head to Uraiyur and reclaim the sword and Thirukkural from Vasantha Theevu. Tracing the sivanadiyar, seeking his counsel and freeing the Maharani were next on their agenda. As both men were exhausted, they resolved to sleep in the mandapam that night and head to Uraiyur at dawn. But how were they to fathom that a severe fever would grip Vikraman, rendering him too feeble to even move by daybreak?

15. The Horse Returns

Kundavai was the cynosure of her father's eyes since childhood. Narasimha Chakravarthi was not just her father, he was also her de facto mother, preceptor and close companion. It was he who offered her solace during times of distress, advice to help resolve her confusions, and one with whom she shared her joys. She would recount to him stories and poems that appealed to her and take him along to galleries to view paintings and sculptures. Father and daughter, despite being two distinct humans, were for long united in spirit.

However, this phase had come to an end three years ago. An invisible curtain had fallen between the father and daughter. Kundavai had not forgotten the Chola Rajakumaran whom Narasimha Chakravarthi had banished. She was unable to do so despite trying hard. Kundavai yearned to speak of the Rajakumaran, but knew of no one with whom she could share her intimate feelings. Till then, she had shared her innermost thoughts and feelings with her father. But she could not bring herself to openly speak to him about the Chola Rajakumaran. When she did occasionally broach this subject with her father, he responded in a rather dismissive manner. It was then Kundavai started feeling the absence of her mother.

Kundavai had wished to befriend Vikraman's mother hoping the latter would be a mother figure to her as well. But Arulmozhi Devi had embarked on a pilgrimage accompanying Paranjyothi Adigal and his wife the very day she had met Kundavai. The trio had camped at Mamallapuram for a few days during their pilgrimage. During that period, Kundavai had often met Arulmozhi Rani, who was very affectionate to her. But given their past, unsurprisingly, the two were unable to forge a bond. While Arulmozhi Rani was enraged with Kundavai's father who had banished her only son to a faraway island, Kundavai believed that her father's conduct was beyond reproach. Kundavai not only loved her father dearly but also held him in high esteem. She believed that it was an honour for the Chola Rajakumaran to accept the suzerainty of her father, whose glory in her view was at par with the emperors of the solar and lunar dynasties of yore, who had led an expedition up to the Narmada river in the north and had annihilated the demonic Pulikesi and his capital city Vatapi. Kundavai was also unable to comprehend the Chola Rajakumaran's insubordination given that the Cholas had ruled as tribute-paying vassals to the Pallava Emperors for two centuries.

The diametrically opposite views the two women held inhibited their ability to communicate candidly. While their mutual affection grew, they did withhold confidences from each other. Arulmozhi Rani relented and divulged to Kundavai that the Pallavas had sought her hand in marriage to Narasimha Chakravarthi, that she had declined and had married Parthiba Maharaja instead. Further, she disclosed to Kundavai that during Vikraman's childhood days she had wished for Vikraman and Kundavai to marry. Hearing this, Kundavai was overwhelmed. However, the Rani continued, 'All that will remain a dream. May you marry a prince who is fortunate to be betrothed to you and live happily ever after!' Kundavai was furious.

'Never, amma! I am not interested in leading a householder's life. I want to renounce the world and lead the life of a Saivite ascetic,' declared Kundavai. The Rani failed to understand the import of Kundavai's pronouncement. At another instance when Kundavai suggested that Ilavarasar Vikraman could still return to rule Chola Nadu if he were agreeable to be a vassal to the Pallava kingdom, Arulmozhi Rani grimaced and exclaimed, 'I would rather receive the news of Vikraman's death!' It was when Arulmozhi Rani was at Mamallapuram that Kundavai ran into the sivanadiyar when he was on his way out after visiting the Maharani. When she had enquired about him to the Rani, the latter replied, 'I don't know who that elderly man is. But he has, akin to our dynasty's deity, been a pillar of strength and support.'

Kundavai thought to herself, 'He is the harbinger of misfortune to your clan and not your dynasty's deity!' When news of Arulmozhi Devi drowning at the Kaveri Sangamam and someone spiriting her away had reached Kundavai, she concluded, 'The fake sivanadiyar must have abducted the Maharani. He must have had evil designs on her all these years!' Kundavai's brother, Mahendran, had returned to Kanchi from a victorious campaign in Lanka shortly before this unfortunate incident. He bore boundless affection for her. Kundavai found it easier to confide in him. Mahendran, understanding his sister's frame of mind, decided to sail to Shenbaga Theevu and fetch Vikraman under some fabricated pretext. He had sought the Chakravarthi's permission to invade the islands in the southern sea including Javaham and Kambojam (present day Java and Cambodia) with this intention in mind. Narasimha Varmar overruled Mahendran stating that he himself was intending to embark on a sea voyage and that Mahendran, in his capacity as the Ilavarasan, ought to govern the Pallava kingdom during his absence. Mahendran could not bring himself to flout his father's command.

Meanwhile, Kundavai had coerced Mahendran to appoint Marappa Bhupathi as the general of the Pallava army and to summon him to Mamallapuram. Marappa Bhupathi was ordered to trace the sivanadiyar and through him, Arulmozhi Devi's whereabouts. Kundavai and Mahendran decided to spend some time at the Uraiyur Vasantha Maligai and instructed that arrangements be made for their journey. As the Chakravarthi had consented to their travel, the siblings accompanied by their retinue embarked on their journey. By noon of the following day, the siblings were a kaada away from the very stream in which Vikraman was trapped and subsequently rescued. Kundavai was travelling in a palanquin, while Mahendran was riding a horse.

Mahendran recounted his voyage to Lanka and the numerous wars he had waged in that island. He also described Lanka's abundant water resources and its verdant land. Though Kundavai listened to Mahendran with great interest, thoughts of the ratna vyapari distracted her intermittently. She wondered why she felt so concerned about the trader's failure to show up. 'Although a little voice in her mind said that the Chola Rajakumaran and the trader resembled each other,' she brushed this idea away. 'If they did indeed resemble each other, wouldn't appa have noticed it? If he had done so, would appa have rescued the trader from highway robbers and sent him to Uraiyur? Their resemblance is a figment of my imagination!' she thought and the urge to meet the young man in Uraiyur gripped her all the more.

The preoccupied Kundavai was taken aback by a sight that suddenly unfolded before the royal retinue. The spectacle was not exactly earth shattering. A riderless, beautifully caparisoned high-breed steed was galloping towards them. She was unable to fathom why this sight shocked her so much.

As the horse neared the retinue, she was certain that the quadruped belonged to her father. She had seen the Chakravarthi ride that steed occasionally. She speculated how the horse could have materialized there and if her father had ridden the horse towards Uraiyur. They had taken leave of their father at Kanchi and it was not possible for him to have overtaken them unbeknownst to them. She then recollected that her father had mentioned lending his horse to the ratna vyapari who was headed to Uraiyur. Kundavai was convinced that this was the horse that the trader had borrowed from her father. She pondered why the horse was all alone and what became of the young man. Kundavai felt choked with worry.

16. At the Riverbank

Mahendran saw the change in Kundavai's countenance and asked, 'What is it, thangai?' Kundavai who was staring at the riderless horse intently could not bring herself to speak. Mahendran asked with concern, 'Thangai! It is just a horse that is galloping towards us, not a lion or a tiger. Why are you scared thus?'

This comment pricked Kundavai, who retorted, 'With you by my side, anna, why would I be frightened of a lion or a tiger?'

'Then why are you staring at it as if it were a ghost?'

'Anna, do you know who owns that horse?'

'No, I don't.'

'It belongs to appa.'

'What!'

'Yes, he owns two such high-breed steeds. This one is called Pushpakam and the other one, Parijatham.'

'Why is the quadruped loitering around without a rider? We had taken leave of appa at Kanchi. He could not have ridden this horse here.'

'Appa had mentioned that he had lent the horse to the ratna vyapari from Shenbaga Theevu.'

'Oh!'

By then, the steed was near the royal retinue. A soldier took hold of it by its reins on Mahendran's order. Kundavai asked the horse to be brought to her and she gently caressed it. The horse shook itself and neighed. Taking the horse with them, the royal retinue moved ahead.

A worried Kundavai enquired, 'Anna, what could have befallen that trader?' That Kundavai suspected the trader to be Vikraman was lost on Mahendran. He laughed and flippantly replied, 'A horse that the Pallava Chakravarthi rides will not deign to convey a mere trader. It must have flung him off into a ditch and returned!' Kundavai was disconcerted. The very next instant a comforting thought struck her. If the horse had indeed shrugged the rider off, then he could not have been Vikraman in disguise. He must be a common trader. But her father had spoken highly of his gallantry and dexterity in wielding the sword. Alas! What could have happened to him? Kundavai rued that the Almighty had failed to endow the astute horse with the ability to speak. The horse would have revealed what became of Vikraman if only it could speak. Kundavai once again caressed the horse wishing that Pushpakam would miraculously acquire the ability to articulate.

The royal retinue soon observed a change in the environment. The ground was damp with puddles dotting the landscape. The foliage was a pristine shade of green.

'There must have been a heavy downpour here yesterday. It did not even drizzle at Kanchi,' remarked Mahendran. His words echoed Kundavai's thoughts. It then dawned on Kundavai that Pushpakam and the trader must have got trapped in the heavy rains that must have suddenly ravaged those parts the previous evening. The horse had managed to get away. The ratna vyapari – the poor man – will she be able to ascertain what became of him? Will Pushpakam indicate the spot at which a mishap might have occurred? Will they chance upon his corpse? Shiva! Shiva!

Kundavai closed her eyes when that unbearable thought struck her. The retinue travelled half a kaada across the damp region and reached the banks of the forest stream a nazhigai ahead of sunset.

The landscape at the banks of the forest stream was in stark contrast to the situation that prevailed the previous evening. The area looked picturesque, akin to the beauty of a newly created realm, following the deluge. The calf-deep water in the forest stream gurgled as it flowed. The golden rays of the setting sun trickled through the verdant branches of the forest trees and caressed the flowing waters, forming colourful patterns on the water surface. Birds chirped mellifluously as they returned to their nests on the trees at the banks of the stream. Beauty, tranquillity and joy pervaded the area.

But Kundavai's mind was in a turmoil similar to the cyclone and rains that had earlier raged in the area. She realized that the forest stream must have been inundated the previous evening. The trunks of the trees beside the forest stream bore knee-height water marks. Hay and sundry objects were tangled in the overhanging branches of the trees. As it was just a stream, the floods must have swelled precipitously. Kundavai could conjecture the trader's fate. He must have either attempted crossing the forest stream unaware of the vigour of the water flow or the stream must have unexpectedly swelled as he was crossing it. The horse must have managed to escape and reach the bank. The poor quadruped must have waited for long at the bank for its rider to return. As he did not return, the horse would have started trotting toward Kanchi. Alas! The ratna vyapari must have become a victim to the flood. He had apparently told the Chakravarthi that he was rushing to Uraiyur to meet his mother. That he met with this fate was pitiable...

As Kundavai was thinking thus, the palanquin neared the stream. Everyone in the retinue stepped into the stream but Pushpakam hesitated. Everyone noticed Pushpakam's growing reluctance. The warrior holding the quadruped by its reins coerced it to enter the stream. It shook itself, extricated itself from the warrior's grip and fled to the stream's banks. The steed did not stop on reaching the bank. Like an arrow shot by Rama, the horse galloped swiftly down the highway leading to Kanchi and soon disappeared from the royal retinue's sight.

17. A Feeble Voice

The royal retinue partook food at the banks of the forest stream. While Mahendran ate enthusiastically, Kundavai had lost her appetite. She felt happy flinging bits of snacks around and watching the crows swoop down and grab them. However, the happiness she felt was superficial. The thought of the ratna vyapari drowning in the forest stream and consequently losing his life weighed down her heart. Kundavai managed to convince herself that it was a trader and not the Chola prince who had lost his life. She was unable to bear the thought that the man who had stolen her heart could have met with such a ghastly fate.

A thought struck Kundavai when, after resting for a while, the retinue was about to resume its journey. She had heard people mention that the ghosts of those who met with untimely death tended to hover around the spot where they had died. Could it be true? Would the young trader's ghost be loitering around the banks of the forest stream? Would the ghost shriek horrendously in the middle of the night? Even as she was thinking along those lines, she thought she heard a feeble voice call out, 'Amma! Amma!' somewhere in the vicinity. Kundavai had goosebumps. Was she hallucinating or was it indeed the trader's ghost calling out? She was reluctant to bring this to Mahendran's notice.

As the palanquin moved ahead, the voice became more audible. Was the ratna vyapari's ghost pursuing them? A little later she could distinctly hear a helpless voice moaning, 'Amma! Amma!'. Kundavai overcame her reticence and asked her brother, 'Anna, do you hear anything?'

'Indeed, thangai! I can hear someone call out, "Amma! Amma!"' replied Mahendran as he looked around, seated on the horse.

'The voice seems to be coming from that mandapam!'

Kundavai instructed the palanquin bearers to redirect

the palanquin to the Mahendra mandapam which was some distance away from the stream. Her heart was beating fast in anticipation. It was indeed Vikraman who was moaning. Ponnan and Vikraman had made plans the previous night to embark on their journey early in the morning and to hire a cart on the way. Earlier, that morning, Ponnan woke up from deep slumber to find Vikraman already awake and sitting. 'May we leave, Ponna?' asked Vikraman.

But he was unable to walk even a step and Ponnan observed that he was quite unsteady. An agitated Ponnan rushed towards Vikraman and enquired, 'Oh! What is it, Maharaja? Are you unwell?'

'My head is throbbing, Ponna! It pounds hard when I try to walk. My feet feel wobbly. I don't know what has beset me!' blurted out Vikraman.

Ponnan felt Vikraman's body and asked, 'Oh, Maharaja! Your body feels hot. Did you sleep well last night?'

'No, I was preoccupied and hence could not sleep well.'

'You're running a high temperature, Maharaja! I am a sinner; I slept like Kumbakarnan. Why didn't you wake me up? You will not be able to walk in this condition, come with me!' He placed Vikraman's arm over his shoulder and led him back into the mandapam. He then ran to the banks of the forest stream, gathered some hay strewn there and brought it back to the mandapam. He spread the hay on the floor and made Vikraman lie down on it.

Th two men pondered what their course of action ought to be. They decided to wait by the roadside, hire a passing cart and head to a nearby village to stay till Vikraman had recovered. There appeared to be no other option. Ponnan thought, 'Alas! What a pity Valli is not with us now. Why can't some miracle bring her here immediately?' He did not know how to attend the fever-stricken Vikraman. Shortly thereafter Vikraman started complaining of extreme thirst. At the rear of the mandapam lay a few pieces of earthenware that travellers had discarded after cooking. Ponnan took a pot from these and fetched water from the forest stream. He was moved to tears to see the Maharaja, who was used to drinking water from golden goblets, quenching his thirst from an old earthen pot.

As time passed, Vikraman's fever became more intense. Ponnan too felt hungry. He was gripped by indecision. He realized that if the Maharaja and he tarried at the mandapam without medical assistance and food, they could probably die. He finally decided to walk to a nearby village, and fetch a local vaidyar, a healer, to the mandapam on a hired cart. He prayed to the deity of the Cholas to protect Vikraman during his absence. Vikraman had no choice but to consent to Ponnan's plan. Ponnan frequently turned around and glanced at the mandapam as he started walking swiftly in the direction of a nearby village. Soon

Vikraman's temperature rose causing him to turn delirious. Struck by confusing thoughts, he started speaking incoherently. He writhed in intense pain and became weaker. Soon he stopped rambling and started calling out in a feeble voice, 'Amma! Amma!'

Kundavai's palanquin came to a halt outside the mandapam. Kundavai hurriedly got off the palanquin, walked to the mandapam's entrance and looked inside. Yes, it was indeed the young ratna vyapari. The excruciating fever had caused his gentle countenance to turn red. He stared at the ceiling for a few moments and then closed his eyes out of weariness. Kundavai struggled to come to terms with the intense and conflicting emotions that welled within her – surprise, joy, sorrow, tenderness and above all, agitation. 'Anna! Anna! He is indeed the trader. He seems to be indisposed. Summon the vaidyar,' she screamed.

The royal vaidyar who was part of the retinue examined Vikraman and said, 'A lethal fever has struck him. He needs to be treated immediately. It will take at least ten days for him to recover.'

'Poor man! Let's take him along with us, anna! I have to ask him about Shenbaga Theevu!' remarked Kundavai.

Arrangements were then made at a feverish pace. The vaidyar applied some medicine on Vikraman's tongue. The guards carried him and placed him in Kundavai's palanquin. Kundavai herself got on to a horse and the retinue resumed its journey.

In the meantime, Ponnan, with great difficulty, got hold of a vaidyar at the village. He hired a cart to bring the vaidyar to the Mahendra mandapam and fretted about the Maharaja's condition all the while. He was thunderstruck on being greeted by a vacant mandapam.

18. At Parantaka Puram

Ponnan combed the area within and outside the empty Mahendra mandapam. He pondered on the Maharaja's mysterious disappearance. Ponnan wondered if the events that had transpired since he rescued the Maharaja the previous evening from the forest stream were a dream. By then the vaidyar and the cartman had started badgering him. Ponnan, who had a few gold coins to meet unforeseen expenses, gave them a gold coin and sent them away. Had the fever induced delirium in the Maharaja? Did he consequently walk away from the mandapam? Ponnan was shaken by these thoughts. Ponnan started wandering around as if he were in a daze. He ran to the stream's banks and then back to the mandapam and searched the place, agitated. He was confused and not conscious of what he was doing. He undid the bed of hay he had made for Vikraman, walked down the road that led to Uraiyur and then returned to the mandapam.

Ponnan repeated his acts of search anxiously. On one such occasion, he was returning to the mandapam when he observed a figure hiding behind a large ilupa tree. The figure appeared to be that of a dwarf. Ponnan was reminded of the menacing characters he had seen by the waterfall at the Kolli Mountains few days ago.

He was reminded of the conversation he had overheard in the dark the previous night. The thought that the Maharaja might have fallen into the hands of barbarians who performed human sacrifice enraged and saddened him immensely. He ran towards the ilupa tree intending to vent his anger on the dwarf, who was oblivious to Ponnan's approach. Ponnan leapt quickly, held his prey tightly and shook him up several times.

The midget, who was initially taken aback, regained his composure and enquired, 'Why are you behaving thus? Why the rage?'

Ponnan shrieked, 'You dwarf! Where is the Maharaja?'

'Maharaja? Who is the Maharaja?'

Ponnan realized the mistake he had made and bit his lip. He then asked, 'Where is the man who was lying down in the mandapam?'

The dwarf undid the knot of the cloth fastened to his waist and brandished it. He mockingly remarked, 'Alas! I had fastened him in this knot but he has gone missing.'

Ponnan, unable to appreciate the untimely wisecrack, raised his hand to hit the dwarf. The midget would have probably not been able to withstand the blow struck by Ponnan, whose hands had turned steely from rowing the boat for a living. But he twisted his body, extricated himself from Ponnan's grip and vanished in a moment. A furious Ponnan ran hither and thither. By then darkness had set in and he was unable to see beyond a short distance. Moreover, the dense growth of bushes in that area made it difficult for him to trace the dwarf. Just as a dejected Ponnan was about to leave the place, he heard a sound that resembled an owl's hoot from atop the ilupa tree. A startled Ponnan looked up to find the midget amidst the tree's lush branches. Gripped by extreme fury, he considered uprooting the tree for a moment. The midget asked, 'You fool! What can you do to a devotee of Maha Bhadra Kali?'

An idea struck Ponnan. Even as he was thinking about it, the dwarf commented, 'You ruffian! Why don't you become a devotee of Maha Bhadra Kali too? All your difficulties will vanish.'

Ponnan laughingly retorted, 'Are you asking me to become Kali's devotee?'

'Why are you laughing? Beware! You will become the target of Kali's rage!'

Ponnan then remarked, 'I have indeed joined the ranks of Kali's devotees. I have! But of what use is it? I have failed to execute the Kabala Bhairavar's orders! Oh my God! What will I tell him?'

An amazed dwarf enquired, 'Is that so? What were his orders for you?'

'He had asked me to safely escort the man who was lying down in the mandapam to the Kolli Mountains. Last night, he

had commanded me to do so at this very spot. Aiyyo! I botched up the mission,' wailed Ponnan.

'Oh, I see! You ought to have told me this before. Shortly before you reached here, the entourage of the Kanchi Ilavarasan and Ilavarasi passed by this mandapam. They came to a halt outside the mandapam, carried a man from within the mandapam and placed him in the palanquin. I don't know who that man was. Do you?'

This question fell on Ponnan's deaf ears. On his way back with the vaidyar and cart, a royal retinue had crossed him. He

had stood by the side of the road and made way for the retinue. Observing Kundavai Devi on horseback, he hid himself behind the cart to escape detection and failed to observe the palanquin. Recollecting that incident, Ponnan realized that there may be a grain of truth in the midget's statement.

The dwarf asked from atop the tree, 'Why are you silent? What are you thinking of?'

Ponnan retorted, 'I'm wondering how I may sacrifice you to Kali,' and then flung a stone at the midget. The latter reacted in the manner he had when Vikraman had aimed his sword at him – he cupped his mouth with his palms and let out a loud howl. Ponnan's hair stood on end on hearing that fearful howl. He fled that place immediately in the direction of Uraiyur. Ponnan ran by the forest stream for around a kaada to reach a place called Parantaka Puram. It was probably a jaamam after sunset. Yet the place wore a festive look, illuminated by torches and resonating with the sounds of musical instruments. On asking around, Ponnan came to know that the Chakravarthi's son and daughter were visiting, that they were being welcomed at the temple and that tents were being erected at the outskirts of the village to accommodate them.

Ponnan hastened to the area where the tents were being pitched intending to complete his reconnaissance when the royals were still at the temple. There was not much of a crowd at the royal camp as Yuvaraja Mahendran and Kundavai Devi were at the temple. A few guards were scattered across the camp. The ladies-in-waiting and ushers were engaged in tasks such as making beds. A high hedge cordoned off one end of the camp. Ponnan positioned himself by the hedge, where he heard two ladies-in-waiting gossiping.

'Hey, Maragatham! Wasn't the initial plan to halt for the night at Thiruvennai Nallur? Why are we staying here?'

'Don't you know? The vaidyar has prescribed complete rest for the invalid and has said that his condition may worsen if he were to travel in a palanquin for long. That's why...'

'Who is this invalid? Why is there so much fuss about him?'

'He is apparently Devasenan, a ratna vyapari from Shenbaga Theevu. He had met our Devi on the streets of Mamallapuram. He had informed her that he was headed to Uraiyur to meet his mother. As he lay unattended to at the mandapam by the stream, our Devi decided to take him along to Uraiyur in the palanquin.'

'Maragatham, there is something fishy afoot!'

'What is fishy?'

'Something is certainly amiss. Why should a desolate man found by the roadside be accorded royal hospitality and treatment, Maragatham? He could have been left behind in this village for treatment. Why should he accompany the royal retinue in a palanquin?'

'There is a reason, Thangam. But I will not divulge it to you.'

'I will not talk to you if you don't share the secret with me.'

'Don't be cross with me; come near me. I'll tell you. No one else should hear about this.'

'Tell me...'

'Apparently, the Uraiyur Rajakumaran resides in Shenbaga Theevu. Aren't you aware that after having encountered him at the streets of Kanchi, our Devi had pleaded with the Chakravarthi to forgive him? It is to enquire about that Rajakumaran that our Devi has commanded that the trader accompany our retinue.'

'Oho! So, this man will continue staying with us at the Vasantha Maligai once we reach Uraiyur?'

'Yes.'

'Maragatham, have you seen the trader?'

'Of course! I am the one who administers his medicines.'

'Is he a young man?'

'Yes, so what?'

'He is apparently very handsome with a pleasing countenance.'

'So...'

'Maragatham, I somehow don't like the idea of our Devi

keeping him in such proximity...'

'You fiend! I will burn your tongue of you speak ill of our Devi.'

'You devil! I did not bad-mouth the Devi!'

'You were on the verge of doing so!'

'I will never speak disparagingly of the Devi. If you were allowed in the vicinity of such a handsome, young man and also asked to administer medicines, you are bound to administer your own medicine to mesmerize him...Aiyyo! Don't pinch me!'

The ladies-in-waiting, conversing thus, walked away from the hedge. Ponnan had heard their conversation with rapt attention. He felt a joy he had not experienced for long. He walked a short distance along the hedge and observed that there was some activity in one tent. He parted the leaves in the bushes and looked inside the tent intently. He could see, in the light cast by the torches, Vikraman reclining on the bed and the vaidyar examining his pulse.

After observing the proceedings in the tent for some time, Ponnan left the camp.

19. Ponnan's Apprehension

Ponnan, who was walking down the streets of Parantaka Puram, encountered the royal retinue on their way from the temple. He stepped aside to make way for it. In the light cast by the torches, he beheld Kundavai Devi seated in the palanquin. He developed an unprecedented sense of devotion and regard for her. It struck Ponnan that the Devi was endowed with divine beauty and character as well. Rescuing an invalid man who lay abandoned on the wayside reflected her kindness, generosity and magnanimity.

As Ponnan retired for the night at the temple's praharam, the area around the main temple structure, he contemplated about his future course of action. The Maharaja was receiving proper care and treatment. Kundavai Devi was far more equipped than Ponnan to nurse him back to health. She was also taking the Maharaja to the very place he had wished to visit. It appeared that the deity of the Chola clan was ensuring that events unfold in Vikraman's favour. The Maharaja might take days to recuperate during which time it might not be possible for Ponnan to visit or speak to him. Ponnan also realized that it was pointless for him to shadow Vikraman or to return to Uraiyur. He decided to apply his efforts towards tracing and freeing Arulmozhi Devi. He was desirous of meeting the sivanadiyar and conferring with him. The sivanadiyar had asked Ponnan to alert him as soon as he received any clue about Arulmozhi Devi's whereabouts and had also specified the location where he could be reached. He had asked Ponnan to locate the sculptor's house cloistered in the dense forests close to Kanchi. Ponnan decided that he would meet the sivanadiyar at the sculptor's house, inform him of the developments and then seek his counsel.

The next morning Ponnan watched from afar as the royal retinue left Parantaka Puram for Uraiyur and prayed, 'May the Almighty protect our Maharaja! May he completely recover by the time I return from Mamallapuram.' Once the retinue had disappeared from sight, Ponnan started walking in the opposite direction. Though his mortal body was moving towards Mamallapuram, his heart was in the palanquin with the Maharaja travelling to Uraiyur. Ponnan was often reminded of the potential perils Vikraman was exposed to on account of being under Kundavai Devi's care. What would happen if Kundavai Devi came to know that the invalid who was being transported in the palanquin was the Chola Rajakumaran? What if the still feverish Maharaja blurted out the truth? What if he, on recuperating, was astonished by the familiar environs of the Vasantha Maligai and divulged his identity? Would any harm befall him? Once Kundavai Devi found out his identity, she was bound to share the news with her brother and also with the Chakravarthi. Wouldn't the Chakravarthi sentence Vikraman to death for daring to visit his homeland in disguise after being banished?

Ponnan consoled himself hoping that Vikraman would not, by God's grace, be exposed to such dangers. He hoped that Kundavai would try to protect Vikraman even if she were to unravel the truth. That she had pleaded with the Chakravarthi to pardon Vikraman when he was banished from the country had reached his ears. The sivanadiyar had waxed eloquent on this matter to Arulmozhi Devi. When Ponnan remembered the sivanadiyar and Kundavai Devi, he could not help but recollect the conversation he had overheard the previous night outside the Mahendra mandapam. An indescribable fear and concern gripped him. He wondered why Kundavai Devi had ordered Marappa Bhupathi to apprehend the sivanadiyar.

Who was the sivanadiyar? Was he indeed a virtuous soul or a fake ascetic? Was he truly a well-wisher of the Chola dynasty or a foe disguised as a friend? Ponnan wondered whether he ought to divulge or to suppress the news of Vikraman's return and his being under Kundavai Devi's care at the Vasantha Maligai? Ponnan regretted not deliberating with Vikraman on these issues. Ponnan was surprised on yet another count. Vikraman had mentioned that after the spymaster had rescued him, the duo had spent the night in a sculptor's house! The sivanadiyar had summoned him to the sculptor's house. It appeared that the sculptor's house Vikraman and he were referring to was the same place. Were the spymaster and the sivanadiyar somehow connected?

Ponnan firmly believed that the sivanadiyar was a great soul. He could never ever forget the ascetic rescuing him from Marappa Bhupathi. It was also evident that Arulmozhi Devi trusted him implicitly. Nevertheless, there were grounds to suspect that he was not an ascetic in reality but was masquerading as a sivanadiyar. Valli had once conjectured that it was Parthiba Maharaja who had disguised himself as the sivanadiyar. She felt that Parthiba Maharaja had not died at the battlefield and disguised himself as a sivanadiyar as he did not wish to reveal that he was the lone survivor at that fateful battle. Though Ponnan had great regard for her intellect, he was unable to agree with her on that issue.

Yet another incident added fuel to his suspicion. Ponnan had been very dejected after Arulmozhi Devi had embarked on the pilgrimage. He had visited the Ayyanar temple in the forest that was a short distance away from the quay. He had noticed that one of the earthen elephants at the sanctum was broken. As he was examining the broken elephant, a cloth bundle in the belly of the nearby earthen horse caught his eye. A surprised Ponnan had unknotted the cloth bundle to find a mat made of tiger skin, rudraksha beads and a wig of matted locks. He was taken aback. He was convinced that those were the accoutrements used by someone to assume a sivanadiyar's get-up. Who was the masquerader – was he a good man or a treacherous person? Was he trustworthy? What had the Maha Kabala Bhairavar whispered about the sivanadiyar into Marappa Bhupathi's ears? Why did Kundavai Devi, who was the very embodiment of kindness, bear so much hatred towards the sivanadiyar?

Ponnan was baffled. But he was determined to question the sivanadiyar about his true identity when they met next. If the sivanadiyar were to provide a satisfactory response, Ponnan decided he would share the news of Vikraman's return and Arulmozhi Devi's whereabouts. In the event of not getting a convincing response, Ponnan decided to leave the sculptor's house without saying anything. Ponnan also resolved to somehow meet Vikraman after the latter had recovered and discuss with him the future course of action.

A pensive and purposeful Ponnan embarked on his journey to the sculptor's abode. He hailed passing carts, each carrying him some distance towards his destination. On reaching the by-road that led to Mamallapuram, Ponnan alighted from the cart and started walking. The sivanadiyar had provided lucid directions to the sculptor's house in the forest. As he walked, meticulously following the sivanadiyar's instructions, he observed a horse riding towards him and quickly turning into the forest. Ponnan was unaware whether the horse rider had noticed him. However, the rider's physical appearance matched with Vikraman's description of the spymaster.

As Ponnan reached the spot where the sivanadiyar had asked him to take a turn, the sound of a horse trotting was audible, even though it was muffled by dense foliage. Ponnan continued walking and after having walked for a nazhigai, he reached a clearing on which stood a beautifully sculpted house. The sivanadiyar came out of the house and greeted him with a smile. Shocked, Ponnan stared at him in amazement.

20. Ponnan and the Sivanadiyar

Ponnan was bewildered. The warrior who had taken the turn and certainly entered the house, seemed to have mysteriously morphed into the sivanadiyar when he emerged from the house. Was it the same person who entered and subsequently stepped out of the house or were they two different people? Though Ponnan's expression gave away his amazement and misgivings, he did not articulate his thoughts. He did not get an opportunity to do so.

The sivanadiyar started talking to him, animatedly, 'Ponna! You have come here at the apt moment! I was just thinking of you. I am headed to Uraiyur. You wouldn't have met me had you come here even slightly later...'

The sivanadiyar sat in the veranda and enquired, 'Ponna! Tell me what you have been up to. Be quick. There is a critical task on hand. I'll tell you about it later. Were you able to get any information about the Maharani?'

Ponnan nodded in agreement and then proceeded to describe his sojourn to the Kolli Mountains, climbing the mountain along the waterfall, and hiding himself on seeing the man with one arm and the dwarf. He also related how he had waited for the duo to return for three days and had then left the area. He refrained from mentioning that he had rescued Vikraman from the forest stream and the subsequent events. Ponnan complied with the sivanadiyar's request to describe the man with one arm in detail and then asked, 'Swami! Who is that man? Do you know him?'

'I'm convinced that Parthiba Maharaja's consort is hidden somewhere in the Kolli Mountains. I now comprehend several matters that had confounded me till now. Do you know who that one-armed man is? In Tamizhagam – home to numerous enlightened souls and ardent devotees of the Almighty – this man is spreading the barbaric practice of human sacrifice. His name is Maha Kabala Bhairavan. Despite my vigorous efforts, I have not been able to meet him in person till today. I harbour another suspicion about him. I can surmise why he is consciously avoiding me. The two of us will soon uncover the truth.

'But we have another important task to complete before pursuing the Maha Kabala Bhairavan. I am about to tell you something that will astonish you. The Ilavarasar of Chola Nadu has returned,' remarked the sivanadiyar while looking at Ponnan pointedly. Ponnan looked a tad surprised, but he exuded no joy or exultation.

'Don't you believe what I'm saying, Ponna?' queried the sivanadiyar.

Ponnan was cautious in reply, 'How can I not trust your words, swami? But I'm concerned. Why did the Ilavarasar have to return braving so many dangers?'

'Some harm must have befallen the Ilavarasan, Ponna, probably when he was en route to Uraiyur. We must go immediately looking for him. We must trace him before locating Arulmozhi Devi!'

Ponnan asked with genuine bewilderment, 'How did you come to know of what transpired, swami? Did you see the Ilavarasar? Where did you see him? What evidence do you have to conclude that the Ilavarasar may be in danger?'

'Ponna! What has become of you? You have started asking me for proof...Never mind, listen to me. I not only saw the Ilavarasar in person but also spoke to him. It was I who sent him off to Uraiyur...'

'Pray why, swami?'

'Why?! I wanted him to see his native land. Ponna! Do you know when a man's love for is motherland reaches its zenith? It is when he returns to his country after having lived in a foreign country for some time. When a man returns to his country after having lived in an alien land for a few years, even a desert in his homeland will appear to be heaven. How ecstatic a man

from the bountiful Chola Nadu will be when he returns to his land! I wanted to honour my word to Parthiba Maharaja on the battlefield. What else can be better than making Vikraman not leave the country ever even in his dreams! I wanted to render him incapable of thinking on the lines of leaving his motherland

and hence helped him to achieve that. But I did not anticipate that harm will befall him on the way. Oh God! I am answerable to Arulmozhi Devi!'

'Sometime ago I noticed that you reached this house on horseback. You seemed to be a different person then. You entered the house and have emerged as another person. But I believe that both these forms are disguises. I have had this suspicion for long. But now it is imperative for me to find out the truth. If you do divulge your true identity...'

'If I do?'

'Swami, I am aware of an important matter, something that is of interest to you. If you reveal your true form, I will share the information with you. If not, I will go my way...'

The sivanadiyar became thoughtful. He saw the resolute expression on Ponnan's visage.

'Ponna! Is it necessary for you to know?'

'Indeed, swami.'

'I will, in that case, tell you. But you must promise me that you will keep this confidential and will not share this with anyone else. You ought to keep the information regarding my identity in utmost confidence.'

'As you wish, swami.'

'Will you swear in the name of Parthiba Maharaja, who attained martyrdom on the battlefield?'

'I give you my word in the name of Parthiba Maharaja, swami!'

'In that case, behold me!' pronounced the sivanadiyar as he removed his matted locks, moustache and beard, just as he had for Parthiba Maharaja on the battlefield.

'Prabhu, is that you?' cried Ponnan as he prostrated before the sivanadiyar.

'Didn't Valli share this with you, Ponna?' asked the sivanadiyar as he wore his matted locks, moustache and beard again.

'Valli is wicked and deceptive. She misled me. When I asked her if she was referring to you, she lied to me saying that you were

Parthiba Maharaja. I will not spare her. I too am in the know of an important secret. I will not divulge this to her,' retorted Ponnan.

Ponnan then related to the sivanadiyar all the events that had transpired from the time he had rescued Vikraman from the flooded forest stream to Kundavai taking the invalid Vikraman along with her to Uraiyur. The usually unflappable sivanadiyar was taken aback on listening to Ponnan's account.

The sivanadiyar then pronounced, 'Ponna, there is no need to worry about Vikraman. He will be safe. We ought to trace Arulmozhi Devi and free her from captivity.'

21. At Vasantha Theevu

For a week, Vikraman's spirits buoyed and ebbed, making him feel as though he was oscillating between heaven and hell. He dreamt that he was in the vicinity of an inferno. Parthiba Maharaja held him by his hand and asked, 'My son! Will you enter this fire for the sake of your motherland?' Arulmozhi Devi was also present, shedding copious tears.

Vikraman courageously replied, 'I will, appa!' His father's grip loosened. As Vikraman entered the fire, he felt like he was being roasted alive. He felt tormented and wondered, 'Aiyyo! How much longer will I be scorched in this fire? Why am I not dying? My body seems to be intact!' Suddenly a tender hand held his and yet another tender palm felt his chest. He beheld a beauteous, lotus-like visage looking at him kindly amidst the raging fire. Shortly thereafter, Vikraman felt that he had emerged from the inferno. He wished to thank the divine damsel who had held him by his hand and ushered him out of the blaze. Alas! There was no sign of her.

In another dream, he was cruising in a warship with the tiger flag hoisted atop. Hundreds of Chola warriors were accompanying him in the vessel. He could hear Parthiba Maharaja and

Arulmozhi Rani blessing him, 'May you return victorious!' and seeing him off at the harbour. Suddenly, a cyclone broke out causing the ship to capsize. Vikraman, who was flung off board, tried to navigate through the savage sea single-handedly. His body turned cold and his limbs numb. Just as Vikraman was convinced that he was going to drown and breathe his last, a boat miraculously appeared. On the deck of the boat stood a maiden with a moon-like countenance. She appeared familiar to him; he had seen her somewhere…sometime…in a previous birth. The damsel offered Vikraman her hand and helped him climb on to the boat. Her face was wet. Vikraman was unable to ascertain if it was the waves or tears that had dampened her face. He was desirous of thanking her. Vikraman tried to speak to her but could not bring himself to do so. He felt choked.

In yet another reverie, Vikraman was wandering aimlessly in an inhospitable desert. It was daytime and sun's rays were beating down mercilessly. His legs appeared to be glued to each other, his body seemed to be ablaze and he felt extremely thirsty. Not a single tree, shrub or sheltered area was seen in the vacant landscape that stretched up to the horizon. There seemed to be a water body far away, towards which Vikraman started moving. Despite walking fast and long, the water body appeared no nearer. He wondered with dismay if it was a mirage. He was able to walk no further. His eyes darkened and he collapsed. As he fell to the ground, he thought: 'I'm undergoing all these tribulations to fulfil my parents' expectations and for the betterment of Chola Nadu!' He felt someone's tender arms lift him off the scorching desert sand.

Vikraman tried opening his eyes to find out who it was. His eyes were open but he was unable to see. 'Aiyyo! Have I lost my eyesight in this blistering heat?' wondered a distraught Vikraman. The person who had lifted him off the sand placed him gently on a soft mattress and gave him water. On sipping the water, Vikraman rejoiced, 'Aha! This water is as refreshing as

the water from the Kaveri!' At that juncture, he felt his environs cooling down. He felt as if he was in a cool grove on the banks of the Kaveri and that the divine being who had rescued him and had quenched his thirst was observing him closely. The fragrance of jasmine enveloped him. Suddenly, he regained his ability to see.

Lo and behold! A maiden with lips as red as the arils of pomegranate and dark, wide eyes was smiling at him with compassion. He had seen her before. She had rescued him from innumerable perils. Vikraman, desirous of touching her mesmerizing face, tried to lift his hand but was unable to do so. His hand felt like lead; his eyes closed as he drifted out of consciousness.

After vacillating between abject misery and delirious joy for days, Vikraman regained his consciousness. He was gradually able to recollect the events of the recent past. He remembered spending the night at the Mahendra mandapam on the banks of the forest stream with Ponnan. He looked around and felt that his surroundings appeared familiar. On further contemplation, he was stunned that he was in Uraiyur – in an island amidst the Kaveri – at Vasantha Maligai.

Vikraman pondered, 'How did I come here? Who brought me here? Who is living in this palace now?' He was reminded of Ponnan and wondered where he was now. He had faint memories of his bittersweet dreams during the time the severe fever had gripped him. He was convinced that the maiden who had appeared in those dreams was real and not a figment of his imagination.

Sometime later, on hearing the sound of anklets, Vikraman eagerly looked around anticipating her arrival. He was disappointed to see a stranger, a lady-in-waiting. A vaidyar accompanied her and examined him. Ushers and ladies-in-waiting frequently attended to his needs. However, Ponnan and the maiden who had appeared in his dreams were nowhere to be seen. Vikraman did not wish to ask the attendants, who went about their daily chores silently. An entire day passed in this manner and Vikraman passed the night in slumber.

On waking up at dawn the following day, Vikraman was unwilling to remain confined to the bed. He felt stronger and started walking around. He felt no fatigue and rather felt sturdy. Vikraman walked out of the room and into the garden. None of the attendants stopped him. As he languidly walked towards the Kaveri riverbank after several years, he took in the sights and sounds of the verdant island nestled in the river.

He was ecstatic. Walking in the shade of the lush green mango trees made him unimaginably happy. Walking at an unhurried pace, he finally reached the banks of the Kaveri and sat under a tree. He was enveloped by a sense of peace and joy.

Vikraman was gazing at the river flowing past, when he observed a maiden's reflection. It was the reflection of the divine maiden. She was the one who had looked at him compassionately at Kanchi and at Mamallapuram. She had appeared in his feverish dreams and offered him peace and solace. Just when Vikraman heaved a deep sigh wondering if he would ever see her again, Kundavai Devi had reached that very spot and now stood behind him, leaning against a tree.

22. Is it Indeed You?

Kundavai stood still under the tree for some time. Vikraman seemed to be completely oblivious to her presence; he appeared to be more interested in gazing at the Kaveri. Kundavai flung a pebble into the water near him, hoping to break his reverie. The pebble plonked into the water, spraying water droplets on his person. Vikraman turned around to see from where the pebble had descended. His eyes widened on seeing her. He could not help staring at her and he helplessly gulped while looking at her. His lips parted slightly but no words came forth. Sighing deeply, he turned around and resumed contemplating. After a while, Kundavai left her perch by the tree and walked over to the riverbank to sit next to Vikraman. As she sat down, Vikraman turned and gazed at her unblinkingly and finally turned away.

Shortly thereafter, Kundavai stood up and said, 'I'm leaving.' Vikraman, who appeared to be taken aback, queried, 'Did you speak…?'

'Yes, I'm not mute!' retorted Kundavai.

Vikraman glanced at her in amazement without saying anything. She started walking away.

'Why are you leaving?' questioned Vikraman in a choked voice.

'You don't seem to be interested in talking to me. Why should I stay?' remarked Kundavai as she retraced her steps and sat next to Vikraman again.

'I'm afraid,' blurted Vikraman.

'Why are you afraid? If you are scared of a fragile girl, you ought not to have travelled by yourself!'

'I'm not scared of you!'

'Then!'

'I was wondering if you are real or a fever-induced hallucination. I am concerned that my dream will come to an end if I speak.'

Kundavai smilingly asked, 'Do you still think I am a dream or a hallucination?'

'I'm still doubtful... If you won't get angry...'

'If I won't...'

'I want to confirm for myself that this is indeed the real you.'

So saying, Vikraman gently touched Kundavai's cheek. Unlike in his feverish reveries, the face did not vanish. Neither did the owner of the face protest at the touch. Vikraman's palm lingered on Kundavai's tender petal-like cheeks and caressed them. At last Kundavai held his palm and gently returned it to his lap.

She mischievously asked him, 'Are your doubts now laid to rest? Are you now certain?'

'My doubts have vanished. I am now certain of several things all at once.'

'What are you certain of?'

'First of all, I am convinced that I'm not hallucinating. It is indeed you who are sitting next to me.'

'Go on...'

'You are not a divine maiden beyond the reach of humans. Neither are you a lifeless golden statue devoid of any feelings. I am convinced that you are a mortal maiden.'

'What next?'

'Henceforth, it is impossible for me to think of a life without you…'

Kundavai looked away and secretly wiped the tears which were welling in her eyes. She then asked Vikraman, 'Do you really remember me?'

'Remember you? The more relevant question would have been if I remembered anything else besides you. It was your countenance that I recollected day and night, during my voyages, at the battlefield and during times of joy and tribulation. Memories of you have haunted me for the last three years, no matter where I went, what I did.'

'Three years? We met at the streets of Mamallapuram barely ten days ago!' remarked Kundavai in a tone tinged with mirth and disbelief.

Vikraman remained silent for some time to cover his slip and remarked innocently, 'Oh! Is it really only ten days since we met?'

'Well! Unless the fever had rendered you bedridden for three years?'

'Well, this fever did create such a delusion. I thought that we have been friends for years!'

'Do you remember seeing me somewhere before we met at Mamallapuram?' asked Kundavai.

Vikraman thought for a while and replied, 'I am unable to recollect much of my past at this juncture. I confess to being confused. And also…'

'Also?' prompted Kundavai.

'Also, I am helpless and completely blank out when I gaze into your wide, dark eyes. I forget myself, the purpose of my visit to Uraiyur and my station in this world! How do you expect me to keep track of days, months and years?'

'You are babbling thus because you're not yet completely rid of the fever. You ought not to have ventured out alone.'

'Not at all. I'm no longer feverish. You may feel my hand!' So

saying, Vikraman extended his hand.

Kundavai touched his hand gently and exclaimed, 'God! Your temperature is still high!'

'Maybe; but that's not because of the fever.'

'Never mind that! Please stop gazing at my eyes. Now do you remember who you are and where you have come from? Are you still having problems with your memory?' queried Kundavai.

'Yes, indeed I remember. I came here, sat on the riverbank and recollected my past. I sailed here from Shenbaga Theevu on a ship to sell precious gems…'

'Don't you remember meeting me at the streets of Mamallapuram?'

'I do.'

'Do you recollect me inviting you to the palace for the Chakravarthi's daughter to buy gems?'

'I now do.'

'Why didn't you visit the palace? Why did you slink away that evening without informing anyone?'

'May I tell you the truth?'

'If ratna vyaparis do indeed speak the truth at times, you may do so.'

'I swear that I was concerned that I would not be able to tear myself away from you should I see you again. Now I realize that my concern was not unfounded.'

'Is it customary for men in Shenbaga Theevu to be sweet tongued with women? Are such skills imparted routinely in your island?' mocked Kundavai.

'You forget that while I currently live in Shenbaga Theevu, I was born and raised in Chola Nadu. In my childhood, I used to run around and play on these very banks of the holy Kaveri. I learnt to swim in this river. I have wandered several days in the mango and coconut groves of the picturesque Chola Nadu. Ah! How much have I yearned for Chola Nadu during the years I lived in Shenbaga Theevu! I've shed copious tears reminiscing the Kaveri! How I pined to visit Chola Nadu again! My desire has been fulfilled and that too, because of you! I am indebted to you,' declared Vikraman animatedly.

'You ought not to thank me but Kundavai Devi.'

'Who?'

'The Chakravarthi's daughter, Kundavai. She was the one who consented to bring you here. You are indeed indebted to her.'

'Is that so? I seem to be ignorant of several facts. I am bewildered. That I have been brought to Vasantha Theevu and I am now sitting on the banks of the Kaveri surprises me no end. I'm unable to comprehend anything else. Please explain to me in detail how I was brought here. Before that, do tell me who you are and what your name is.'

'I introduced myself at Mamallapuram; don't you remember?'

'I only recollect meeting you; nothing else.'

'My name is Rohini. I'm Ilavarasi Kundavai's companion.'

Actually, Kundavai had introduced herself as Madhavi when she met Vikraman at Mamallapuram. As she had thought of the name in haste, she had now forgotten what she had said earlier.

Vikraman replied, 'Rohini... What a beautiful name! I often used to gaze at the night sky at Shenbaga Theevu. The sight of the Rohini star (astronomical name: Aldebaran) glittering near the crescent moon captivated me. But the Rohini star pales when compared to the twinkle in your eyes.'

'I see through your façade...' remarked Kundavai.

Vikraman, who was taken aback, echoed, 'Façade?'

'You are not, in reality, a trader. You are a poet; a wandering minstrel. I cannot for a moment believe that you brought bundles of gems here for trading!'

Vikraman paused before replying, 'I do not have the wherewithal to convince you now. But one day I will prove to you that I did carry a bundle of gems. I am certainly not a poet. If I have suddenly sprouted some poetic talent, it is because you are my muse. The radiance of your moon-like visage...'

'Enough! Please stop! Your chicanery is not amusing!' exclaimed Kundavai.

'Chicanery?' repeated Vikraman and heaved a deep sigh. He then remarked, 'I will refrain from speaking, if that is what you desire. But I will be grateful if you could tell me how I reached this place.'

'You were running a high temperature and lay unconscious at a Mahendra mandapam on the Kanchi–Uraiyur route. If you tell me first of the events that transpired from the time of your departure from Mamallapuram to your reaching the mandapam, I will divulge what happened subsequently.'

Vikraman provided Kundavai a succinct account of his journey from Mamallapuram to the Mahendra mandapam. She then remarked, 'Ilavarasar Mahendran and Ilavarasi Kundavai were travelling from Kanchi to Uraiyur. I accompanied Kundavai Devi. As we were crossing that Mahendra mandapam, we heard a voice call out "Amma! Amma!" from within. I came to the mandapam and realized that you, the trader I had met at Mamallapuram, lay there ill. I then sought Kundavai Devi's permission to bring you along. She was kind enough to acquiesce. She also permitted you to stay here till you completely recover.'

'I imagined I saw you often when I was down with fever. I now realize that those were not dreams and that you had visited me in reality.'

'It may be so. I indeed visited you often when you were beset with fever. But it was Kundavai Devi's graciousness that facilitated your recovery.'

Vikraman was lost in thought. Kundavai questioned him, 'Despite my explaining at length about Kundavai Devi's kindness, you are not keen to express your gratitude. Are you so ungrateful?'

'I'm incapable of feeling beholden to a member of the Pallava dynasty!'

'You would feel differently if you were to meet Kundavai Devi in person. You will forget me too!'

'I certainly will not! A thousand Kundavai Devis will not match up to you! Never mind. Is the duo staying at Vasantha Maligai?'

'Which duo are you referring to?'

'The siblings.'

'Yuvaraja Mahendran has returned to Kanchi. A Chinese traveller who has extensively travelled across Bharata Nadu has finally visited Kanchi. His has a strange name – Hiuen Tsang. As the Chakravarthi was occupied with important matters of the state, he had sent a missive to Ilavarasar Mahendran asking him to return to Kanchi forthwith and to receive and attend to the Chinese traveller. Ilavarasar Mahendran returned to Kanchi within two days of coming to Uraiyur. Our Chakravarthi's fame has spread far and wide to nations beyond the seas. Is this the case in the countries you visited too?' enquired Kundavai.

'True. The Pallava Chakravarthi is well regarded even in the countries I visited.'

'Isn't it an honour for Chola Nadu to be a vassal state to such a Chakravarthi? Why should the Chola Ilavarasar refuse to pay tribute to the Chakravarthi and fritter away his time at Shenbaga Theevu? Is this right? What do you think?' enquired Kundavai and she looked at Vikraman's face eagerly.

Vikraman looked at her in the eye and said, 'I prefer being a free denizen at Shenbaga Theevu to being a slave in Chola Nadu.'

'Are you certain? Wouldn't you tarry here for my sake?'

Vikraman looked at her tenderly and remarked, 'Please do not put me in such a disconcerting situation!'

Though Kundavai and Vikraman had become aware of each other's identity, they pretended otherwise. How long could this charade last!

23. The Trail by the Waterfall

The golden rays of the rising sun enhanced the beauty of the Kolli Mountains. While the sun rays illuminated one side of the rocks and bushes, the long, dark shadows that enveloped the other side made for a strange sight. The cheerful chirping of numerous birds along with the mellifluous sounds of the waterfall briskly cascading down the mountain was mesmerizing. The sivanadiyar and Ponnan, mounted on two high-breed white steeds, were riding towards the mountain down the path that hugged the forest stream.

The sivanadiyar, pointing out to a bare rock that lay some distance away, asked, ‘Ponna, look at that rock. What does it remind you of?’

‘Nothing, swami! I only see a bare rock.’

‘Do you know what that rock reminds me of? It reminds me of Nandi Bhagavan, the bull-mount of Lord Shiva, genuflecting. Behold the rock’s shadow.’

Ponnan was shocked observing the rock’s shadow. He remarked, ‘Swami! It does resemble Nandi’.

‘This is the difference between the eye of a lay person and that of a sculptor, Ponna! On seeing a rock, a sculptor will be able to perceive an elephant, a lion or the form of a deity. He immediately understands how the image in his mind may be culled out of the rock...'

Ponnan interjected, 'Swami! Are you...?'

'Yes! I am indeed a sculptor! That's the vocation I'm most passionate about...Once I complete the task I've undertaken... Never mind, Ponna! Have you seen the sculptures at Mamallapuram?' enquired the sivanadiyar.

'I have seen them just once, swami!'

'What feelings did those sculptures evoke?'

'I was transported to a dream world...'

'But those sculptures are no figment of imagination! They are more real than our very existence. Those sculptures carved out of stone are going to outlive us for ages. A millennium later our descendants will continue admiring those sculptures. Aha! Ponna! I once aspired to transform the whole of Tamizhagam into a sculpture paradise like Mamallapuram...'

'What, you too had aspirations?' asked Ponnan.

'Yes. Do you think it was just your Parthiba Maharaja who had a grandiose vision? His aspirations were restricted to the glory of the Cholas. I aspired to enhance the glory of Tamizhagam...Ponna! Our divine country is divided into Uthara Bharata and Dakshina Bharata. It is Uthara Bharata that has been extolled since time immemorial in literature and history.

'Emperors of Uthara Bharata like Chandragupta of Pataliputra, Ashoka Chakravarthi and Vikramadityan have earned unparalleled fame. Which king in Dakshina Bharata is as renowned? Even in our times, Mahendra Pallavar's fame was not as widespread as Harshavardana Chakravarthi's. The latter was world renowned. Why is the southern country lagging behind? It is because this country has been fragmented into Chola Nadu, Chera Nadu and Pandya Nadu since times of yore. Ruling over a vast kingdom is essential to scale greater heights and thus, attain widespread fame. The length and width of Harsha Chakravarthi's empire span a distance of two hundred kaada each. In the southern country, we traverse three kingdoms within a distance of ten kaada. Tamizhagam must unite into one large kingdom. Mahendra Pallavar wished Tamizhagam's eminence to spread across the entire world. I too harboured such ambitions and was optimistic of achieving this goal during my lifetime. But one man's sheer valour dashed all my aspirations to the ground.'

'Swami! Who are you referring to?' enquired Ponnan.

'He is none other than your Parthiba Maharaja! Aha! I am able to recall the battle on the banks of the Vennaru River even today. It was an unforgettable war! The water in the Vennaru turned red. That battlefield was horrific even in the light cast by the full moon. Can you imagine how fierce that war must have been if there was not a single survivor amongst the ten thousand strong force that had marched from Uraiyur to wage the war!' averred the sivanadiyar passionately.

'Aiyyo! I was not fortunate to be amongst those ten thousand warriors!' exclaimed Ponnan.

'While it is gallant to give up one's life on the battlefield, great fortitude is required to lead a steadfast life. You possess that fortitude and Valli's fortitude exceeds yours. You are a fortunate couple!' remarked the sivanadiyar.

'Swami, tell me more about the Vennaru War!' asked Ponnan. Ponnan did not tire of asking the sivanadiyar to narrate the events of the Vennaru War and the final moments of Parthiba Maharaja's life nor did the sivanadiyar's eagerness wane in relating those recollections. He narrated the tale in great detail to Ponnan again.

Soon they reached a point beyond which taking their horses on the uphill ascent was impossible. The duo left their horses at a spot where there was a dense growth of trees.

Ponnan asked, 'Shouldn't we tether the horses to the trees?'

The sivanadiyar replied, 'No need, Ponna. These high-breed steeds are endowed with a much sharper intellect than most humans! It was Pushpakam that alerted me to Vikraman being swept away in the flooded forest stream before you did. If we leave the horses here untethered, they will not wander away. But if we were to tether them, they will not be able to escape if wild animals attacked them.' He then caressed the backs of both the horses. Ponnan and the sivanadiyar then started climbing the rocky landscape upwards towards the foot of the waterfall.

The uphill path was steep, bumpy and strewn with small and large boulders. The sivanadiyar, very deftly and effortlessly, leapt from rock to rock and waded through the water as he climbed. Ponnan struggled to follow him. He asked, 'Swami! Is there any skill that you lack?'

'There is one skill I do not possess, Ponna. I find it impossible not to keep my word,' shot back the sivanadiyar. Even as Ponnan was trying to comprehend the import of the sivanadiyar's statement, the ascetic continued, 'Yes, indeed! The promise I made to your Parthiba Maharaja was instrumental in my life's aspirations being dashed to the ground!'

Ponnan countered, 'Why is that so, swami? You mentioned this earlier too! How is Parthiba Maharaja responsible for you not achieving your ambitions?'

'On returning from Vatapi, I aspired to unite the southern country into one large kingdom. I firmly believed that Tamizhagam was large enough to accommodate just one kingdom with one ruler. I had vowed to annihilate the Cholas, Cheras and Pandyas and to bring the whole of Tamizhagam under the Pallava reign. But Parthiban's valour rendered me incapable of fulfilling my aspiration. I had promised him that I will bring his son up as an independent and fearless man. I myself was obliged to take the initiative to establish an independent Chola kingdom! I now wonder what prompted me to head to the battlefield on that

Puraṭṭāsi full moon night and to look for Parthiban. Is this what people refer to as fate's machination?'

Conversing thus, the sivanadiyar and Ponnan continued their uphill trek. By noon, they reached the foot of the roaring waterfall. The waters cascaded down with great force into a turbulent pool which in turn was the source of the forest stream. Ponnan told the sivanadiyar that it was not possible to ascend further by following the course of the waterfall. On hearing that, the sivanadiyar started examining the terrain around them carefully, all the while in serious contemplation. There appeared to be no path around the area where the cascade fell to the ground. The waterfall was flanked by the perpendicular and uneven mountain wall and thorny bushes and creepers that grew in its vicinity. He stepped into the pool, waded further, and soon reached the spot where the cascade fell to the ground. The depth of the pool here was difficult to determine. The turbulence caused by the waters falling with full force to the ground was unnerving. The perpendicular mountain walls that flanked the waterfall made it seemingly impossible for anyone to near the waterfall.

However, the sivanadiyar went about accomplishing the seemingly impossible task. He grasped the uneven walls of the rocky mountain at the edge of the pool, leapt from one rock to another, waded through parts of the pond and swam in others and finally disappeared behind the waterfall. Ponnan was awestruck observing this. When the sivanadiyar went out of sight, he shrieked, 'Aiyyo!' He was consumed by dread and regret wondering if the sivanadiyar had met with his end. Ponnan became increasingly anxious as time passed by. He felt giddy envisaging the disastrous events that might pan out should the sivanadiyar come in harm's way. Ponnan wondered, 'I cannot bring myself to leave the sivanadiyar behind and return. I must follow him, come what may!' He boldly set foot in the tumultuous pond.

24. Ponnan's Departure

Just as Ponnan stepped into the waters of the pool, the sivanadiyar – much to his delight – emerged from behind the waterfall. As Ponnan stood hesitant, wondering whether he ought to walk towards the sivanadiyar or stay put, the sivanadiyar said something to him and beckoned him. The roar of the cascade drowned the sivanadiyar's voice, but Ponnan understood his gesture. He, like the sivanadiyar, walked falteringly by the edge of the pond, holding on to the rocks, finally reached the spot where the latter was standing. Ponnan realized that the cascade, which appeared narrow from a distance, was actually around thirty feet wide. The ascetic held Ponnan by his hand and led him down a passage that was flanked by rocks on one side and the waterfall on the other. This dimly lit narrow passageway was slippery. If a man were to momentarily lose his balance in the passage, the cascade would sweep him away into deep pond below! The two men walked slowly and carefully, placing their feet firmly on the ground. After walking in this manner for four to five feet, the sivanadiyar pointed out a large, almost square, aperture on the rockwall. There lay an inclined passage that ran from the aperture to some place above. The opening was large enough for one person to enter. The duo was unable to ascertain how long the passage was and where it led to. They could not see beyond some distance into the hole.

The sivanadiyar gestured to Ponnan to follow him, entered the aperture and started walking up. He used his arms and legs to scale the upwardly inclined passage. Ponnan followed suit. An indescribable fear caused Ponnan's heart to beat fast. After climbing thus for some time, the passage turned pitch dark. Ponnan became even more apprehensive and anxious. He however felt somewhat reassured on realizing that the rocks were intermittently incised so that he could hold on to the walls and place his feet without losing balance while navigating upwards. After hiking thus for some time, they could see light streaming into the passage from a cave above. The passage became progressively better illuminated. The sivanadiyar climbed up and made way for Ponnan. Following the sivanadiyar and hoisting himself up, Ponnan was in the open, standing on a plateau. The two men were spellbound by the wondrous scene around them.

The duo stood close to the spot where the waterfall started cascading down the mountain's steep face. At the centre of a square, well-like pit culled out of a nearby rock was a passage that led to an underground cave. To the right of this pit, the waterfall raucously fell off the cliff. The landscape here was breathtaking. Lush golden hued konrai, or golden shower, flowers carpeted the plateau, which was flanked on three sides by mountains.

'What a breathtaking spot, Ponna! I wonder why the Almighty chose to conceal this place in such a remote location!' exclaimed the sivanadiyar.

'Indeed, swami! This place is as inaccessible as Parthiba Maharaja's Chithra Mandapam!'

The sivanadiyar smiled slightly and continued, 'Ponna, this picturesque locale that God chose to so carefully hide, is the site of unmentionable and barbaric atrocities.'

'Aiyyo! Swami! Why do you say so?'

'It's true! I have today unravelled the mystery that has confounded me for long. Maha Kabala Bhairavar's abode is somewhere in this mountainous region. I will return once I trace his hideout. You…'

'So will I, swami! Do you believe that I will leave you alone in this place and return?'

'No, Ponna! You must leave. There is an extremely important matter you need to attend to.'

'What can be more important for me that tracing our Rani?'

'That's the reason for my coming here, Ponna. But is it enough if we rescue the Rani? What will we tell her when she enquires about Vikraman? The Ilavarasar is also in great danger. Recollect the conversation between Marappan and Maha Kabala Bhairavan. Imagine what Marappan will do if he came to know of the Ilavarasar's whereabouts...'

'What can happen in contravention to Mahendra Ilavarasar's wishes?'

'Anything can happen! Mahendran is not in Uraiyur now, Ponna! Marappan, who has now set his sights on the Chakravarthi's throne, will go to any length. Should Kundavai come to know that the ratna vyapari is in fact the Chola Ilavarasar, she may herself hand him over to Marappan.'

'Aiyyo!'

'It is, hence, imperative for you to head to Uraiyur forthwith!'

'But how can I leave you here alone? I now understand the reason for the Maha Kabala Bhairavar wanting you beheaded.'

'Don't worry about me, Ponna! I have countered several such hazards in my lifetime. I wish to meet the Kabala Bhairavan face to face and confirm my suspicion about him.'

'What is your suspicion, swami?'

'I will divulge that at the apt moment, Ponna. You must now return to Uraiyur. Vikraman may continue staying at Vasantha Theevu if there is no suspicion about him. If you believe that he is likely to be in danger, fetch him to the sculptor's house near Mamallapuram. I will meet you two there.'

'If you don't come…'

'If I don't return to Uraiyur or the sculptor's house the next full moon day, you may come in search of me.'

Ponnan reluctantly replied, 'As you say, swami!' and retraced his steps downhill. On crossing the pool, he looked up towards the plateau. The sivanadiyar stood by the brink of the waterfall, watching him. Ponnan brought his palms together and took leave of the sivanadiyar, who stretched his hand and blessed him. He then swiftly walked by the waterfall to the foot of the mountain.

25. Valli's Tidings

Ponnan returned to Uraiyur safely and headed to his in-laws' house, where Valli was staying during his absence. Unusual for her, Valli was in a sombre frame of mind. Sorrow had debilitated her body and soul. Members of the Chola royal family, whom she held in high regard, meeting one misfortune after another and her being separated from Ponnan had rendered her listless. When she saw Ponnan after several days, she smiled a bit, held both his hands and ushered him in. Without pausing for breath, she started speaking.

'Come in! I was worried that you too, like our Ilavarasar, had sailed away to a foreign shore or were beheaded at a Kali temple. I visited the Kali temple in Uraiyur every day and prayed to the deity to spare you. Now I'm so happy you have returned. What news do you bear? I hope it's good news!'

'I bear both good and bad tidings, Valli. But I cannot talk now. I am famished! It's ages since I ate your kambu adais. I had to eat what I could lay my hands on…'

'Notwithstanding the fact that you starved, you have put on weight, you wretched man! That's only to be expected given your worries,' she remarked as she looked at Ponnan from head to toe.

'Is that so? While I have become fatter, you have lost weight, Valli! Were you fretting about me?' retorted Ponnan.

'Yes, I was. But now I realize that all my apprehension was unnecessary. If you tell me what transpired during your journeys first, I will share an important piece of information with you.'

'I will tell you briefly. Vikrama Maharaja has returned.'

'What! Is that true?' asked Valli eagerly.

'I met him in person and spoke to him.'

'Where is he now?'

'That is a secret I cannot divulge.'

'Fine. Has there been any other development?'

'We have more or less traced the place where our Rani has been hidden. The sivanadiyar is now looking for our Rani. He must have traced her by now.'

'Aha! The sivanadiyar...'

'Wicked Valli! You had misled me by not divulging the sivanadiyar's true identity. I grabbed his wig of matted locks, flung it away and ascertained his identity!'

'Is that so? Who is he?'

'He is none other than your late grandfather, Veerabhadra Achari, reincarnated!' Ponnan quipped.

Valli smilingly replied, 'This skimpy account will not do. You must relate to me in detail, without omitting anything, what transpired since the day you left Uraiyur!'

'I will, if you light the stove!'

Valli started cooking a meal for Ponnan, who related at length the events that unfolded during his journey. He finally asked Valli, 'You said that you had some news for me. What is it?'

Valli replied, 'Marappa Bhupathi visited this house five times during the last four days. Apparently, he has now been appointed as the general of Chola Nadu. He is throwing his weight around, which is intolerable. He pressed me for information about a ratna vyapari from Shenbaga Theevu who is staying at the Vasantha Maligai. I swore I knew nothing. He then enquired if you had returned. He may come here today.'

Ponnan, after listening to Valli's account, became pensive. He asked, 'Valli, we don't have the time to tarry here. I must head to Vasantha Theevu this very evening. Haven't you kept the boat in our hut and locked the hut?'

'Yes, I have. But under what pretext will you visit Vasantha Theevu?' she countered.

'Hadn't the Chakravarthi mentioned earlier that I ought to ply Kundavai Devi across the river? I will inform the guards that I wanted to find out if she requires my services.'

'But I don't understand why the ascetic is still creating such challenging circumstances. When does he propose to discard his disguise?'

'I posed this very question to him. He said that it was to keep his word to Parthiba Maharaja that he has disguised himself.'

Ponnan and Valli, soon finished eating, and walked along the Kaveri to their home at the quay. As soon as the couple reached their hut, they fetched the boat from inside and placed it on the river. Ponnan reassured Valli, 'I will return before dusk. Don't worry!'

Ponnan's spirits lifted as he rowed across the Kaveri after many days. However, his eyes turned misty recollecting his rowing the royal family during Parthiba Maharaja's time. He wondered whether Vikraman had recuperated. If the Ilavarasar had recovered, would he be able to speak to the Ilavarasar alone? Ponnan, who was preoccupied while rowing, suddenly realized that he had neared Vasantha Theevu. He rowed his boat towards a remote, isolated cove of the island. He wanted to tether the boat and walk around the island discreetly and enquire about Vikraman. However, as he surveyed the riverbank, he was in for a pleasant surprise. Vikrama Maharaja was standing some distance away, with one foot in the river and the other on the ground, eagerly looking at Ponnan and his boat. Ponnan swiftly rowed towards Vikraman.

26. The Boat that Drifted Away

Once the boat reached the riverbank, Ponnan leapt to the ground. Vikraman embraced him eagerly. A joyous Ponnan shed tears as he remarked, 'Maharaja! I'm indeed fortunate to meet you again!'

Vikraman replied, 'Ponna, you have a knack of arriving at the right place at the right time. I have been observing your hut for the last two to three days. If I had not sighted your boat today, I would have tried to swim across the river and come to your house. Look, Ponna! The boat is moving. Tether it right away.'

Ponnan rushed to the boat and fastened it to the aerial root of a tree on the riverbank. The two men sat under the tree. Vikraman then asked, 'Tell me what happened after we were separated. I wonder whether the events that occurred near the forest stream are a dream. Even now, I am uncertain if I am really at the banks of my beloved Kaveri or in a reverie! When did you leave me? Why did you leave me?'

'Aiyyo, Maharaja! I strove hard to find a vaidyar. By the time I fetched one to the Mahendra mandapam, you were not there.'

'When did you fetch a vaidyar? Ponna, explain what happened in detail.'

'Do you recollect us spending the night at the Mahendra mandapam, Maharaja?'

'I do. Even thinking of that night is so unsettling.'

'We had decided to travel to Uraiyur the following morning. You were up at dawn but could not even walk. You were beset with high temperature. You tried walking a short distance, then came back and lay down. As time passed, your temperature intensified. I was in torment! I could not bring myself to leave you alone at the mandapam and fetch a vaidyar. But I also realized that it was futile to idly sit by your side. I resolved to walk to the nearest village looking for help. By the time I found a vaidyar, you were missing from the mandapam. I thought I would go crazy!'

'What happened after that?' prodded Vikraman.

Ponnan related how he had started running around looking for Vikraman, his meeting the dwarf and his coming to know that Kundavai Devi had arranged for Vikraman to accompany the Chola royal retinue to Uraiyur. He informed Vikraman that he had shadowed the royal retinue up to Parantaka Puram, had met the sivanadiyar at the sculptor's abode after which the two men had headed to the Kolli Mountains, and had discovered the hidden route close to the cascade. Ponnan concluded his account with him parting ways with the sivanadiyar at the Kolli Mountains and returning to Uraiyur.

Vikraman, taken aback on hearing that Ponnan had met the sivanadiyar at the sculptor's house, remarked, 'The sculptor's residence where I had spent the night with the spymaster, Veerasenan, was where you met the sivanadiyar! I wonder…'

'What is your suspicion, Maharaja?'

'Has the spymaster been masquerading as the sivanadiyar?'

'Indeed, Maharaja! Veerasenan and the sivanadiyar are one and the same person. As I was walking down the by-road to Mamallapuram, I saw a warrior riding a horse ahead of me. I surmised that he was Veerasenar based on your description of the spymaster. He went towards the sculptor's house and emerged from it after sometime as the sivanadiyar!'

'Aiyyo! The Pallava Chakravarthi's spymaster knows who I am… But he has been so supportive of us for years. Will he now expose me?'

'He will never do so, swami! Notwithstanding his position as the Pallava Chakravarthi's spymaster, he had given your father his word at the battlefield. He will not put you in peril. But…'

'But what, Ponna?'

'There lurks another major hazard here. Marappa Bhupathi has now been appointed the general of Chola Nadu. He suspects that you may be at Vasantha Theevu, Maharaja! It is imperative for us to leave this place immediately.'

Ponnan observed Vikraman's joyful expression as he remarked, 'There lurks a danger here that far exceeds the one posed by Marappa Bhupathi, Ponna! We must indeed leave this place soon.'

'What is that, Maharaja?'

'The danger that lurks in a maiden's dark eyes,' stated Vikraman as he gazed at the Kaveri. Silence prevailed for some time. He then remarked, 'Who else am I going to share my innermost thoughts with, Ponna? Three years ago, when I was imprisoned and taken to Kanchi, a maiden in a palanquin saw me in shackles being led to the court. She again appeared on the seashore when I was onboard the ship bound for Shenbaga Theevu and regarded me compassionately. Despite living in Shenbaga Theevu for three years, I was unable to forget her. You

will be surprised to hear this, Ponna! It was that damsel who, on seeing me afflicted with fever at the Mahendra mandapam, brought me here.'

'Who is that virtuous woman, Maharaja? I am eager to meet that Devi and express my gratitude!'

'Ponna, you wouldn't feel grateful if you knew the truth.'

'Aiyyo! What is that?'

'I have been subjected to much turmoil for the last three days, Ponna. Folklore and epics are replete with instances of women luring men to their downfall. It appears that I will be subject to the same fate. Wasn't Viswamitra's penance disrupted due to his infatuation with Menaka? I am scared I will meet with a similar fate. That maiden has lured me!'

'Maharaja, I am an illiterate, ignorant person. Nevertheless, I seek your consent to submit my view.'

'Do so, Ponna. You don't need my consent.'

'You mention that Menaka led to Viswamitra's downfall. But Maharaja, there are women who helped men achieve greatness. Didn't Seetha play an important role in Rama attaining greatness? Why did Krishna abduct Rukmini? What harm did Subhadra cause Arjuna? Why did Lord Muruga seek Valli's hand? Did that lead to his downfall?'

'Well said! It was not only Seetha, Rukmini and Subhadra who were instrumental in Rama, Krishna and Arjuna attaining greater heights. Arulmozhi Rani supported Parthiba Maharaja while Valli supported you, Ponna.'

'Exactly! Then why do you say that falling in love with a woman is debilitating?'

'Heed me, Ponna. A woman's love has caused mere mortals to acquire divine qualities and has also resulted in a few Gods deteriorating into the basest of men. I, unfortunately, belong to the second category. The woman I am in love with will be instrumental in my reneging my duty and my life's aspirations. Ever since I recovered from my fever, all I can think of is her. I believe that I will not be able to live even for a moment away from her. I am concerned that I may relinquish my quest for Chola Nadu's independence for her sake. I might even happily wed her and become a vassal of Kanchi Narasimha Pallava Chakravarthi!'

Ponnan was shell-shocked and recollected the sivanadiyar saying that this phase of Vikraman's life will be his ultimate test. 'Aiyyo! Why do you speak thus? Do you remember the promise you made to Parthiba Maharaja at the Uraiyur Chithra Mandapam?' questioned Ponnan.

'I do remember that, Ponna! But I don't think I will remember my promise for much longer. My resolve is weakening by the day. This is the reason for my wanting to leave this place immediately. I am ready to leave with you now. Shall we?' asked Vikraman.

'We may, Maharaja, but we have a task to accomplish in this island. I had buried the casket Maharani gave me here.'

'I told you so! I have forgotten even that! If I spend a few more days here, I will forget the reason for my visiting Uraiyur and myself too. We must leave before I run into that maiden today. Where have you buried the casket?' queried an agitated Vikraman.

'I have buried it close by, swami.'

'Don't we have to dig out the casket?'

'I have come prepared with a spade and a crowbar,' said Ponnan as he fetched the tools from his boat. The two men walked swiftly into the mango grove.

Shortly after they left, Kundavai emerged from behind a nearby tree. She looked around and then walked towards the tethered boat. She looked around surreptitiously once again and unfastened the rope that tied the boat to the tree. The boat started gliding away and then, caught in the river's swirling current, moved away rapidly. Kundavai stood there for a while with a grin on her face.

27. Buried Treasure

Ponnan led the way, followed by Vikraman, into the verdant mango grove whose overgrowth blocked the sunlight. Ponnan craned his neck up and observed the branches while walking into the grove. He came to a halt under a tree, which bore the figure of a tiger etched on the bark of one of its low hanging branches. Ponnan removed the dry leaves and twigs that had fallen under that tree and started digging the ground. When Vikraman enthusiastically grabbed the spade to follow suit, Ponnan restrained him from doing so by saying, 'Maharaja! You are yet to completely recover. You have much to accomplish. I implore you to sit under a tree for some time.'

Vikraman, in acquiescence to Ponnan's request, sat under a tree. Numerous thoughts rose like waves in his mind, 'I've spent several joyful days at this very Vasantha Theevu as a child. But I am here today as a guest of a foreign maiden. Thank God! This ignominy will come to an end today. We must leave as soon as we retrieve the casket. I must not tarry here even a moment longer.'

Vikraman was bemused recollecting his eagerness to visit his motherland while at Shenbaga Theevu, and his current haste to leave Vasantha Theevu. He wondered, 'Why did I come here? This is sheer insanity. This wasn't the independent Chola Nadu that Parthiba Maharaja had ruled over. This now is a nation, devoid of honour, under the authority of the Pallava Chakravarthi. This is a nation whose general is a man who has betrayed both his country and his clan – Marappa Bhupathi. I am better off leaving this country at the earliest.'

Then, a contrarian thought struck Vikraman, 'How is the nation at fault if its denizens have lost their valour?' He sighed deeply. Vikraman recollected Parthiba Maharaja taking him to the Chithra Mandapam on the eve of his departure to the battlefield and showing him the paintings that depicted his aspirations. He wondered if those aspirations will see the light of day or remain castles built in the air. Everyone at Chola Nadu was enthralled by the Pallava Chakravarthi's fame. A messenger from the Kanchi court had visited Uraiyur the previous day and had described the reception accorded to an envoy from China. Vikraman was enraged listening to the messenger's account. The envoy was bound to spread the Pallava Chakravarthi's fame in all the nations he would subsequently visit and in China. Chola Nadu and the brave Parthiba Maharaja, who gave up his life defending his country's independence, will languish in anonymity.

Vikraman stood up with a start on hearing Ponnan call out. Ponnan was standing in the pit he had dug, holding a casket wrapped in a hide. He removed the hide to reveal the ancient, carved casket. Vikraman rushed to Ponnan, eagerly took the casket and opened it. He touched the carefully preserved palm leaf manuscripts with his eyes in reverence and put them back in the casket. He then held the sword in his hand and remarked, 'Ponna, improper and cowardly thoughts had occurred to me some time ago. I developed an aversion to Chola Nadu itself. I wondered when this nation would be liberated and if it is destined to be a vassal of the Pallavas for eternity. I regretted returning to my motherland in the face of grave danger. This sword has cut through the veil of my misconceptions.

'This was the sword that ruled the world during times of yore. Karikala Chola and Nedumudi Killi embarked on overseas expeditions with this sword in hand and established the great Chola empire. The current residents of Shenbaga Theevu are the descendants of those Tamils who had migrated to that island during the times of Karikala Chola. I, the descendant of a clan of illustrious warriors, am now holding the sword they once wielded. Why wouldn't I scale the heights they did? Ponna, the Thirukkural my father bequeathed to me along with this sword says, "Effort doth lead to victory sweet!" Aha! I had forgotten that hallowed precept! Chola Nadu is now like a sick person; the very breeze that blows across this nation renders one feeble. I will not tarry here a moment more. Come, let's go!'

Ponnan, who was dumbstruck hearing Vikraman speak thus, gawked at him. It was the valour shining through on Vikraman's face that astounded him. Ponnan snapped out of his shock and quickly covered the pit with mud. After covering the spot with dry leaves and twigs, the two men rushed to the Kaveri. They were taken aback on reaching the spot where the boat was tethered. 'What is this, Ponna? Where is the boat?' exclaimed Vikraman.

'Have we come to the wrong spot?' responded a dazed Ponnan as he looked around. On sighting the rope that tethered the boat to the tree, the two men concluded that the end of the rope that was fastened to the boat was somehow unknotted and that the boat had drifted away.

'Ponna, what are you thinking of? Shall we swim across the river?' asked Vikraman.

'Please wait for some time, Maharaja. I will run down the riverbank and check if the boat has come to a halt in the vicinity,' replied Ponnan as he sprinted away.

28. Kundavai's Stipulation

The instant Ponnan disappeared from sight, Vikraman heard the rustling of dry leaves, and looked around. Kundavai emerged from behind a tree. The two of them gazed at each other silently for some time. Kundavai remarked, 'It is evident that the natives of Chola Nadu are a thankless lot. How could you bring yourself to leave without informing me?'

Vikraman refrained from replying. Kundavai said, 'Valluvar Peruman who stated, "Effort doth lead to victory sweet!", also avowed "It does not bode well to be ungrateful!"'

Vikraman, who was taken aback, stuttered, 'How did you come to know? Did you…?' He struggled to speak further.

'Yes, I watched the two of you dig out the casket. I also overheard your conversation.'

'Really?'

'Indeed! I am now aware of your identity.'

Vikraman thought for some time and remarked, 'In that case, my leaving without informing ought not to have surprised you. Isn't it natural for a man who has been banished from his country and who has returned braving a death sentence, to leave surreptitiously?'

'So, you're scared of losing your life?'

'Yes, I'm keen to live for some more time to fulfil my promise to my father and to discharge my duties to my motherland.'

'But your life no longer belongs to you. You lost ownership of your life at the Mahendra mandapam. It was I who nursed you back to health. Doesn't your life now belong to me?' observed Kundavai.

Vikraman became thoughtful again and pronounced, 'Your statement is true in more ways than one. My life belongs to you not just because you offered me succour. My life became yours when you set your eyes on me at Kanchi and at Mamallapuram

three years ago...'

'Ah! Are you speaking the truth now?' queried Kundavai.

'Indeed! My life being yours, haven't you saved your own life?'

'If what you say is true, is it fair for you to sneak away?' questioned Kundavai in a harsh tone.

'While I am guilty of that lapse, don't you understand why I tried to do so? I was concerned that I would not be able to leave bidding farewell to you. If you denied giving me leave, I could not have brought myself to leave...'

'Why do you think of me so poorly? Why would I prevent you

from leaving? Why would I stand in the way of you discharging your duty?'

'I now realize that I had misjudged you. I ought to have divulged my identity at the very beginning and sought your assistance. It was wrong of me to conceal my motives.'

'Let bygones be bygones. Let's talk about what needs to be accomplished. Please sit here till your boatman returns,' stated Kundavai.

When Kundavai referred to the boatman, Vikraman's suspicions were raised, 'Do you know what became of the boat that was tethered here?'

'Yes, it drifted away in the river. The boatman is searching for it in vain.'

'How did it drift away? Was it you...?'

'Yes! I unfastened the boat as a punishment for your attempting to leave without informing me!'

Vikraman fell silent for some time and then remarked, 'As I already mentioned, I was concerned that I cannot bring myself to leave after bidding farewell to you in person.'

'Your ancestor, Karikala Chola, could not have conquered islands across the seas had he been as meek as you are!' quipped Kundavai.

'I agree. I will now courageously take your leave and will also seek your assistance. Kindly provide me with a boat to cross the river and a horse to ride to Mamallapuram.'

'I will, on one condition.'

'Condition?'

'Yes, an unequivocal condition. You ought not to leave me behind and sail to Shenbaga Theevu, like you did three years ago. You must take me along with you.'

Vikraman was shell-shocked. He held Kundavai's tender hands and said in a choked voice, 'What did you say, Devi? Did I hear right? What have I done to deserve such a fortune? Will you, the only daughter of the world renowned Pallava Chakravarthi, accompany me, the one who has been banished from this country, to Shenbaga Theevu?'

Kundavai replied, as she gazed at the Kaveri, 'Don't you believe me? Does your distrust stem from your poor opinion of women?'

'Not at all! I, the son of Arulmozhi Devi, will never ever be contemptuous of women. But how is it possible for you to accompany me? Will your father... the Chakravarthi... consent to this?'

'My father has never ever not fulfilled my desires. He will not do so now.'

The couple were taken aback hearing someone call out, 'Maharaja!' and looked around. It was Ponnan. When Vikraman and Kundavai, oblivious to their surroundings, were conversing, Ponnan had returned and was silently standing behind them. He had heard the concluding part of their conversation.

Vikraman stated, 'When did you come, Ponna? You couldn't find the boat, could you? This Devi had unfastened the boat. She has promised to give us another boat.'

'I heard, Maharaja. But I fail to understand why you have to undergo such difficulties. The Chakravarthi is bound to acquiesce to the Devi's requests. If she were to intercede on your behalf...'

An enraged Kundavai stood up, faced Ponnan, and pronounced, 'Mind your words, boatman! Do you want me to ask the Chakravarthi to forgive your Maharaja? I committed that mistake once. I will not repeat it. If your Maharaja, by the might of his sword, conquers one span of land, I will become the queen of that territory. Even if he plies a boat like you, for a living and puts me up in a hut, I will, like your wife Valli, reign over that hut. I will never ever ask the Chakravarthi to forgive him or to return the Chola kingdom to him. While I am happy to beseech my father for my sake, I will never intercede on your Maharaja's behalf and sully his honour!'

Ponnan started replying, 'Devi...'

Kundavai cut him short stating, 'Yes indeed! Even if his true identity becomes known and he is sentenced to death, I will not plead with the Chakravarthi to spare him. I will request the Chakravarthi to solemnize my wedding with your Maharaja before the sentence is carried out!'

'Devi! It appears that you may indeed have to ask the Chakravarthi for such a boon. Look there! Warrior-laden boats are sailing towards Vasantha Theevu,' remarked Ponnan.

Vikraman and Kundavai were taken aback. They looked in the direction Ponnan was pointing to. Four boats filled with warriors were sailing from the direction of Uraiyur towards Vasantha Theevu. The dense growth of trees had obstructed the approaching boats from the couple's line of vision. As the boats sailed around the island's corner, the couple were able to perceive them. The boats, filled with warriors carrying spears, were swiftly sailing towards Vasantha Theevu.

29. The Chakravarthi's Command

Vikraman stood rooted to the spot, astounded at the sight of the approaching boats. He snapped back to consciousness and called out, 'Ponna, grab the sword!' Ponnan, who was preoccupied till then, rushed to Vikraman on hearing his voice and entreated, 'Maharaja! I seek a boon!'

'What an apt time to seek a boon, Ponna. Ask me quickly. But what do I have to give you, anyway?' asked Vikraman, a tad surprised.

'Maharaja, please do not engage in combat with Marappa Bhupathi's men. The two of us are outnumbered...'

'Ponna, is it indeed you speaking like this? Have you too imbibed Chola Nadu's valorous character!' demanded a sarcastic Vikraman.

'No, Maharaja, I am not scared of dying. I am prepared to sacrifice this worthless life of mine any time. But my reasons for asking you to desist from fighting are different. How will we meet your mother if you clash with these soldiers now? There's another important aspect. Do you intend to wield the hoary sword of your ancestors for the very first time to decimate your subjects?'

Vikraman appeared crestfallen on hearing this. 'Alright, Ponna. There is no need to discuss this further. I will not wield the sword,' declared Vikraman. He then told Kundavai, 'Devi, kindly safeguard this casket and return it to me, should we chance to meet again.'

It was not clear whether Kundavai registered what Vikraman was saying. She was glaring at the approaching boats like one possessed. Marappa Bhupathi was the first to get off the boat once

the boats reached the riverbank. He deferentially approached Kundavai and stated, 'Your Majesty! I seek your apology to visit this island without your prior consent. I am here to execute the Chakravarthi's command.'

Kundavai, who was enraged, demanded, 'Which Chakravarthi? What command?'

Marappan extended a missive to Kundavai remarking, 'Your brother, Mahendra Pallavar, has commanded that the spy from

Shenbaga Theevu be apprehended and transported to Kanchi with utmost security. Please do read this.'

The missive, which bore Mahendran's insignia, did carry the aforesaid edict. Kundavai read the missive and questioned, 'Who is the spy from Shenbaga Theevu?'

'The man standing here is the spy, Devi!'

'No, he is not a spy. You may return!'

'Devi! I beseech you to tell me who he is if he is not the spy!' replied Marappan with an assumed air of obsequiousness.

'Bhupathi! How dare you question me? Have you forgotten your station?' demanded a furious Kundavai.

'No, I have not forgotten my station. Forgetfulness is not a failing of mine. He does appear familiar. I now remember! I recollect that the peerless defender of justice, Narasimha Pallava Chakravarthi had banished this man! If he is not a spy, he is the man who was exiled from this country. You must be aware of the punishment meted out to a banished man who dares to return to this country. Devi! I must perform my duty. I must carry out the command accorded to me. The Pallava Chakravarthi will find my failure to comply with his command, even at the behest of his sister, unacceptable.'

Kundavai shivered. She heaved a deep sigh. 'General! He is my guest. He is under my protection. If he were to be harmed...' As Kundavai spoke thus, she moved towards Vikraman and stood in front of him as if to camouflage him.

Marappan burst out laughing and quipped, 'Ah! The tiger who will be upholding the Chola dynasty's glory is hiding behind a woman!'

Vikraman, overcome by embarrassment and rage, charged ahead of Kundavai and remarked, 'Chithappa! I am ready to accompany you. Imprison me!'

Marappan mockingly said to Kundavai, 'Please don't make a poor man like me the target of your rage. All you have to do to save him is to intercede on his behalf with your father or your brother. The Chakravarthi is a compassionate man. If he were to prostrate before the Chakravarthi seeking his pardon and agree to pay tribute, the Chakravarthi is bound to forgive him.' Marappan was delighted to observe that his words had the desired effect on Vikraman and Kundavai – the duo was distraught.

Vikraman quickly walked away and sat in one of the boats. Kundavai observed him keenly. She might have hoped that he would turn around and look at her and that she could communicate her support for him through her eyes. However, Vikraman did not look around. Marappan after observing the goings-on, turned his attention to Ponnan. He commanded, 'Boatman! Go and sit in the boat!'

'Why should he come? Do you carry an order to detain him too?' demanded Kundavai as she shot a scorching look at Marappan.

Marappan, unable to withstand her gaze, submitted, 'I do not carry an order, Devi. But he assists this spy, this man who has been banished from our country…'

'Ponnan is in my employ. He plies the boat for me. You do not have the authority to arrest him. Beware!' declared Kundavai.

Marappan hesitated on hearing her authoritative tone. Kundavai continued, 'I too am guilty of aiding a man who was banished from this country. Imprison me!'

'I will, Devi, if the Chakravarthi commands me to do so!' replied Marappan. He then asked the boatmen to start rowing.

The boats sailed swiftly towards Uraiyur.

30. In the Dead of the Night

After the boats had sailed away, Kundavai enquired, 'Boatman! Where is your wife now?' Ponnan informed her that Valli was staying at their hut across the river. Kundavai continued speaking, 'Fetch her here forthwith. We have a lot to accomplish. We need to free your Maharaja and dispatch him to Mamallapuram in utmost secrecy. We may rest only after we ensure he is on board the ship headed to Shenbaga Theevu this amavasai.'

'Devi! I don't understand!' replied a surprised Ponnan.

'It was from your Maharaja's unconscious whining in his fever-ridden state that I discovered his identity and the purpose of his visit. The ship from Shenbaga Theevu awaits his return at the Mamallapuram harbour every amavasai. We must free him before the next amavasai and ensure he boards the ship covertly.'

'Ammani (a respectful way to address a woman)! Please do not get angry with me. I still do not understand why we have to go to such lengths. Wouldn't it suffice if your father were apprised of the situation?' asked Ponnan.

'Ponna, while you have not understood my father, Marappan

has. He dispenses justice impartially. Your Maharaja may escape only if he boards the ship before the Chakravarthi becomes aware of what transpired. Fortunately, my father is not in Kanchi now. He is travelling across the country incognito for some reason. It is an opportune moment for us.' As Kundavai spoke her mind, Ponnan felt inclined for a moment to divulge all what he knew. He then recollected that he had given his word to the sivanadiyar. Moreover, Ponnan was not aware of the sivanadiyar's motives for carrying out his activities under the cloak of secrecy. Resolving that he ought not be instrumental in thwarting the sivanadiyar from achieving his goals, Ponnan heeded Kundavai patiently.

Ponnan finally remarked, 'Devi, Vikrama Maharaja's well-being is of utmost importance to me. I am willing to carry out your commands, whatever they may be.'

'I am happy to hear that. I will return to the palace. You may first fetch your wife here,' replied Kundavai.

Ponnan was given a boat and he rowed across the river. By then, it was pitch dark. While he was rowing, his mind wandered. He felt distressed reminiscing that Vikrama Maharaja, who ought to have been seated on the Uraiyur throne ruling over Chola Nadu, was spending the night in the Uraiyur prison. Ponnan even considered spreading the news of Vikraman's imprisonment in Uraiyur and thus, organizing an uprising. But he realized that his efforts would be futile as the denizens of Chola Nadu had lost their gallantry and had become cowards. They had accepted a foreign king's suzerainty and were keen, like Marappan, to conform with the Pallava Chakravarthi's commands.

Ponnan felt embarrassed wondering if he too was like the rest of the denizens of Chola Nadu. He wondered if he could completely trust the sivanadiyar's disguise and his words. How could he be certain that the sivanadiyar spoke the truth. The sivanadiyar may be deceiving him . . . He was convinced that Kundavai, out of genuine affection for Vikraman, was striving to save him. She had saved Vikraman from death. After analysing the problem at hand from several angles, Ponnan decided to abide by Kundavai's wishes.

On reaching the opposite bank, Ponnan was surprised to see that the door to their hut was bolted. He knocked on the door. Valli called out, 'Who is it?' Only after confirming that it was Ponnan did she open the door. When he asked her why she had locked the door, her response surprised and horrified him.

It was dusk, when Valli heard the sound of people talking and went inside the hut, closing the door behind her. The voices became progressively louder as the men neared the hut. She heard a horrific voice command, 'You stay here and fetch Bhupathi! I am heading to the temple.'

Another voice responded, 'Maha Prabhu! We could stay in this hut!'

The ghastly voice that initially spoke replied, 'You tarry here and fetch him to this spot as soon as he comes!'

Valli waited for some time before gingerly opening the door and stepping out. She observed two men walk away at a distance in the dim light of twilight. Observing that one of the men was tall and had only one arm, the normally courageous Valli lost her nerve. Her fear intensified recollecting that this was the man who had spirited away Arulmozhi Devi at the Kaveri Sangamam on the day of the solar eclipse. The second man appeared to be a dwarf. The one-armed man appeared even taller while walking beside the dwarf.

The tall one-armed man had walked away eastwards, while the dwarf sat under a roadside tree. Valli walked into the hut and bolted the door. After relating what had transpired, she looked around. Grabbing Ponnan's hand, she said, 'Look there!' Ponnan observed the dwarf sitting under a roadside tree. It appeared that the dwarf was staring intently in the direction of their hut. Ponnan said, 'Valli, come with me! We have tasks to accomplish tonight.'

'Are we headed to Uraiyur?' queried Valli.

'No, we're headed to Vasantha Theevu. Kundavai Devi asked me to fetch you.'

'Is that so? Is the Ilavarasar – Maharaja – keeping well? Does the Devi know of his true identity?' asked Valli eagerly.

'I have a lot to share with you. I will tell you everything while rowing across the river!' replied Ponnan.

The couple headed to the riverbank. Ponnan purposely created much noise while unfastening his boat and rowing the boat. He observed the dwarf watch them sail across the river. Around one nazhigai past midnight, Ponnan rowed the boat back to the southern bank of the Kaveri. He did not row back to the quay; instead he noiselessly plied the boat slightly eastwards and tethered the boat there. He saw that the dwarf continued to sit under the roadside tree. Ponnan sat by the hut and observed the road leading to Uraiyur, agitated in anticipation of the events that may unfold. On hearing the sound of horse hooves, he became alert and sat erect. The sound was coming from the direction of Uraiyur. Shortly thereafter Ponnan observed Marappa Bhupathi riding towards the quay. The horse came to a halt in the middle of the road, where the dwarf was standing to receive Marappa Bhupathi.

31. Bhairavar and Bhupathi

Ponnan noiselessly walked in the dark shadows cast by the foliage along the road and hid himself behind a tree. He heard Marappan ask, 'Chitragupta! Where is Mahaprabhu?'

The dwarf replied, 'He is at the Ayyanar temple. He asked me to stay here, show you the way and lead you to the temple. Where is he?'

'Who are you referring to?'

'The one with several names . . . ratna vyapari . . . Devasenan . . . your contender,' quipped the dwarf and chuckled in a high-pitched tone.

'Him?' asked Marappan and burst out laughing uproariously.

In the dead of the night, the echoes of their laughter sounded horrific. Some of the birds that were sleeping in their nests on the trees woke up and flapped their wings. A few others chirped in fear.

'He is safe. You don't have to worry. Are you going to show me the way today in the same manner as you had to the trader a few weeks ago?' mocked Marappan and laughed loudly again. Ponnan was unable to hear Chitraguptan's response.

Marappan remarked again, 'Didn't Prabhu ask you to

show me the way? Walk ahead. Let's see how you show me the way.' He then wielded the whip he was carrying, the tip struck Chitraguptan. The horse, on hearing the sound of the whip, sped. The dwarf murmured something as he swiftly pursued Marappan. Ponnan was taken aback observing the speed at which the dwarf walked. Ponnan, walked and ran, for almost a nazhigai eastwards in pursuit of the dwarf. He then observed Marappan standing beside the horse on the road.

Chitraguptan asked Marappan, 'Why did you stop? You ought to have proceeded further!'

Marappan retorted, 'You wild cat! I can go further only if you, the nocturnal king, show me the way.'

'I will show you the way by all means. But you ought to be wary of the wild cat, failing which it may attack and injure you!' warned the dwarf. He then turned to the right and made his way amidst the dense overgrowth of bushes and creepers into the forest. Ponnan understood that the duo was headed to the Ayyanar temple that lay in ruins. He realized that if he were to closely shadow the two men, the sounds of the creepers and bushes grazing him would alert them. He waited for around quarter a nazhigai to pass before following them. He felt nervous about walking through the forest in the middle of the night. The hooting of owls and howling of foxes heightened Ponnan's dread. He felt distinctly ill at ease upon hearing the rustling of trees and bushes and the dry leaves crumbling under his feet. At the same time, he sensed that something crucial was about to happen and that he would unravel a vital secret. The resultant excitement bolstered his spirit as he made his way to the Ayyanar temple.

After walking in this manner for some time, Ponnan beheld an illuminated torch at a distance. It was the Ayyanar temple. He continued walking towards the temple. The massive statues of warriors, elephants and horses presented a ghastly sight in the torchlight. People get unnerved visiting this dilapidated temple even in broad daylight. One can only imagine how Ponnan must have felt heading to the temple in the dead of the night. The sight that awaited Ponnan at the temple entrance intensified his terror by a hundred times. A man resembling the hideous demons described in legends stood there, holding aloft a torch. The tall, sturdy and majestic looking Maha Kabala Bhairavar was standing next to him. In the red light cast by the torch, the sandalwood paste and vermillion smeared on Bhairavar's forehead resembled blood. Ponnan felt extremely apprehensive observing the garland of skulls the Bhairavar had donned. He walked to the rear of the temple and hid himself behind a neem tree close to the temple's rear entrance. It was then that Chitraguptan and Marappan presented themselves to the Maha Kabala Bhairavar.

'Maha Prabhu! Supreme Lord!' exclaimed Marappan as he prostrated to the Bhairavar.

'General! Have you complied with Mata's command? Where is the man to be sacrificed?' bellowed the Bhairavar in a ghostly voice. That voice – the same voice that was heard outside the Mahendra mandapam – caused the already fear-stricken Ponnan's hair to stand on end.

Marappan replied, 'Maha Prabhu! The man to be sacrificed is safe.'

'Where is he? Why have you not produced him here? Are you flouting Kali Mata's command, General?'

'Not at all, Maha Prabhu! I arrested the Ilavarasar just this evening. Fetching him here immediately would have been dangerous, Prabhu. That boatman is lurking around.'

Ponnan, who was hiding behind the tree, was startled. His heart leapt to his mouth. He felt somewhat reassured when Marappa Bhupathi continued, 'I was unable to arrest him. The Chakravarthi's daughter forbade me from doing so, Maha Prabhu. Kundavai Devi is still in Uraiyur. I am certain they are striving to free the Ilavarasar. We ought to be extremely cautious, failing which our efforts will come to naught.'

Maha Kabala Bhairavar burst out laughing. That ghastly sound echoed in all four directions and sounded akin to a hundred ghosts laughing in unison.

'General! Is it you who speak thus? Are you reluctant to carry out Kali Mata's orders that too in the face of obstacles posed by a mere woman and a boatman?'

'Not at all, swami! I am only concerned that there may be impediments in executing Kali Mata's command. Maha Prabhu! I will strive my utmost to comply with your order. I will ensure that the Ilavarasar is produced here before the night of amavasai.'

'If you fail to do so…?' asked the Kabala Bhairavar harshly.

'I will offer myself as sacrifice to Kali Mata.'

'Don't do that, Bhupathi! Kali Mata has chosen you to perform several tasks for her. You will be the general of the kingdom Kali Mata establishes in prosperous Tamizhagam.'

'It is my bounden duty to accomplish your and Kali Mata's commands.'

'Marappa, Kali Mata has chosen you as the recipient of her unreserved compassion. She will bless you with progressively more powerful roles…Let that be! Where will you fetch the Ilavarasar?'

'I will bring him to the Mahendra mandapam that lies beyond Parantaka Puram during the early hours of amavasai. I beseech you to send your men there and take possession of him.'

'Why are you assigning that task to me?'

'Maha Prabhu, I don't entirely trust the guards. I will inform them that I am sending the Ilavarasar to Kanchi in deference to the Chakravarthi's order. I will follow them at a distance. Kindly arrange for your men to ambush the contingent and abduct the Ilavarasar. However, the men I will be sending are unlikely to be particularly adroit. Once they hear your name, they are likely to meekly drop their swords.'

'So be it, general. But beware! Kali Mata will be expecting a sacrifice next amavasai.'

'There is yet another matter I wish to convey to you, Maha Prabhu.'

'Tell me quickly. I need to cross the river before dawn.'

'Ponnan, the boatman, had been absconding for the last few days. I came to know that he is searching for the Maharani. I had arranged for a man to spy on him. My spy informed me only yesterday that Ponnan and another man rode on horseback by the forest stream towards the Kolli Mountains.'

'You had earlier mentioned that the boatman was here.'

'Yes, he returned today.'

'Is that all?'

'Prabhu, do you know who had accompanied Ponnan?'

'Who?'

'Our sworn enemy.'

'What! Tell me who it was!'

'The fake sivanadiyar who sports matted locks.'

Ponnan was alarmed seeing the horrendous transformation in the Maha Kabala Bhairavar's expression on hearing this. Intense rage, fear and hostility contorted the Bhairavar's already unsightly face. Ponnan screamed, 'Aiyyo!' Fear fortunately muffled his voice, rendering him inaudible.

The Kabala Bhairavar, Chitraguptan and Marappa Bhupathi left the Ayyanar temple. The demonic looking man holding the torch walked ahead of the trio. Soon the light disappeared from Ponnan's sight and the crescent moon appeared on the horizon. Ponnan waited for some time before leaving the dilapidated temple. Though he was quite fatigued, he also felt excited. He was keen to ensure that Vikrama Maharaja did not fall into the hands of this mob that engaged in human sacrifice. He understood Marappan's ruse.

Marappan planned to dispatch the Ilavarasar to the Maha Kabala Bhairavar so that the latter could decapitate him. But he planned to execute this task in a crafty manner so that he could emerge blameless. It was imperative that Ponnan rescued Vikrama Maharaja at the earliest and escorted him to the Mamallapuram harbour. He could accomplish this task only with Kundavai Devi's assistance. Preoccupied with such thoughts, Ponnan made his way back to the quay when the sun was rising in the horizon.

32. The Uraiyur Prison

Vikraman was cloistered in a solitary cell at the Uraiyur prison. The irony of being imprisoned in a country that he was supposed to reign saddened and amused him. He often recollected the period of his father's reign. He could vividly recall his father in a warrior's attire headed to the battlefield and showing him his aspirational paintings in the concealed chamber of the Uraiyur Chithra Mandapam. Vikraman, who was keen to realize his father's aspirations, was dismayed at the thought that Parthiba Maharaja's dreams might remain just that. He was despondent and wondered for how long he would have to languish in jail awaiting the Pallava Chakravarthi's sentence and what that sentence would entail. Vikraman was convinced that he was likely to be sentenced to death and that Marappan would be prepared to execute that sentence. The denizens of Chola Nadu were likely to remember Parthiba Maharaja's exploits at the battlefield for a few years. But no one would know how Vikraman had met his end. The few people who still remembered him were also likely to forget his very name soon.

Vikraman often wondered why he had returned from Shenbaga Theevu. Notwithstanding its small size, he was delighted to rule the island as an independent king. Returning to Uraiyur all by himself was sheer insanity. He pondered over his objectives for returning to his motherland and if he had achieved them. While at Shenbaga Theevu, he pined to visit the Ponni river and the verdant Chola Nadu, his love for his motherland had not blinded him to the fact that the denizens of Chola Nadu had lost their thirst for independence and that they were content being subjects of the Pallava Chakravarthi. This enraged him and this anger grew manifold inside the prison cell. It was ironic that the denizens went about their lives oblivious to the gallant Parthiba Maharaja's son being imprisoned at Uraiyur itself.

Vikraman's desire to meet his mother did not materialize. He wondered whether he would die without even seeing his mother. Then, Kundavai...Vikraman tried hard not to think of her but he failed. A realization struck Vikraman the moment he remembered Kundavai. He might ascribe several reasons for returning from Shenbaga Theevu but deep down he realized that it was his desire to see Kundavai that drove him to return to his motherland. Vikraman likened his association with Kundavai to the bond between iron and magnet. Kundavai's genuine affection for him was the magnet that drew the iron-hearted Vikraman from Shenbaga Theevu.

Vikraman was furious with Kundavai, even after coming to know that it was she who rescued him at the Mahendra mandapam and nursed him back to health. He had expected her to pose impediments to his endeavour of liberating Chola Nadu. But the manner in which Kundavai spoke to Ponnan and Marappa Bhupathi made him realize that he had misunderstood her. She had so majestically stated, 'I will not plead with the Chakravarthi to spare him. I will request the Chakravarthi to solemnize my wedding with your Maharaja before the sentence is carried out!'

It was worthwhile leaving not just Shenbaga Theevu but heaven itself for the love of such a maiden. Vikraman rued that

Marappan's intervention had scuttled the couple's plans to sail to Shenbaga Theevu on amavasai.

Vikraman became increasingly agitated as amavasai approached. The ship from Shenbaga Theevu would call on the Mamallapuram harbour on the new moon day and would anchor there for two days waiting for him to board. Vikraman wished to somehow break out of the prison and head to Mamallapuram. Every passing moment appeared to be an aeon to him. Finally, Marappa Bhupathi met him on the evening preceding amavasai. He laughingly remarked, 'Respected ratna vyapari! We have received the directive from Kanchi.' Vikraman froze thinking that the directive would entail a death sentence. Though he was not scared of death, Vikraman found the idea of falling to an executioner's axe repulsive.

However, Marappan stated, 'We have been directed to safely transport you to Kanchi. We're leaving tonight during the second jaamam. Be prepared.' Vikraman rejoiced thinking there might be several opportunities en route to escape or to die valiantly while trying to escape. He rationalized that even if he were unable to achieve either of these outcomes, he would get another opportunity to declare to the Chakravarthi, 'I would rather die as a free man than live as a slave.' Could there be greater honour than uttering these words in Kundavai's presence?

33. The Night of the New Moon

One jaamam into the night, the prison gates were flung open. Marappan and a few armed guards arrived. Vikraman, who was shackled by chains, was escorted outside. A bullock cart was waiting at the prison entrance. Flanked by guards on both sides, the prisoner sat in the bullock cart. A few guards stood in front of and behind the cart. Marappan beckoned the guard who appeared to be the chief and whispered something into his ear. He then loudly ordered the cartman to embark on the journey, with guards marching both ahead of and behind the cart. As the cart traversed the streets of Uraiyur, Vikraman observed that, unlike during the reign of Parthiba Maharaja, the streetlights remained unlit. He was saddened that Uraiyur, the capital city of Chola Nadu, was plunged in darkness both metaphorically and literally.

Vikraman was taken aback when the cartman asked in a loud voice, 'Aiyya! Who is this boy? Where are you taking him?' His voice sounded like Ponnan's. One of the guards replied, 'Why do you want to get involved in this? Keep quiet and ride the cart!'

The cartman replied, 'Why should I care? But everyone in Uraiyur is talking about a spy from Shenbaga Theevu who had disguised himself as a ratna vyapari and had deceived the Chakravarthi's daughter, Kundavai Devi, herself. Apparently, it was our general who tracked him down. I was wondering if this boy is the spy from Shenbaga Theevu.'

One of the guards replied, 'You may assume he is the one!'

'Where is he being taken?' enquired the cartman.

'Kanchi,' was the response.

'Good lord! Do you have to travel such a long distance? Are the eight of you enough to provide adequate security? What if someone were to help him escape en route?' quipped the cartman.

Vikraman ruminated, 'Has Ponnan disguised himself as the cartman? Is he signalling that he will help me escape en route?'

Meanwhile, the chief of the guards rebuked the talkative guard, 'Why this unnecessary chatter?'

Silence ensued. Neither the cartman nor the guards spoke further. The cart came to a halt on reaching the banks of the Kaveri. Vikraman and the guards seated in the cart alighted. A boat had been arranged to transport the contingent across the river and a man stood close to it holding aloft a torch.

The cartman, while turning his cart around after everyone had alighted, called out, 'Have a safe trip! Do carefully escort the spy to the Chakravarthi's court, aiyya! Watch out for the forest stream on the way!'

The light of the torch fell on the cartman's face. Vikraman observed him and was disappointed; it was not Ponnan. But the cartman's eyes gleamed and his face appeared familiar. Vikraman realized in a flash that it was Ponnan indeed; he was sporting a false moustache. He wondered, 'Was Ponnan trying to convey to me that he will help me escape near the forest stream?' Vikraman felt extremely enthused speculating thus. The contingent crossed the river and continued their journey on foot till midnight. They then slept at a roadside mandapam, hired a bullock cart at dawn and continued travelling. It was dusk by the time the contingent crossed Parantaka Puram.

Vikraman had conjectured that the forest stream lay a short distance away. He thought that if it was Ponnan who had disguised himself as the cartman, then it is around here he is likely to receive help. He felt unsettled wondering who might come to help him and when the person was likely to come. Around two nazhigai had passed since sunset. Vikraman was taken aback observing that the road was buzzing with human traffic that amavasai night. People were walking in groups. They appeared to be headed to a temple. They were singing and dancing like those possessed. Some of them were wearing yellow-coloured robes. One person in each group was holding a torch aloft. Vikraman was perturbed to observe that a few people were carrying long swords. He wondered where these people were headed to and why they were carrying swords.

The guards, on witnessing the goings-on, whispered amongst themselves. Vikraman caught snippets of their conversation. He was shocked and petrified on hearing words such as 'Bhadra Kali', 'human sacrifice' and 'Maha Kabala Bhairavar'. He recalled the conversation that took place between the Maha Kabala Bhairavar and Marappa Bhupathi outside the Mahendra mandapam. It dawned on Vikraman that it was amavasai and that Marappan, under the pretext of sending him to Kanchi, could be dispatching him to the Maha Kabala Bhairavar to be decapitated. Coincidentally, he heard several people chant loudly in unison, 'Om Kali! Jai Kali!'

The very next instant a mob surrounded the cart Vikraman was travelling in. The long, sharp swords the mob carried glittered in the starry night. As the mob continued chanting, 'Om Kali! Jai Kali!', a ghastly voice asked, 'Where is the man to be sacrificed?' The guards who were walking ahead of and behind the cart had fled by then. Those sitting in the cart, flanking Vikraman, jumped off and took flight.

Vikraman's hands were fettered to the cart with chains, rendering him incapable of jumping off the cart. It was then he heard a voice call out from the rear of the cart, 'Maharaja! Fear not. It's me.' Ponnan jumped on to the cart and unfastened the chains. Getting off the cart, Vikraman observed that there stood two high-breed steeds in the vicinity. Ponnan remarked, 'Maharaja! Get on to the horse. We cannot delay even for a moment!'

34. Ah! What is this?

Vikraman and Ponnan leapt on to the waiting horses and started riding. 'Ponna! It was you who came disguised as the cartman, sporting a turban and moustache, wasn't it?' asked Vikraman as the two men rode away.

'Yes, Maharaja!'

'I wondered if you had forgotten me when I was in prison.'

'Even if I were to forget you, there is one person who will not allow me to do so!'

'Who is that?'

'Who else could it be? The Devi who snatched you from the jaws of death!'

Vikraman, who was delighted to hear this, was keen to enquire about Kundavai. But he felt bashful.

The two men continued riding for some time, after which Vikraman enquired, 'Where are we headed to now?'

'Mamallapuram, Maharaja.'

'Ponna.'

'What is it, Maharaja?'

'It is imperative that we reach Mamallapuram by dawn tomorrow.'

'Indeed, Maharaja. That's the reason I said we should not tarry for even a moment.'

'The ship will be anchored at Mamallapuram only till tomorrow afternoon.'

'We will reach Mamallapuram well before noon, Maharaja. Don't worry.'

Vikraman paused for some time and then remarked, 'Where is the Devi now, Ponna? I would have been happy if I could have taken leave of her before I left.'

'That's not possible, Maharaja!'

'What is not possible?'

'You bidding farewell to the Devi before leaving.'

'True. There's no way I can return to Uraiyur.'

'The Devi is not at Uraiyur, Maharaja.'

'Where is she now?'

'She is at Mamallapuram!'

'Ah!' murmured Vikraman.

The news of Kundavai waiting for him at Mamallapuram, the experience of riding on horseback on a cool, pleasant night, and the freedom after a few nights in prison – all rendered Vikraman ecstatic.

'Then why did you say that it was not possible to take leave of her, Ponna? I must meet her to express my gratitude and also give her the responsibility of finding my mother.'

'That is not possible, Maharaja,' repeated Ponnan.

'Why are you so certain it's not possible?'

'I am certain because the Devi has no intention of bidding you farewell. She is determined to accompany you.'

'Really! Why didn't you share this important information with me before?'

'I ought not to have told you even now. The Devi had intended to surprise you after you had boarded the ship. I spilled the beans in haste.'

Vikraman was lost in thought for some time when Ponnan

suddenly called out, 'Look there, Maharaja!' Vikraman returned to consciousness with a start. He looked in the direction Ponnan was pointing to. Ten-twelve men were standing by the road under a tree. One of them was holding a torch aloft. The men appeared intimidating in the light cast by the torch. They sported garlands of skulls, had smeared sandalwood paste and vermillion on their foreheads and were carrying swords.

As Vikraman rode past these men, he involuntarily shivered. Once Vikraman and Ponnan had covered some distance, Ponnan said, 'Maharaja, it is for you that they were waiting. Marappa Bhupathi's final instruction to his men was to hand you over to this mob. I pre-empted them. These men would not have expected you to ride past them on horseback all by yourself. They are likely to wait here for some more time and then inform the Kabala Bhairavar that you did not show up. The Kabala Bhairavar is bound to be furious with Marappa Bhupathi today!'

'Ponna! You have saved me from the Chakravarthi's death sentence and the kabalikas beheading me. You also rescued me from drowning in the forest stream. You are the very incarnation of the Chola dynasty's guardian deity. I am forever indebted to you. We will part ways tomorrow. I wonder when I will meet you again.'

'How wonderful!' quipped Ponnan.

'Why do you say so?'

'Do you think I will stay here while you sail away? What will I do here? Valli has accompanied Kundavai Devi to Mamallapuram. The two of us are coming with you.'

Vikraman was silent for some time. Then he remarked, 'Ponna, your words delight me. You and Valli accompanying me is akin to the whole of Chola Nadu coming with me. But one thing troubles me. What has happened to my mother? Who will find her? Who will inform her about me? I returned to Chola Nadu primarily to meet the Maharani. I am returning without even seeing her. Shouldn't someone stay back to inform her about me?'

Ponnan shared Vikraman's concern. He had promised the

sivanadiyar to accomplish certain tasks, which he had failed to do. He wondered what became of the sivanadiyar and if he had traced the Maharani. Though Ponnan himself was not at ease with the situation, he consoled Vikraman saying, 'Maharaja, please don't worry about the Maharani. The sivanadiyar will find her. No task is beyond him. He is endowed with several powers.'

'But you did mention that he would meet us at the sculptor's house in Mamallapuram.'

'But that is not possible now. If we were to stay back to meet the sivanadiyar, we will not be able to board the ship!'

'True, but I'm sad to leave without meeting my mother and the sivanadiyar,' lamented Vikraman.

'Ah! What's this?' exclaimed a surprised Ponnan.

By then the duo had reached the Mahendra mandapam on the banks of the forest stream. Seven to eight armed men stood outside the mandapam, while two men stood holding aloft illuminated torches. A palanquin was placed at the corner of the mandapam's entrance.

Ponnan murmured, 'Quite a few incredible incidents are occurring tonight.'

'Who is passing by this place at this time of the night, Ponna?' asked Vikraman.

'I don't know, Maharaja.'

'They are certainly not kabalikas. Who else could they be?'

'Perhaps Kundavai Devi sent more men to assist us? But why the palanquin?'

They had reached the Mahendra mandapam as they were conversing thus and brought the horses to a halt. Ponnan thought that one of the men who stood outside looked familiar. He then realized that he had seen that man at Thiruchengattankudi. He was Kumarappan, one of Paranjyothi Adigal's men. Kumarappan, who also recognized Ponnan, called out in a surprised tone, 'Oh Ponna! Are you aware that the Uraiyur Maharani has been found? She is inside this mandapam. She was enquiring about you.'

35. Mother and Son

Vikraman and Ponnan were overwhelmed on hearing that the Maharani had been found. As they leapt down from their horses, a female voice called out from within the mandapam, 'Kumarappa! Who is it? I thought I heard Ponnan's voice!' The speaker was none other than Maharani Arulmozhi Devi.

'Amma!' shrieked Vikraman as he ran into the Mahendra mandapam followed by Ponnan. Arulmozhi Devi emerged from the darkened mandapam. When Vikraman had last met her, she was a youthful beauty. Now, she was unrecognizable. She appeared to have grown older by thirty years in the past three years.

Vikraman rushed to his mother, prostrated before her and held her feet. Arulmozhi Devi sat on the floor, placed her son's head on her lap and shed tears of joy. Ponnan who had followed Vikraman into the mandapam watched the mother and son reunite. As he casually glanced around the mandapam, he observed a figure in shackles. In the dim light of the torch, Ponnan realized that it was the dwarf. As soon as he set his eyes on the dwarf, the later chuckled aloud. Hearing the chuckle, Vikraman looked up. Shocked on seeing the dwarf, Vikraman exclaimed, 'Ponna!'

'Yes, Maharaja! He is the dwarf who was supposed to show you the way from Mamallapuram to Uraiyur.'

The dwarf chuckled aloud again. Arulmozhi Devi looked alternately at Vikraman and Ponnan, unable to decide to whom she ought to pose her numerous questions. She finally asked, 'Ponna, I don't understand anything. I'm completely in the dark. I lost count of time when I was imprisoned in the mountain cave. When I finally decided to commit suicide by jumping into the waterfall, the sivanadiyar prevented me from doing so and saved me. He informed me that Vikraman had returned and reassured me saying that I will be reunited with my son soon. Ponna, was

it you who had saved Vikraman from drowning in the flooded forest stream?'

Vikraman interjected, 'He not only saved me from drowning but also from the Chakravarthi's death sentence, being decapitated at Kali's altar, and several other dangers.'

Arulmozhi trembled as she echoed, 'Decapitated at Kali's altar?'

The dwarf laughed in a ghastly manner and pronounced, 'Sacrifice! Tonight, an important person is going to be decapitated. Kali's thirst is going to be quenched.' Everyone looked at him with rapt attention. 'At the stroke of midnight

today, the sivanadiyar is to be beheaded! Maha Bhadra Kali's kingdom is about to be established. Then... then... there will be no scarcity of skulls,' quipped the dwarf as he burst out laughing.

Vikraman leapt up and questioned, 'Ponna! What is he blabbering about the sivanadiyar...?'

The dwarf chuckled as he retorted, 'I am not blabbering. I am stating the truth. By now, the arms and legs of that fake ascetic would have been bound and he would have been brought to the sacrificial altar. At the stroke of midnight, the executioner's sword will strike the sivanadiyar's neck.'

Arulmozhi Devi shrieked, 'My child! He had been speaking like this for long. I escaped from the cave five-six days ago and was about to jump into the cascade. The sivanadiyar, after saving my life, handed me over to his men. He said they will take me to safety. He then left on an urgent mission. On our way here, the men guarding me apprehended this dwarf, who was hiding, and brought him along. Ever since we reached this place, he has been saying that the kabalikas will behead the sivanadiyar on the night of amavasai. Aiyyo! That great soul has helped us so much... Does such a horrific end await him?'

'Ponna, what do you say? It is pointless for us to continue living if we are unable to stop this atrocity,' remarked Vikraman.

'How is that possible, Maharaja? You forget your precarious situation. If we fail to reach Mamallapuram by dawn...'

'The ship will leave the harbour. So what?'

Ponnan then reasoned with Arulmozhi Devi, 'Amma! He is in great danger. Aren't you aware what punishment will be meted out if a man banished from the country were to return? Marappa Bhupathi, on coming to know of Maharaja's return, tipped off the Kanchi Chakravarthi. If Vikrama Maharaja fails to reach Mamallapuram by dawn and board the ship, escaping will be practically impossible. His life will be in danger if he were to head to the forest to save the sivanadiyar. Do tell us what you think Vikrama Maharaja ought to do.'

Arulmozhi Devi was shell shocked. Vikraman remarked, 'Amma! You are the brave consort of Parthiba Maharaja. Pray do tell me the course of action I must pursue in this situation. When the great soul who has been of immense help to us is in danger, should I flee fearing for my life? Would my father, had he been alive, approve of such behaviour?'

'Vikrama Maharaja's life is of paramount importance. How else will Parthiba Maharaja's dream come true?' countered Ponnan.

Arulmozhi Devi looked alternately at Vikraman and Ponnan and finally stated, 'Ponna, you may think that I am a stone-hearted woman who bears no affection for her son. But I will state what I believe is right. I do not wish to hear people say that my son fled fearing for his life when the person who has been so supportive of our family is in danger.'

Vikraman immediately prostrated before his mother, stood up and ardently declared, 'Amma! You are a brave mother and indeed the valorous consort of Parthiba Maharaja.'

The dwarf laughed and called out, 'I will show you the way. Untie me.'

The dwarf was set free and given a torch. Vikraman and Ponnan climbed on to their horses. The dwarf, holding the torch aloft, swiftly walked westwards towards the forest. Vikraman and Ponnan followed him.

36. The Sacrificial Altar

After travelling for about two nazhigai westwards along the banks of the forest stream, the dwarf turned southwards and entered a dense forest. Beyond the forest lay a high embankment, which the dwarf scaled with dexterity. The horses struggled to climb the embankment. On reaching the top of the embankment, Vikraman and Ponnan realized that a dam lay on the other side. The dwarf pointed to a place and said, 'Look there!' Vikraman and Ponnan complied. Flat-topped hillocks surrounded by a dense growth of short trees were partially visible in the light cast by hundreds of torches. The people who had flocked the forest at the base of the hillocks appeared like ghosts from a distance. Drums and udukku (an hourglass-shaped hand-held drum) were being played, rendering the scene even more eerie.

Though Vikraman and Ponnan were frightened, they did not show their apprehension and followed the dwarf down the banks of the dam. The pace at which the dwarf walked accelerated. On reaching a point where the water in the dam had dried up, the dwarf walked across the riverbed. Vikraman and Ponnan manoeuvred their horses to follow the dwarf. The horses too seemed to be trembling in fear. The trio reached the forest at the foot of the hillock in another quarter nazhigai. The horses trembled even more and Vikraman and Ponnan jumped off them and tethered them to trees.

As the two men walked into the forest, they observed some people dancing like ones who are possessed, certain others wearing yellow robes and meditating, a group of people cooking pongal (a confection made of rice and jaggery), yet another group sharpening their knives by rubbing them against rocks and a few people playing udukkus. Vikraman, Ponnan and the dwarf suddenly reached a clearing, to the right of which was a flat-topped hillock. An imposing and intimidating figure of Kali was carved out of that hillock and painted in bright hues. Kali's eyes appeared to be glaring at the onlookers. A group of people stood beside the Kali's figure. Standing amidst this group was a tall man with red locks sporting a garland of skulls, with sandalwood paste and vermillion smeared on his forehead. He was Maha Kabala Bhairavar. A man stood behind the Bhairavar playing the udukku. Kabala Bhairavar's eyes were shut. He was swaying gently back and forth to the rhythm of the udukku.

There lay a rock in front of the image of Kali that was naturally shaped like a sacrificial altar. The sivanadiyar lay on the altar with ropes tied across his arms, legs and torso. His eyes were wide open and he was vigilantly looking around. A demonic figure stood next to the altar holding a massive sword. He was waiting for the Maha Kabala Bhairavar to open his eyes and command him to execute the sivanadiyar. Vikraman took a moment to scan the area and to grasp the situation. He then leapt into action. Swirling his sword around, he raced to the altar and firmly struck the executioner's sword with his. The sword slipped from the executioner's hand and fell far away from the altar. Vikraman then positioned himself next to the sivanadiyar and instructed Ponnan, who had followed him, 'Ponna! Why are you standing still? Untie the sivanadiyar.'

All this happened within the blink of an eye. Listening to

the shocked gasps of the people surrounding him, the Maha Kabala Bhairavar opened his eyes. After observing what had transpired, he walked in a measured pace towards the altar and looked sharply at Vikraman. He burst out laughing; the sound of his laughter echoed in all directions across the hillocks, rocks and dense forests. Those who heard the laughter, got goosebumps. Realizing that something untoward was happening, those who were standing some distance away started rushing towards the altar. Observing this, the Maha Kabala Bhairavar raised

his sole arm and roared, 'Hmm!' The crowd stepped back. The executioner, who by then had retrieved the sword, also stood some distance away in response to the Bhairavar's roar. Ponnan too stood still.

The Maha Kabala Bhairavar, while continuing to survey Vikraman, remarked, 'My boy! Aren't you Parthiba Chola's son,

the right time. Hail the Mata!' Vikraman, mesmerized by the Bhairavar's reddened eyes, struggled to move away from his line of vision. 'I came to Mamallapuram in search of you. That lunatic, Marappan, intervened and thwarted my efforts. Nevertheless, I was anticipating your arrival here tonight!'

Vikraman, like a snake hypnotized by black magic, asked in a choked voice, 'Who are you? Why were you expecting me?'

'Why? Kali Mata's kingdom is to be established in Dakshina Bharata tonight. The Mata has commanded that you be coronated the Ilavarasar of her kingdom!' pronounced the Bhairavar.

Someone laughed in derision. Everyone who had assembled there including Vikraman and the Kabala Bhairavar looked around. But there was no means to find out who had laughed.

Vikraman, who seemed to be in a trance till then, snapped back into his senses on hearing that laughter. He shot a glance at the sivanadiyar, then faced the Kabala Bhairavar and pronounced, 'I am unable to comprehend your words. You say that you are going to crown me Ilavarasar. If that were true, you ought not to stand in my way. This elderly man who lies shackled at the altar is a friend of the Cholas. He has been extremely helpful to me and my mother. It is my duty to free him. I will not allow him to be executed as long as I am able to wield a sword and I am alive!' declared Vikraman as he walked to the altar and attempted to cut through the ropes that shackled the sivanadiyar.

The Kabala Bhairavar roared, 'Halt!'

Even the fearless Vikraman felt a tad alarmed on hearing that roar. He stood rooted to the spot. The arm he had stretched to cut through the sivanadiyar's shackles remained outstretched.

The Kabala Bhairavar bellowed, 'My boy, Vikrama! You will not speak thus if you knew who this fake sivanadiyar, this wicked masquerader who sports a wig of matted locks truly is! You will not strive so much to save him.' The fury and decisiveness in the Bhairavar's voice stunned Vikraman. He recollected that he had suspected that the spymaster of the Pallavas had disguised himself as the sivanadiyar.

The Kabala Bhairavar screamed in a guttural tone, 'Ask this masquerader who he is. Let's see if he is courageous enough to state the truth!' Vikraman looked at the sivanadiyar, who was smiling.

Just then, another voice thundered, 'Vikrama! Do ask first who this wicked masquerader sporting a garland of skulls is. Let's see if he is courageous enough to state the truth!' A man emerged from behind a nearby rock. Everyone assembled there turned towards him. When the glow from the torches fell on his face, everyone gasped in surprise. Vikraman, on seeing the elderly man donning rudraksha beads with thiruneeru smeared on him, his face exuding wisdom, felt a sense of devotion he had never felt before.

It was none other than the former general of the Pallava kingdom and the brave warrior who had conquered Vatapi – Siruthondar.

37. Neelakesi

As soon as Siruthondar emerged from behind a rock, certain surprising incidents occurred. Armed soldiers miraculously started emerging from behind the rocks, trees and all other nooks and crannies. There was an even more astounding event. The sivanadiyar who lay shackled at the altar suddenly extricated himself from the ropes that bound him and jumped off the altar. By then, Siruthondar started walking towards the Maha Kabala Bhairavar, whose face incredibly betrayed fear. As the veteran warrior neared the Bhairavar, the latter started trembling. Siruthondar came close to the Bhairavar, looked up to him, and demanded, 'You masquerading kabalika! State who you really are at Kali Mata's sanctum!' The Bhairavar took two steps backwards and then fell to the ground as if he had lost the strength to walk or even stand.

The devotees of Kali who had congregated there gasped in surprise. Vikraman was concerned that the fanatical kabalikas may wreak havoc. Ponnan, overcome by amazement and devotion, stood still. As soon as the Kabala Bhairavar fell down, the kabalikas started running towards the sanctum from all directions. Siruthondar quickly climbed on to the altar and addressed the gathering, 'Respected denizens! Devotees of Kali Mata! Come closer to me. I will now state the truth about the one-armed man who has been deceiving you for long under the pseudonym of Maha Kabala Bhairavar.'

Realizing that Siruthondar was addressing them, the perplexed kabalikas surrounded the altar and gazed at him. The former general spoke majestically and his voice echoed across the forest and hillocks.

'Heed me! The place of our birth, Tamizhagam, is extremely sacred. Several great souls were born here. They have preached to us about the nature of the true God and the means of reaching this God. Thirumoola Maharishi said "Love and Shiva are synonymous." A Vaishnavite elder has sung:

Love moulded into lamp
Devotion being the fuel
Wisdom fashioned into a wick
With affection I light the lamp
To feel you intimately!

'In a land where such compassionate faiths flourish, some people have been lately spreading barbaric faiths such as Kabalikam and Bhairavam and repulsive practices such as human sacrifice and cannibalism. Isn't it ignorance that prompts people to believe that Shiva, the very embodiment of love, and Parasakthi, the very embodiment of mercy, desire human sacrifice? Our elders have explained the philosophy underlining mythological depictions of Shiva carrying a skull and Parasakthi sporting a garland of skulls. Why has a brutal practice like human sacrifice gained acceptance in this sacred land? Where does the root of this evil propaganda lie? My friend, the sivanadiyar who lay shackled at the sacrificial altar, and I have been striving hard to find answers to these questions. Finally, my friend, the sivanadiyar was successful. He uncovered the truth...'

One person asked, 'Who is he?' Several others questioned,

'Where is he?' In the commotion that ensued following Siruthondar's sudden appearance, the sivanadiyar had slipped away discreetly without anyone noticing. Siruthondar continued speaking, 'You will come to know who the great soul is if you attend the proceedings at the Uraiyur Royal Court in another two days. You ought to know who this Kabala Bhairavar, the man who now lies on the ground trembling in fear, is. Do you remember the King of Vatapi, Pulikesi, invading Tamizhagam during the reign of our glorious Mahendra Chakravarthi twenty-five years ago?'

When Siruthondar paused, several voices replied, 'We do!'

'Also etched in your memory must be the treacherous conduct of the demonic Pulikesi and his forces and the atrocities they had perpetrated in our cities and villages. You are aware that the just King of Kings, Narasimha Pallavar, and I had mobilized a massive army and had invaded Vatapi in retaliation after the demise of Mahendra Chakravarthi. Our valiant forces had annihilated Pulikesi's army in the bloody war that occurred outside the city of Vatapi. Our Chakravarthi had commanded that we ought not to spare even one Chalukya warrior. I disregarded the Chakravarthi's order and spared one person. I could not bring myself to kill a man who had lost an arm in the war and had surrendered at my feet; I allowed him to escape. That one-armed man, Neelakesi, is the one who now lies sprawled on the ground. He is far more brutal than his sibling, Pulikesi.'

Hearing this, there was commotion amongst those assembled. People expressed their shock by gasping and talking amongst themselves about Neelakesi's treacherous behaviour. As the noise subsided, Siruthondar continued his account, 'On coming to know that I had spared Neelakesi, the Chakravarthi had remarked, "You committed a blunder; this decision of yours is bound to have disastrous consequences." He was right. Neelakesi disguised himself as a kabalika and started propagating Kabalikam and human sacrifice, thereby exploiting the people who were distressed by the famine that had struck the holy land of Tamizhagam. What was his motive? He wanted to achieve through treachery what he could not achieve through valour. He aimed to instigate you against our Narasimha Chakravarthi, whose fame has even spread to far-flung nations across the seas. It is to this end he had hoarded thousands of swords and axes in caves atop the Kolli Mountains.'

The Kabala Bhairavar exclaimed with anger, 'Ah!'

'Indeed! Those weapons were confiscated today, as commanded by the Chakravarthi. Neelakesi also wished to manipulate Vikrama Ilavarasar to achieve his evil objectives. So, he had abducted and imprisoned Parthiba Maharaja's brave consort, Arulmozhi Devi.'

At this juncture, the Maha Kabala Bhairavar briskly stood up and demanded, 'He is lying. All what he says is a figment of his imagination. Where is the proof to substantiate his claims?' The Bhairavar appeared to have overcome his fears.

But a voice called out, 'Here I am. I am a witness!' Marappa Bhupathi suddenly emerged from behind a mimosa tree. 'Yes, I will bear witness. This Kabala Bhairavar, also known as Neelakesi, is not a kabalika in reality. He is a masquerader. He conspired against the Great King of Kings, Narasimha Pallava Chakravarthi. He had asked me to join hands with him in that conspiracy. I refused to do so. He subsequently wished to align himself with this banished Ilavarasar. He arranged to waylay this Ilavarasar, whom I had dispatched to Kanchi in accordance with the Chakravarthi's command, and to bring him to this place.'

Siruthondar interjected, 'That's enough, Marappa! Enough of your testimony.'

There were several reasons for Marappan performing this volte face. Marappan might have been enraged by the Maha Kabala Bhairavar sidelining him and preferring to coronate Vikraman as Ilavarasar. The possibility of being accused of conspiring against the Chakravarthi might have unnerved him. Whatever be his motive, he subsequently acted in the most unexpected manner. He walked towards the Maha Kabala Bhairavar with his sword unsheathed and pronounced, 'May this traitor who dared to conspire against the Chakravarthi be sacrificed to Kali Mata!' Marappan abruptly and swiftly aimed his sword at the Kabala Bhairavar's neck. The man lay beheaded.

Everyone was stunned. Marappan walked to the altar on which Siruthondar stood. He prostrated before him and said, 'Prabhu! I acted in rage. Please forgive me if I have erred.' Yet another shocking incident happened. Chitraguptan, who was nowhere to be seen till then, rushed to the altar holding a sword. He decapitated Marappan, who lay prostrated before Siruthondar! A few Pallava warriors immediately nabbed the dwarf, who was chuckling sardonically. Vikraman was repulsed by these ghastly incidents that occurred in quick succession. While he believed that warriors combatting and killing each other face to face on the battlefield was fair, he felt distressed watching people murder on the sly. He quickly turned to Ponnan, who was standing next to him, and said, 'Ponna, come! Let's go!' It was then that he observed that the Pallava warriors had surrounded him and Ponnan.

The chief of the warriors handed over a missive to Vikraman. It bore Narasimha Chakravarthi's insignia and carried his edict. The missive directed the warriors, who were transporting Vikraman from Uraiyur to Kanchi, to take him back to Uraiyur. It further stated that Vikraman's trial will be held in Uraiyur. Vikraman, on reading the missive, looked around even as his hand reached his sword. Ponnan remarked, 'Maharaja! Pray do not act in haste!'

Siruthondar, who observed the goings-on, enquired, 'What is in this missive?'

The chief of the warriors handed over the missive to Siruthondar, who read it. He then stated, 'Vikrama, do comply with this command and go to Uraiyur. I will bring your mother there. The Chakravarthi is bound to change his mind once he comes to know of the valorous deeds you performed today. Don't act in haste!'

The very next moment, Vikraman and Ponnan, escorted by the Pallava warriors left the forest. Siruthondar then sermonized to those congregated about the Almighty's merciful nature as against the savagery inherent in human sacrifices. After listening to him, those who had come to offer themselves as sacrifice and those who had intended to perform sacrifices changed their minds, thanked the great soul who had reformed them and returned to their villages. They speculated at length about the sivanadiyar's identity on their way back.

38. The Sentencing

At dawn on the day after amavasai, an extremely restive Kundavai was up and about at the Mamallapuram palace. She climbed to the upper storey of the palace, looked around in all four directions, rushed down, issued instructions to the palace retainers and chatted intermittently with Valli, who had accompanied her from Uraiyur. Amidst the frenzied, self-inflicted activities she engaged in, she kept an ear out to the sounds of horses entering the palace complex. While speaking to the retainers, she would abruptly stop talking and check if the sounds of hooves were heard. Such was her zeal to meet Vikraman and Ponnan.

Kundavai had decided what she ought to do as soon as Vikraman and Ponnan arrived. She had given up the idea of accompanying Vikraman to Shenbaga Theevu for she felt that the sly act would give rise to suspicions and pave the way for his being captured again. She also could not bring herself to elope with Vikraman keeping her father in the dark. She was unwilling to act in a manner that would sully her father's eminence. Kundavai now believed that the correct behaviour on her part would be to allow Vikraman to sail to Shenbaga Theevu first and then seek her father's consent after informing him of all the events that led to her accepting Vikraman as her life-partner. She was convinced that the Chakravarthi would forgive her and arrange for her to sail to Shenbaga Theevu. Her father had often mentioned that he did not intend to arrange her wedding and that she ought to choose her husband herself. Hence, it was unlikely for him not to acquiesce to her wishes.

It was in this frame of mind that Kundavai was anticipating Vikraman's arrival. Kundavai's agitation increased as the day progressed. At noon, when the sounds of hooves were indeed heard, Kundavai's heart leapt to her mouth. She started having second thoughts. She wondered if it was right for Vikraman to sail to Shenbaga Theevu leaving her behind. After all, hadn't women in epics acted boldly in similar situations? Subhadra had eloped with Arjuna and Rukmini with Krishna. Kundavai wondered why she had to be separated, albeit temporarily, from Vikraman. She felt it would be torturous to bid farewell to him.

Finally, when horses did enter the palace complex, Kundavai became impatient. The horses came to a halt at the palace entrance. Kundavai had instructed the palace guards to usher on arrival the ratna vyapari, Devasenan, to her presence. On hearing footsteps, Kundavai was excited and convinced that she was about to meet Vikraman and Ponnan. Her shock knew no bounds on seeing the Chakravarthi entering her chamber. She felt faint and exercised great effort to maintain her composure.

Kundavai enquired haltingly, 'Appa... Welcome! Where were you all these days?'

An exuberant Chakravarthi walked to Kundavai and embraced her. He then asked her in a concerned tone, 'What is it, my child? Why are you trembling thus?'

'It's nothing, appa! Your sudden arrival caught me by surprise.' replied Kundavai.

'Is that all? I'm relieved. Sit down, my child. When did you come here from Uraiyur? Why did you leave Uraiyur in such a hurry?' asked the Chakravarthi as he sat down.

Kundavai felt anguished thinking, 'What if he comes when appa is here? He must be reaching here any time now! How can I send him a message asking him to head directly to the ship and not visit the palace?'

The Chakravarthi, who appeared not to observe her anguish, remarked, 'My child, I'm leaving for Uraiyur this evening. Why don't you accompany me? Or are you bored with Uraiyur?'

'Why are you headed to Uraiyur, appa?' asked Kundavai.

'There are some extremely important developments, my child. Arulmozhi Devi has been found!'

'Aha!' exclaimed Kundavai.

'Do you know who traced Arulmozhi Devi? It is that sivanadiyar whom you claimed was a masquerader and used to ill-mouth often!'

'What! Where was the Devi? Who had abducted her? Probably that fake sivanadiyar…'

The Chakravarthi was amused. He replied, 'You continue to be suspicious of him, my child! It wasn't the sivanadiyar who had spirited Arulmozhi Devi away. It was a man about whom I had told you before; the leader of the kabalikas – Maha Kabala Bhairavan. Apparently, the sivanadiyar's life was in danger as a consequence of his rescuing Arulmozhi Devi. Last night, the Maha Kabala Bhairavan was about to behead the sivanadiyar at Kali's sanctum. The kabalikas had tied up the sivanadiyar with ropes and had produced him at the sacrificial altar. Do you know who saved the sivanadiyar in the nick of time?'

'Who was it, appa?'

'The ratna vyapari from Shenbaga Theevu, Devasenan, and the boatman, Ponnan! They saved the sivanadiyar's life just as he was about to be sacrificed.'

Kundavai opened her mouth to say something but no words came out of her mouth. Her beautiful lips remained parted like the aril of a pomegranate.

'Hear this shocking news, my child. The trader, Devasenan, too is a masquerader! The Chola Ilavarasan, Vikraman, whom I had banished, disguised himself as Devasenan and returned to meet his mother and see his motherland! What an audacious man, my child!'

Kundavai asked in a choked voice, 'Where are they, appa?'

'Are you asking about Vikraman and Ponnan? I have asked our soldiers to take them to Uraiyur. I have decided to conduct the inquest myself. This is the primary reason for my visiting Uraiyur now. Will you come with me?'

Kundavai was unable to hide her turmoil any longer. She put her head on her father's lap and simply burst into tears. Tears welled in the eyes of the Chakravarthi too. He caressed Kundavai's hair and face affectionately and enquired, 'My child! Why are you so forlorn? There is something you are hiding from me. Tell me what is troubling you.'

Amidst sobs, Kundavai revealed to the Chakravarthi that it was love at first sight for her when she beheld Vikraman in shackles on the streets on Kanchi. She narrated everything that had occurred from the time she found him in delirium at the Mahendra mandapam, his recovery under her care, their coming close to each other and her intention of helping him board the ship bound for Shenbaga Theevu that very day. She then vehemently declared, 'Appa, I have, in my heart, accepted the Chola Ilavarasan as my consort. I will no longer think of any other man.'

The Chakravarthi remarked affectionately, 'Love is the only eternal phenomenon in this world, my child. Everything else is transient. The love that unites two young souls becomes the sanctum of the Almighty, who is the embodiment of love. No one, including the couple's parents, have the right to come in the way of two people whose souls are united in love. I will never ever pose impediments to your decision to marry the Ilavarasan of Chola Nadu. However, my child, our Pallava dynasty is renowned for upholding justice. In the Pallava kingdom, royalty and commoners are on a par in the eyes of law. Hence the trial of the Chola Ilavarasan will be conducted in accordance with the laws of the land. The severity of his sentence will depend on the gravity of his offences.'

Kundavai enquired, 'Appa, what is the punishment when a man banished from the country returns to his motherland?'

'It is usually a death sentence, my child. But there may be mitigating factors in the Chola Ilavarasan's case.'

'What are those, appa?'

'Didn't you frequently mention that the Ilavarasan was not entirely responsible for his actions and that it was the fake sivanadiyar who led the Ilavarasan astray? What you said may be true. The sivanadiyar has been nabbed. He too needs to be interrogated to ascertain the truth.'

Kundavai pondered, 'Indeed! All mishaps occurred on account of that fake ascetic. If he hadn't unnecessarily courted danger last night, the brave Ilavarasar would have boarded the ship by now.'

'There is yet another matter to consider. Do you remember who had lent a horse to the ratna vyapari from Shenbaga Theevu and sent him off to Chola Nadu, Kundavai?'

'Appa!' exclaimed Kundavai in a tone that betrayed delight born out of understanding. She recollected that it was the Chakravarthi disguised as the spymaster who had lent his horse to Vikraman and dispatched him to Chola Nadu.

'Then how can he be punished, appa?' asked Kundavai mischievously.

'Let's conduct the enquiry, my child. An appropriate verdict will be pronounced on completion of the enquiry. An unjust course of action will never ever be pursued in the Pallava kingdom,' emphasized the Chakravarthi.

39. The Sentence

The Chola capital of Uraiyur had shrugged off its indolence and was beautifully decorated that day. It seemed as if Lakshmi, the Goddess of wealth and prosperity, who had left the city with Parthiba Maharaja, when he had headed to the fateful battle on the banks of the Vennaru river, had returned. The residents of Uraiyur were ecstatic and effervescent after long. The denizens of Chola Nadu living in other cities and villages thronged the capital in bullock carts and by foot. People stood in groups on the streets and conversed animatedly. A proclamation had been made that Narasimha Pallava Chakravarthi would hold a public durbar at Uraiyur for which the prominent subjects from the cities and villages of Chola Nadu were invited. People were agog with expectations of the unravelling of several mysteries and the occurrence of unforeseen events at the durbar. News of Arulmozhi Devi and Ilavarasar Vikraman returning to Uraiyur had spread across the city.

There were rumours of Ilavarasar Vikraman staying at the Vasantha Maligai disguised as a ratna vyapari, him and Kundavai Devi falling in love and the likelihood of their marriage being solemnized soon, thus forging a permanent bond between

Uraiyur and Kanchi. The naysayers felt that the Chakravarthi would interrogate the Ilavarasar, who had returned to Chola Nadu despite being banished, and take into account the views of the public while passing a verdict. People also avidly discussed, not without embellishing and downplaying, the incidents that occurred four days ago on the night of amavasai and Marappan's death.

When Ponnan and Valli walked down the streets of Uraiyur, people accosted them and asked the boatman about what he thought was going to happen. Ponnan professed complete ignorance and Valli replied likewise to the women who asked her. Ponnan and Valli were a sought-after couple that day; their pride knew no bounds.

No mortal has ever returned to earth after visiting the court of the King of the Gods, Indra, in the heavens to be able to describe it. But those who were present at Mamalla Narasimha Chakravarthi's court at Uraiyur unanimously declared, 'Devendran's (another name for Indra) durbar must be similar to this!' The denizens' court congregated at a lavishly decorated sabha mandapam. Everyone but the Chakravarthi walked in noiselessly and took their seats at the appointed time. The sivanadiyar and Siruthondar, akin to the mythological sages – Vasishta and Vamadeva – were seated on one side of the Chakravarthi's throne. On the other side of the throne were seated Ilavarasar Mahendran, Ilavarasi Kundavai, Arulmozhi Devi and Siruthondar's consort, Thiruvengadu Nangai. The apple of Siruthondar's eye, his son Seerala Devan, sat amidst the four of them looking around wide-eyed. Ponnan and Valli stood behind them deferentially. Vikraman, surrounded by the Pallava general and soldiers, sat majestically right opposite to the throne.

Though Vikraman was determined not to look at Kundavai, his eyes did flit involuntarily in her direction. Kundavai's behaviour mirrored Vikraman's. When their eyes met, they hurriedly looked down in embarrassment. Ministers, army chiefs, treasurers, scholars, artists, poets, prominent traders and village chieftains were all present at the assembly. One man seated behind Ilavarasar Mahendran garnered disproportionate attention. His appearance and attire indicated that he was not native to Tamizhagam. Those at the assembly pointed out to him and whispered, 'He is the traveller from China!' People mispronounced his name, Hiuen Tsang, in several ways.

Also, in attendance at the Court were a few other foreign dignitaries. Though their outfits indicated that they were foreigners, they spoke in Tamil. They were the delegation that had accompanied the ratna vyapari, Devasenan, from Shenbaga Theevu to Mamallapuram. They were keen to know the fate that awaited their Maharaja at the end of the trial. Ushers and ladies-in-waiting were dispersed across the sabha mandapam waving hand-held fans and offering trays with sandalwood paste, thus ensuring the physical comfort of those assembled.

There was much murmuring amongst those assembled when the Chakravarthi did not turn up at the appointed time. When it appeared that this murmuring may reach a crescendo, Siruthondar stood up and announced in a thundering voice, 'Courtiers! We have received news that the Chakravarthi may take some time to come to Court. The Chakravarthi has commanded me to, in the meanwhile, explain to you the reason for all of us congregating here today.' There was absolute silence. Everyone looked at Siruthondar with devotion.

Siruthondar continued his address, 'Vikrama Chola, the son of my dear friend who embraced martyrdom, Parthiba Chola, has been produced in this Court for interrogation. Despite being banished from the country, he was found here and hence was caught by the state. The Chakravarthi wishes to enquire about the reasons for his returning to Bharata Kandam in contravention to the Chakravarthi's command, seek your opinions and pronounce a fair verdict. This is the reason for all of us congregating here today. It is essential for you to be aware of all the facts before enunciating your opinion. Though Vikrama Chola is guilty of flouting the Chakravarthi's diktat, he is not solely responsible for his wrongdoing. My friend who is sitting right next to me has volunteered to accept most of the blame for Vikraman's conduct.' When Siruthondar uttered these words, the congregation's attention turned to the sivanadiyar. Everyone was stunned by his charismatic personality.

'Who is this great soul? Appar Peruman has attained the feet of the Almighty. Sambandar Swami is young. The great Siruthondar is in our midst. Who is he? Why should he take responsibility for Vikraman's actions?' pondered those present in the sabha mandapam.

Siruthondar then reminded the assembly of Parthiba Maharaja setting forth from Uraiyur to wage a battle and the bloody clash that occurred on the banks of Vennaru a decade ago. Those assembled got goosebumps when he stated that not a single warrior from the ten thousand strong Chola force that accompanied Parthiba Maharaja survived. Siruthondar narrated how the sivanadiyar, keen to pay his respects to the King who died fighting so gallantly on the battlefield, sought out Parthiba Maharaja's corpse that fateful pournami night of Puraṭṭāsi. After much searching, the sivanadiyar had stumbled on a barely alive Parthiba Maharaja, whose last wish was that the sivanadiyar ought to raise Vikraman as a brave and independent man. The sivanadiyar had acceded to Parthiba Maharaja's death wish. Those assembled gasped admiringly and tears welled in their eyes listening to this account.

Siruthondar narrated in detail the sivanadiyar visiting Uraiyur and consoling Arulmozhi Devi, Vikraman attempting to hoist the Chola flag on the Chirapalli Mountain, the Chakravarthi banishing Vikraman, his subsequent coronation as the King of Shenbaga Theevu, his returning to Chola Nadu prompted by the desire to see his mother and motherland and the dangers Vikraman had faced.

Siruthondar also recounted the seditious activities of Neelakesi disguised as the Maha Kabala Bhairavar, his abducting and confining Arulmozhi Devi in a cave, the sivanadiyar's relentless efforts in exposing his treachery, the incidents that had occurred on the amavasai night and Vikraman staking his life to rescue the sivanadiyar.

Siruthondar concluded his account by asking, 'Respected people gathered in this Court! I wish to pose a question. Do you believe that my friend, this sivanadiyar, fulfilled the promise he had made to Parthiba Maharaja on the battlefield? Has Vikraman grown into a brave and independent man?'

The uproar caused when everyone assembled called out, 'Yes! Indeed!' was heard within and outside the expansive mandapam. Once the din died down, Siruthondar continued speaking, 'I overlooked sharing an important matter with you. After this great soul had given Parthiba Maharaja his word, the latter asked him, "Swami! Who are you?" This masquerader had removed his fake matted locks and revealed his true persona. After realizing who this sivanadiyar truly was, Parthiba Maharaja peacefully breathed his last, confident that his wish will be fulfilled.' Commotion ensued in the assembly.

Siruthondar quipped, 'Now behold the man who lies beneath this façade!' as he turned to the sivanadiyar and used both his hands to tug the latter's wig and fake moustache and beard. There stood the resplendent and majestic Mamalla Narasimha Chakravarthi. The congregation turned tumultuous. Kundavai shrieked, 'Appa!' as she ran towards the Chakravarthi, still partially disguised as a sivanadiyar, and embraced him. Siruthondar's wife bolstered Arulmozhi Devi, who was so overcome by emotion that she almost swooned. Vikraman stood up and kept staring without batting an eyelid. Ponnan, not knowing how to handle his elation, clasped Valli's hands and shook them.

Those assembled cheered in unison, 'Long live the just King

of Kings, Mamalla Narasimha Pallava Chakravarthi!' and 'Jaya Vijayi Bhava!' This cheering continued for some time, after which Ponnan struck by an afterthought called out, 'Long live Vikrama Chola Maharaja!' The people in the Court hailed, 'Jaya Vijayi Bhava!' in acceptance. It was only when the chaos and exultation had subsided did people observe that the seat occupied by the sivanadiyar lay vacant. Siruthondar announced, 'Respected denizens, there is one task to accomplish before you disperse. Mamalla Chakravarthi will sit on the throne and pronounce the verdict on Vikrama Chola's wrongdoing!'

Shortly thereafter, Narasimha Chakravarthi sporting the attire and ornaments of a sovereign regally made his way into the Court. Once he sat on his throne, the sounds of those assembled cheering, 'Jaya Vijayi Bhava!' reached the skies. The Chakravarthi, on the commotion subsiding, stood up and enunciated, 'I am now aware of your opinion of Vikrama Chola. A man who returns to his country after being banished is usually beheaded. Hence, I command that Vikrama Chola's head be weighed down by the ancient Chola crown and that he ought to endure its weight independently! From today, Chola Nadu is an independent kingdom. The responsibility of ruling Chola Nadu lies entirely with Vikrama Chola and his descendants.'

The uproar and cheering that followed this verdict was so profuse that only the thousand-tongued snake on whom Lord Vishnu rests, Adisesha, could have done justice to narrating the response to Mamalla Chakravarthi's verdict.

40. Dream Comes True

Vikraman was coronated the independent monarch of Chola Nadu at an auspicious time. During another such propitious time, the marriage between Vikraman and Kundavai was solemnized. When Vikraman sought Narasimha Pallavar's blessings after the marriage, the latter remarked, 'My child, may you always conduct yourself in a manner that does not taint the glory of being Parthiba Maharaja's son. May the Almighty give you the strength to lead an honourable life!'

When Kundavai prostrated before Arulmozhi Devi, she blessed Kundavai saying, 'Amma! May you be blessed with all fortune. Do lead your life in a manner that behoves you being Narasimha Chakravarthi's daughter and Parthiba Maharaja's daughter-in-law!'

During Vikraman's and Kundavai's reign, Chola Nadu prospered on all fronts. There was timely rainfall and harvests were abundant. Temples dedicated to Shiva and Vishnu were built. Fine sculptures and paintings emerged. Thirumagal, or Lakshmi – the Goddess of wealth and prosperity, and Kalaimagal, or Saraswathi – the Goddess of knowledge and arts, graced the banks of the Kaveri, hand in hand.

However, Parthiba Maharaja's dream did not come true in its entirety during Vikraman's reign. Just as the luminosity of the planets waned in the sun's presence, Kanchi Narasimha Pallava Chakravarthi's eminence overshadowed Vikraman's. Parthiba Maharaja's martyrdom and Vikraman's valorous deeds served to enhance Mamallar's renown. The Pallavas reigned supreme for long after Narasimha Varmar's demise while Chola Nadu's influence was restricted to a small territory. But Vikraman and his descendants never ever forgot Parthiba Maharaja's aspiration. For generations, they extolled Parthiba Maharaja's gallant death and displayed his paintings at the Uraiyur Chithra Mandapam.

It was during the reigns of Raja Raja Chola and his son, Rajendra Chola, almost three centuries later, that Chola Nadu attained suzerainty overcoming the Pallavas who had by then considerably weakened. Chola warriors waged successful campaigns and hoisted the tiger flag from river Ganga in the north to Singhala (Sri Lanka) in the south and Kadaram (present day Kedah in Malaysia) in the east. The Chola naval forces successfully conquered the islands of Javaham and Pushpakam (present day Java and Sumatra in Indonesia) that lay across the seas. Chola emperors also built across the country magnificent temples and temple towers, which like their glory, grazed the skies. These monuments stand tall even today and are a testimony to the greatness of the ancient Chola kings. It was thus that Parthiba Chola's dream came true three centuries after he attained martyrdom.

Notes

1. Units of distance in ancient Tamil Nadu –
   One kaada equals 10 miles or 16 kilometres
   One yojanai is approximately 8 to 9 miles
2. Units of time in ancient Tamil Nadu –
   1 nazhigai equals 24 minutes
   1 muhurtham equals 48 minutes
   1 jaamam equals 2 hours 24 minutes
   Ten jaamams equal 1 day
3. *Thiruneeru* – Vibhuti, the sacred ash distributed in Shiva temples.
4. Saktars and Kabalikas – Kabalikas were cannibals. Saktars worshipped Shakti, an incarnation of Parvati. Both were belligerent Saivite sects.
5. *Sivakami's Oath* (*Sivakamiyin Sabadham* in Tamil) is the prequel to *Parthiban's Dream* (*Parthiban Kanavu*). Kalki, interestingly, penned *Sivakamiyin Sabadham* after he wrote *Parthiban Kanavu*. *Sivakamiyin Sabadham* is a fictional account of the romance between Crown Prince Narasimha Varma Pallava and danseuse Sivakami set against the backdrop of an actual historical occurrence, i.e. the Chalukya King Pulikesi's invasion of the Pallava empire.

Months in Tamil Calendar

S.No.	Month	Gregorian equivalent
1.	சித்திரை (*Chittirai*)	mid-April to mid-May
2.	வைகாசி (*Vaikāsi*)	mid-May to mid-June
3.	ஆனி *(Āni)*	mid-June to mid-July
4.	ஆடி *(Āadi)*	mid-July to mid-August
5.	ஆவணி *(Āavaṇi)*	mid-August to mid-September
6.	புரட்டாசி *(Puraṭṭāsi)*	mid-September to mid-October
7.	ஐப்பசி *(Aippasi)*	mid-October to mid-November
8.	கார்த்திகை *(Kārtthikgai)*	mid-November to mid-December
9.	மார்கழி *(Mārkazhi)*	mid-December to mid-January
10.	தை *(Thai)*	mid-January to mid-February
11.	மாசி *(Māsi)*	mid-February to mid-March
12.	பங்குனி *(Paṅkuni)*	mid-March to mid-April

Acknowledgements

History enthusiasts owe a debt of gratitude to the (late) Kalki R. Krishnamurthy. Indians who were exposed to a Delhi-centric interpretation of history through school texts became aware of Chola, Pallava and, to a limited extent, of Sinhala and Pandya histories thanks to Kalki's meticulous research and engaging narration.

The Government of Tamil Nadu nationalized the works of certain Tamil authors, including Kalki. This gave multiple publishers the opportunity to print his bestselling novels. Over time, certain discrepancies in the chapter titles, character names and locations crept in. My translation is based on the novel as published by Pavai Publications (August 2009) and www.projectmadurai.org.

***

My friends and mentors – Mrs Rajam Anand and Mr Narayan Anand – edited this book and translated the poetry. Veteran artist, Shri S. Gopalan aka Gopulu, illustrated an edition of *Parthiban Kanavu*. The illustrations in this translation are reproductions of his work. I consider myself blessed to have met the then nonagenarian Gopulu barely four months before his demise in April 2015. He graciously permitted me to use his illustrations in *Parthiban's Dream* and my other forthcoming translation of 'Washingtonil Thirumanam' (The Washington Wedding).

This work is dedicated to the (late) Shri P.S. Ranganathan, whose nom de plumes include 'Kadugu' (Tamil for mustard seed) and 'Agasthiyan'. A fine humourist, thinker and aesthete, PSR mama, as he was fondly known, loved life and the beauties contained within it. In addition to his literary endeavours, he was a scholar of repute. PSR mama and his wife and muse, Kamala mami, published an edition of the *Nalayira Divya Prabandham*, a first millennium Sri Vaishnava text, to great acclaim from pandits and laymen alike. His admiration for Kalki and Kalki's works manifested along with his polymathy, as seen in his invention of new fonts for Tamil and naming them after Kalki's female characters. Ponni, Kundavi and Vanathi are some of the Tamil fonts he invented. PSR mama was a great source of support and affection in my efforts to understand and translate Kalki. I dedicate this labour of love to a man whose labours, in every sense of the word, were founded upon love.

NANDINI VIJAYARAGHAVAN

About the Author

Kalki Krishnamurthy (1899–1954) is among the most renowned Tamil writers. He was a novelist, journalist and music critic. This polymath, who also participated in India's independence movement, was a recipient of India's highest literary honour, the Sahitya Akademi Award, which he received for his social novel *Alai Osai* (*The Sound of Waves*). His writings include over 120 short stories, ten novellas, five novels, three historical romances, editorial and political writings and hundreds of film and music reviews.

About the Translator

Nandini Vijayaraghavan – analyst, columnist, author and translator – was born and raised in Chennai and lives in Singapore. As of 2021, she is the Head of Research at Korea Development Bank. *Parthiban's Dream* is Nandini's second translation. The novel's prequel, *Sivakamiyin Sabadham* (*Sivakami's Oath*) was her first. Nandini co-authored with former Thomson Reuters' fixed-income specialist, Umesh Desai, Singapore's first corporate biography, *The Singapore Blue Chips*. Her columns on finance and the economy have appeared in *Business Line*, *The Hindu* and *Financial Express*. Nandini holds postgraduate degrees in economics and finance from Tufts University and London Business School, respectively and is a CFA charter holder. She blogs at www.litintrans.com.

The HarperCollins–Ratna Sagar Translation Series

Ratna Sagar is an Indian publishing company founded in 1982; Ratna Books, its translations-only imprint, was launched in 2017. The aim of the Ratna Sagar translation list has been to bring acclaimed works written in the Indian languages to a wider readership in English translation, and the focus has been to ensure the quality of the translations, to provide the reader with a seamless reading experience.

Forty-two books have been published in the Ratna Sagar translation list so far, all in hardback. The books have been received well by readers and have met with critical acclaim from the media; many of the books have also won or been nominated for literary awards.

HarperCollins is proud to partner with Ratna Sagar to bring this list of high-quality translations to readers in paperback editions, publishing under HarperCollins's prestigious Perennial imprint.

READ MORE

Havan by Mallikarjun Hiremath
Leaf, Water and Flow by Avadhoot Dongare
Parthiban's Dream by Kalki Krishnamurthy
Prison Notes of a Woman Activist by Bellapu Anuradha
The Bells Are Ringing in Haridwar by M. Mukundan
Dukhi Dadiba by Dadi Edulji Taraporewala
After Yesterday and Other Stories by Appaduari Muttulingam
The Sixth Finger by Malayatoor Ramakrishnan
A Faceless Evening and Other Stories by Gangadhar Gadgil
If a River and Other Stories by Kula Saikia
On a River's Bank by A. Madhavan
Echoes of the Veena and Other Stories by R. Chudamani
Here I Am and Other Stories by P. Sathyavathi
The Rock That Was Not and Other Stories by Githanjali
The Story of Being Useless and Three Contexts of a Writer by Avadhoot Dongare
Mirror in the Hall and Other Stories by Prakash Bal Joshi
The Songs of Life and Other Stories by Vijaya Rajadhyaksha
Jalasamadhi and Other Stories by A. Sethumadhavan
Kadambari - The Flower Girl by A. Sethumadhavan
The Scent of Happiness by R. Vatsala
Asprishya Ganga and Other Stories by Kolakaluri Enoch
Alka and Other Stories by Goutam Das
If there is a God and Other Stories by Imayam
Ananta Jeevanam by Kolakaluri Enoch
The Stepmother and Other Stories by Laxmibai Abhyankar
Cracked Glass Jar and Other Stories by Chandra Latha
A Fine Thread and Other Stories by B. Jeyamohan
Forever Yours, Krishna by Indira Parthasarathy
Mayaloka by Poornachandra Tejaswi
The Go-Between and Other Stories by Ghanshyam Desai
The Masked Face and Two Other Stories by Vaasanthi
Vasudeva ... The Wanderer Prince by Sanghadasagani Vacaka
Randhi: Of Power and Desire by Kolakaluri Enoch